The Brain at School

The Brain at School

Educational neuroscience in the classroom

John G. Geake

 Open University Press

Open University Press
McGraw-Hill Education
McGraw-Hill House
Shoppenhangers Road
Maidenhead
Berkshire
England
SL6 2QL

email: enquiries@openup.co.uk
world wide web: www.openup.co.uk

and
Two Penn Plaza, New York, NY 10121-2289, USA

First published 2009

A catalogue record of this book is available from the British Library

ISBN10: 0 335 23421 6 (pb) 0 335 23420 8 (hb)
ISBN13: 978 0 335 23421 9 (pb) 978 0 335 23420 2 (hb)

Library of Congress Cataloging-in-Publication Data
CIP data has been applied for

Typeset by Aptara Inc., India
Printed in the UK by Bell and Bain Ltd., Glasgow

Fictitous names of companies, products, people, characters and/or data that may be used herein (in case studies or in examples) are not intended to represent any real individual, company, product or event.

Mixed Sources
Product group from well-managed forests and other controlled sources
www.fsc.org Cert no. TT-COC-002769
© 1996 Forest Stewardship Council
FSC

The *McGraw·Hill* Companies

Contents

List of figures

Preface

Young brains come to school to learn: older brains come to school to teach them. At least, that's the ideal. The rationale for writing this book was the question: Can cognitive neuroscience tell us anything about how young brains learn from older brains, and therefore how older brains should teach younger brains for optimal effect?

Cognitive neuroscience entails a century-long worldwide research endeavour to understand how the human brain functions. The intensity of this scientific enquiry has notably increased during the past decades with the widespread use of functional neuroimaging technology. With a concomitant increase in public interest in possible applications of brain research beyond the laboratory and hospital, neuroscientists and educators have asked: How can cognitive neuroscience usefully inform education and, for that matter, how can education usefully inform cognitive neuroscience?

The learning brain has been a focus of many neuroscientific studies utilizing the full repertoire of brain-imaging technologies. In contrast to date, the teaching brain, as an explicit subject of research, has been almost completely neglected. Educational neuroscience, as a recent emergent sub-discipline of cognitive neuroscience, has a strong bias towards learning as a brain function, with the implicit assumption that if learning can be well understood, then good teaching will follow. Here I have attempted to go beyond this assumption by examining some of the implications of educational neuroscientific research for pedagogy.

This book has been written especially for teachers in all sectors: early years, primary, secondary and tertiary, together with those currently studying for a career in the teaching profession. Additionally, the book is for parents of school children, headteachers, members of school governing bodies, education policymakers and administrators, education academics and researchers, education psychologists, politicians and education commentators – in fact, everyone concerned with and involved in education.

As an educator who has had the privilege of teaching in the primary, secondary, further education and university sectors, I sometimes reflect on what these different teaching experiences have in common: Are there generic attributes of teaching, regardless of the age or sophistication of the students? I think there are, and undoubtedly you will have your list. Mine includes subject knowledge, demonstrative articulateness, wisdom, compassion and, most importantly, a seemingly instinctive ability to make (public) sense of initial incomprehension. And about these characteristics, neuroscience does have much to say. But, it must be acknowledged, there is much about education of which neuroscience is silent. Either the relevant research has not (yet) been done, or the educational phenomena are not able to be captured within a neuroscientific paradigm. An example of the latter would be the effects on learning of different seating arrangements in a classroom. Nevertheless, what can be said, and is being said by neuroscience about education, expands each year.

More importantly, from an education perspective, initial teacher training (ITT) programmes in universities are increasingly embracing some educational neuroscience input. Educational neuroscience is also becoming the focus of a range of teacher professional development courses throughout the world, including several at Masters' level. This book is especially intended for anyone embarking on any such programme.

The idea for this book was conceived a decade ago. Since then, I have embarked on a part-time career as a cognitive neuroscientist. This involved a great deal of learning on my part. The book is the result of taking my brain to (neuroscience) school.

Acknowledgements

Any collection of thoughts committed to written form has been influenced, informed and unconsciously plagiarized from the thinking of others too numerous to list. But the following might well recognize their input: Jan Atkinson, Christopher Ball, Karen Brody, Sally Burdon, Gemma Calvert, Sheila Cameron, Tom Campbell, Paul Cooper, Ann Dowker, Lynn Erler, Kurt Fisher, Don Fitzgerald, Tobe Freeman, Usha Goswami, Robert Gregson, Peter Hansen, Paul Howard-Jones, Morten Kringelbach, Roger Lindsay, Sarah Maidlow, Michael O'Boyle, Jonah Oliver, Tomas Paus, John Pegg, Jonathan Sharples, John Stein, David Whitebread. The interpretations, extrapolations and errors are, of course, my responsibility.

Some of the content has been presented previously in academic journal articles, conference addresses, seminar papers, university lectures and teacher professional development sessions. This has been noted where appropriate. In any case, the material has been updated and expanded here.

The genesis of this book occurred in 1998 during a period of sabbatical leave from my then Australian university, Southern Cross, which was spent as a visiting fellow at the Department of Education, University of Cambridge. A particular source of ideas and inspiration over the ensuing decade has been the Oxford Cognitive Neuroscience Education Forum, which I co-founded with UK neuroscientist Colin Blakemore in 2001. My thanks and gratitude are extended to the Oxford Cognitive Neuroscience Centre for support of the Forum, particularly the use of the Sherrington Room, Department of Physiology, Anatomy and Genetics, University of Oxford, as a place to meet, and to the Westminster Institute of Education, Oxford Brookes University for hosting the Forum's website.

Special thanks for to Fiona Richman, Donna Edwards and Claire Munce and the production staff at Open University Press for their unflagging editorial advice and guidance.

And most importantly, my deep gratitude to Ann for her inspiring support.

Introduction

The main reason for writing this book stems from my belief that it is important for teachers to know about how cognitive neuroscience might inform their work. But why this book now, at a time when educational neuroscience, despite its flowering, could still be regarded to be in its infancy? To pre-empt some critics: Is this book premature? This Introduction offers a rationale, and attempts to set the scene for such an endeavour.

In 1998, the *Daily Telegraph* newspaper in the UK reported Paul Fletcher, a neuroscientist in the Functional Imaging Laboratory, University of London, as predicting that 'one day enough might be known about brain functioning that brain scanners could monitor the pupil's learning to assess if it was taking place effectively'. The key words were 'one day', 'enough' and 'might'. That day has certainly not arrived yet, but equally, it is closer than it was back in 1998.

There are several persuasive reasons to answer the question, 'Why this topic at this time?' First, teachers use implicit models of brain functioning in their daily work with students in classrooms, so knowledge of brain functioning should be of professional interest. In recent years, some teachers have adopted explicit models of brain functioning which have often been called 'brain-based' in an attempt to affect a scientific legitimacy which regrettably usually exceeds their claims. That we only use 10 per cent of our brain is a classic claim, but the suggestion that there are left- and right-brained people is just as ridiculous. These and other neuromythologies, such as visual–auditory–kinaesthetic (VAK) learning styles and neurokinaesthetics (brain gym), are now themselves a topic of academic research. How did they arise? What is their appeal? What other neuromythologies have recently hit the airwaves? Undoubtedly the most prolific generator of neuromyths has been the learning styles industry. The assumption that individual differences in personality or management can be attributed to a preference for one of (usually) four styles has been extended into education where academic success is accounted for by a pupil's learning style. The most popular version at present is VAK, discussed in Chapter 4. It must be acknowledged that these learning style inventories have considerable intuitive appeal if we are to judge by the number that have been devised – 170 at last count, and rising. There seems to be no limit to the many ways in which personality or learning style can be divided up and appealingly labelled. The evidence from independent researchers, however, tells a different story. No improvements in learning outcomes have been found from teaching approaches which focus on differences in pupils' learning styles, save for an initial positive rise due to the teacher's enthusiasm for a new approach. Importantly, there is no neuroscientific evidence for the existence of learning styles. Before a school buys a brain-based programme, the old saw, 'Look before you leap' comes to mind.

A second rationale for this book emerges from the shortcomings of contemporary educational research and behaviourist education policies to satisfactorily address many of the challenges, some long-standing, of modern universal education. Whereas, on the one hand, behaviourist policy drivers, such as outcome measures, ignore the personal and social dimensions of education so valued by teachers, on the other hand, the antiscientific postmodernism of much academic discourse about education seems to have deserted the chalk face for a far distant 'reality'. Perhaps some neuroscientific understandings of learning and teaching might help fill this conceptual vacuum. To this end, some findings from neuroscience might reinforce particular aspects of existing practice, providing a boost to teacher confidence about their intuitive sense of effective pedagogy. Other findings from neuroscience might provide some evidence to use in deciding between competing claims. For example, it's a commonplace to hear teachers extolled as 'a guide on the side, not a sage on the stage'. But is this always a sound approach, for all students, in all educational circumstances? In 2006 an international critique of minimal instruction pedagogies flew in the face of 20 years of academic theorizing about how children learn best, by condemning constructivism, discovery learning and inquiry style teaching. Wouldn't it be informative to have some neuroscientific evidence of how children's brains respond to direct instruction compared with discovery learning?

A third reason for writing now is that there is already an existing literature advocating, at least in principle, that neuroscience offers some useful applications for educational practice. Consequently, neuroscientists have been citing educational benefits in their funding applications for some years. This in itself is, of course, no good reason for another book for teachers, but one of the 'take-home' messages is that teachers have an important potential contribution to make to the cognitive neuroscience research agenda in order to steer that agenda towards educationally relevant neuroscience. To this end, the Oxford Cognitive Neuroscience Education Forum, which I've had the privilege of convening since its inception in 2001, has hosted regular meetings at which teachers, psychologists and neuroscientists interested in education have engaged in interdisciplinary dialogue to explore how such an agenda can be usefully prosecuted. Many of the Forum's deliberations are included in the following chapters. My experience with teacher professional development presentations over many years has been that teachers have wanted to be brought up to date on brain research findings relevant to their professional practice. A recent project of the Oxford Forum has been to solicit a raft of questions about brain function from teachers, and to provide some neuroscientific responses. For example, teachers are very interested in being informed about the role of genetics in learning potentials; whether there are neurological bases for the different learning styles of boys and girls; about the relationships between intelligence and emotions, especially in learning situations. However, overinterpretation of neuroscience by some commentators has led to unsubstantiated recommendations for teachers, for example, to educate half of their pupils' brains (usually the right half) in isolation. I hope that the rumour of teachers in America issuing eye patches to their pupils in a misguided attempt to limit visual input to one hemisphere is just an urban myth. Anyone with 'half a brain' knows that each eye sends visual input to both hemispheres. Such overinterpretations and misinterpretations only serve to underscore the point that teacher professional knowledge needs to be informed by accurate and current reviews of the neuroscience literature. Here I've attempted to progress that in-principle position by considering some actual educational issues and looking at what cognitive neuroscientific evidence could be brought to bear on their resolution.

Historically, neuroscience has been driven by the more immediate concerns of neuropathology, where 'deficit functioning' has informed various models of cognition. Recent improvements in the spatial and temporal resolution of various neuroimaging technologies have informed models of cognition with 'normal-functioning' data. Nevertheless, a map of the neural correlates of many characteristics of higher order cognition, for example, subjective beauty, awaits completion, despite informative results from recent neuroimaging research. It must be said that some distinguished commentators argue theoretically, and practically, against the attainment of a complete description of human brain function. Our brains certainly did not evolve to do neuroscience and, perhaps, as clever as they are, our brains are not up to the task of fully understanding how they function. However, neither in-principle nor actual limitations to the determination of neural correlates affect our consideration of what cognitive neuroscience has achieved and what those achievements might suggest for education. With time-honoured educational pragmatism we can remain agnostic over whether neural correlates of all human thought will ever be found.

Nevertheless, the search is attracting an increasingly attentive general audience, reflected by the plethora of populist books by neuroscientists which have graced the shelves of 'good' bookshops over the past decades.

A pioneer work was Jean-Pierre Changeux (1985) *Neuronal Man*. Some of my favourites from the 1990s include: Gerald Edelman (1992) *Bright Air, Brilliant Fire*; Steven Rose (1992) *The Making of Memory*; Antonio Damasio (1994) *Descartes' Error*; William Calvin (1996) *How Brains Think*; Joe LeDoux (1996) *The Emotional Brain*; Susan Greenfield (1997) *The Human Brain: A Guided Tour*; Richard Cytowic (1998) *The Man Who Tasted Shapes*; Edmund Rolls (1998) *The Brain and Emotion*; Rita Carter (1999) *Mapping the Mind*; and Walter J. Freeman (1999) *How Brains Make Up Their Minds*. And from the 2000s: Joaquin Fuster (2003) *Cortex and Mind*; Steven Rose (2006) *The 21st-Century Brain*; Chris Frith (2007) *Making Up the Mind*; and Sergio Della Sala (2007) *Tall Tales About the Mind & Brain*.

It is an interesting exercise, as a teacher, to consult the indexes of these books. There are multiple references to learning, knowledge, memory, motivation, cognitive development and so on, but none whatsoever to education, schooling, children as pupils or pedagogy. An early and welcome exception is Ann and Richard Barnet (1998) *The Youngest Minds*, at least with respect to cognitive neuroscience and pre-schooling. More recently, several scientists have proved the rule by turning their attention to the neuroscience–education nexus, including James Byrnes (2001) *Minds, Brains and Learning*, James Zull (2002) *The Art of Changing the Brain*; and Sarah-Jane Blakemore and Uta Frith *The Learning Brain*. These authors make the case that as cognitive neuroscience advances our understanding of the neural basis of learning, so teachers, as professional educators, should engage with this research in professional development to influence their teaching practice in school classrooms.

Could such a return to the fundamentals of teaching and learning help to reclaim the education agenda from those politicians and boardroom directors whose predominantly instrumental objectives for schooling and further education have caused such dismay within the teaching profession of late? In other words, one possible reason for teachers to embrace educational neuroscience might be that such an endeavour could address an increasing marginalization of teachers as professionally independent pedagogues. This may be all the more urgent given current trends to increasingly replace human teaching with online information retrieval. I want education to remain largely a human endeavour, one where teachers will always be interested in gaining a better understanding of the multitude of factors which govern the learning of their charges. Is it too fanciful to imagine a day when teachers are accorded a similar social status (and pay) as doctors because of their demonstrably science-based professionalism?

In fact, cognitive neuroscientific research into learning, especially literacy and numeracy, is well into its third decade. The potential benefits to education, particularly for pupils with special educational needs (SEN), were also noted over ten years ago where it was suggested that cognitive neuroscience might offer new data and fresh perspectives on some hitherto intractable educational problems such as: Why do some students not learn to read as easily as most; Why doesn't every child 'get' fractions? The responses of the education profession, especially in the UK, have been mixed. Here I argue that the way forward is through the education profession shaping a professionally informative educational neuroscience research agenda of the future. As American neuroscientist John Bruer has argued:

> We send our children to school to learn things they might not learn without formal instruction so that they can function more intelligently outside school. If so, recommendations for school reform should explicitly appeal to and implement our best, current understanding of what learning and intelligence are. In the public debate on school reform, this is seldom the case. Common recommendations – raising standards, increasing accountability, testing more, creating markets in educational services – are psychologically atheoretical, based at best on common sense and at worst on naive or dated conceptions of learning.[1]

Some ten years ago I put forward five arguments in favour of the development of an educational neuroscience. Each argument has caveats – this is not blind ideology.

A case for educational neuroscience

The 'in principle' argument

Humans are biological entities – at appropriate levels, human behaviour is biological. Human brains are biological entities – brain behaviour is neurobiological. Brain behaviour includes learning memorization, epistemology, literacy, numeracy, creativity, reasoning, intelligence, emotion . . . the stuff of education is neurobiological. But, and it's a big 'but', a neuroscience account of learning may not always be the most appropriate perspective for classroom application.

The professional imperative argument

School teachers are interested in brain functioning relevant to learning and development in children. There are many education policy questions which might one day profitably be asked of cognitive neuroscience, for example:

- What is the best age to begin formal schooling?
- What is the best age for early education?
- What are the 'right' things for a parent to be doing at home before their child commences school?
- Is there a natural order of intellectual development for verbal and non-verbal reasoning?
- Is there a critical age beyond which the foundations for adolescent literacy and numeracy are passed?
- For pupils who suffer an educational disadvantage of some kind, e.g., socio-economic and/or genetic, what sorts of specific interventions will be effective?

But for the education profession to benefit from such research, teachers must be able to make appropriately informed interpretations of the science.

The 'in practice' argument

It *is* possible to draw implications and suggest applications for education from the research to date. Cognitive neuroscience research has produced evidence for brain function along a number of non-exclusive polarities:

- modularization and connectionism;
- localization and distribution;
- cellular reductionism and adaptive plasticity;
- genetic determinism and non-linear indeterminism;
- phylogenic similarity and individual differences.

The current conceptual synthesis is that the brain operates through dynamic, task-appropriate neural systems. This includes learning at school. Many examples of educational applications of neuroscience research are presented in the chapters that follow.

The self-interest argument

Although neuroscientists have for some time been active in researching learning, memory in general, and literacy and numeracy in particular, teachers have not thus far been widely consulted. The education profession therefore needs to extend its dialogue with neuroscientists to enable educational applications to be realized.

I hardly need to point out that educational research is under some political pressure for greater explicit relevance. Is it too Panglossian to hope for the development of pedagogy from its current heuristic base to a scientifically valid evidence base? This argument is admittedly one of educational self-interest, but, why not, especially if education is to remain the lynch pin of most political agendas for social improvement? And if teachers don't become involved in the educational neuroscientific enterprise, could they find themselves even further professionally marginalized than some politicians and education bureaucrats seem intent on pushing them? In other words, applying evidence from neuroscience to education could provide a means for teachers to reclaim eroded professional autonomy.

The opportunistic argument

There are many more neuroscientists alive and experimenting today (one estimate is 200,000) than the cumulative total over the entire history of neuroscience. Each year, neuroscience conferences feature hundreds of presentations on educational applications and implications. Of course, such fecundity is not without its limitations. With thousands of new research articles published each year, can anyone keep up to date? The Society for Neuroscience holds its annual conference in one of the few American cities that can comfortably host a conference of 30,000 delegates. Each year, these neuroscientists present some 20,000 papers and posters of new work. At any one time, some 20 papers are being read, while in the poster hall, several thousand posters are simultaneously on display. One can imagine that the information presented on one particular poster down one end of the hall on, say, the Tuesday contains the vital link missing for another piece of research presented on, say, the Wednesday, but the researchers might never know. And the possibility of anyone gaining a coherent overview? And that's at one (admittedly the largest) neuroscience conference. Worldwide, there are dozens of annual neuroscience conferences. Then there are numerous brain and learning conferences where thousands of teachers, mostly at their own expense, hear the latest findings from leading neuroscientists about learning difficulties, especially dyslexia and ADHD. This has gone beyond talk; there are neuroscience-based learning labs in the USA and in the UK for dyslexic children. The technology for ex-laboratory school-friendly neuroimaging is currently being designed and trialled.

To summarize these arguments, the education profession could benefit from embracing rather than ignoring cognitive neuroscience. Moreover, teachers should be actively contributing to the research agenda of future neuroscientific research. That is, a cognitive neuroscience–education nexus should not be a one way street. Whereas neuroscience could inform education by providing additional evidence that confirms good practice, helps resolve educational dilemmas or suggests new possibilities in pedagogy or curriculum design, education could inform neuroscience by providing a source of complementary behavioural data, especially on pupils, as well as posing new worthwhile lines of investigation.

This is reflected in the growing number of organizations and research centres concerned with educational neuroscience. The oldest (1994) is the Brain, Neuroscience and Education Special Interest Group (SIG) of the American Education Research Association (AERA). In the UK, since the year 2000, we have seen the establishment of the Oxford Cognitive Neuroscience Education Forum; the Teaching and Learning Research Programme Seminar Series on Neuroscience and Education; the British Educational Research Association SIG in Neuroscience and Education; the Institute for the Future of the Mind at the University of Oxford, supporting the House of Lords All-Party Parliamentary Group on Scientific Research in Learning and Education, whose first focus issue in 2006 was on the implications of educational neuroscience and the potential dangers for schools of neuromythologies. Several scientific organizations have held specialist educational neuroscience sessions at their annual conferences. These include the Society for Neuroscience (in the USA), and the British Association for Cognitive Neuroscience (BACN). Government organizations have also been interested, with the Organisation for Economic Co-operation and Development (OECD) producing two extensive reports (2002, 2007), and the governments of the United States (through its National Science Foundation (NSF)), Germany (through the Ministry of Education and Science) and Japan (through its Centers of Excellence (COE) in the twenty-first century) budgeting specific educational neuroscience funding programmes. In the USA, the NSF currently supports six Science of Learning Centers – multi-institutional interdisciplinary cooperative research endeavours based in Seattle, Boston, Pittsburgh, Washington (DC), Philadelphia and San Diego. In the UK, the University of Cambridge opened its Centre of Education and Neuroscience in its Faculty of Education in 2005, with the Centre of Learning Science at the University of Nottingham following in 2006. In recognition of this diverse, growing international effort, the International Mind, Brain and Education Society was formed in 2006. It is based in the Graduate School of Education, Harvard University, Boston, USA. Websites and contact information for these organizations are listed in the References and Further Reading.

In December 2007, the National Science Foundation (USA) held a Neuroscience and Education Workshop in Washington, DC, to which leading researchers in the field of educational neuroscience were invited. The object was to take stock of where this new field had reached, and to recommend where it should go next. The report focused on areas of educational neuroscience research that seemed especially promising. The workshop participants agreed that the most promising area for future educational neuroscience research would be to gain a better understanding of the development of multiple neural systems (NB: not multiple intelligences) necessary for learning. For example, which multiple learning systems enable the emergence of necessary expertise in concomitant skills within a particular school subject such as computation and estimation in arithmetic? And if such neural systems can be identified, then what are some potential applications for curriculum design, for example, the ordering of presentations of new concepts?

Caveats and disclaimers

No matter how carefully I try and set out my aims, and note their limitations, I have every confidence that some of my academic colleagues will leap upon this endeavour and attribute all manner of claims to my efforts (does raising this concern indicate that I've been in universities for too long?). So, mostly for them, here are some upfront caveats and disclaimers.

I know that there is a vast literature on educational research about these educational issues *and* that there is a vast literature on behavioural and cognitive psychological research about these issues. I have no wish to repeat what others have more articulately said before. It is assumed that the reader is either acquainted with this literature or can become so through further reading, and to that end I have provided endnotes and references for each chapter at the end of the book.

I know that neuroscience is several descriptive levels removed from the educational interface. Furthermore, *I know* that there is no simple one-to-one mapping between neurophysiological measures and cognitive states. But this does not mean that no connections can be made between neurophysiology and cognitive behaviours typically found in educational settings. Rather, it means that claims for causal links are necessarily made with due reservation.

I am not saying that educational neuroscience can now provide all the answers. Neuroscience is a relatively new discipline in terms of its current level of intensity. Its object of research – the human brain – has often been described as the most complex object in the universe. Whether or not such hyperbole will stand up in time, it is commonly believed by many neuroscientists that a complete understanding of brain functioning is beyond, and will remain beyond, the experimental capacities of human researchers. And even if cognitive neuroscientific accounts of brain functioning become orders of greater magnitude than those available at present, cognitive neuroscience can never provide all the answers. In a matter as complex as education, no one field can provide a complete account of all of the variance.

Nevertheless, some progress in understanding the human brain has been made, especially during the last decade. Given the substantial increase in the potential for data gathering afforded by new neuroimaging technologies, especially functional magnetic resonance imaging, more of the mysteries of brain functioning will undoubtedly become clearer in the not too distant future. An obvious challenge to providing an up-to-date account of how our brain enables us to learn at school is that the relevant science does not stand still. There is every chance that some of the science reported in this book will be superseded by new discoveries by the time it is published. In fact, I rather hope this will happen. Science is discovery, not dogma. But while pointing out the considerable shortcomings of the current state of play, consistent with my belief that teachers should contribute to this most exciting endeavour, I offer some suggestions for where cognitive neuroscientific research could proceed in the future.

However, in doing so, *I am not recommending* that all teachers train as neuroscientists, as was (deliberately?) misinterpreted by a reviewer of one of my earlier papers. *I am suggesting*, obviously by writing this book, that neuroscientific findings, appropriately filtered and interpreted, can be, and possibly should be, of professional interest to educators, especially school teachers and teacher-educators.

Finally, whereas the principal focus here is on the individual learner and teacher, it is fully acknowledged that all formal learning occurs within an educational policy milieu. It is obviously a long stretch from the laboratory to the committee room. Nevertheless, the suggestion here is that many of questions of policy (e.g., Is there an optimal age for school commencement? Is there an optimal age to begin reading lessons?) might profitably be addressed by relevant scientific data, rather than *a priori* ideology. At least, that's my hope. As science writer Rita Carter optimistically prophesies, future generations will use our increasing knowledge of the brain to:

> enhance those mental qualities that give sweetness and meaning
> to our lives, and to eradicate those that are destructive.[2]

The belief underpinning this book is that relevant and useful professional and classroom applications of educational neuroscience will increasingly become available as we gradually come to understand more about brain function through neuroscience research which answers educational questions about learning, memory, motivation, and so on.

All that said, the chapters are fairly independent, and can be read in any order. However, the later curriculum-focused chapters assume some acquaintance with the neuroscience of the earlier chapters. There are no lesson plans, no busy sheets for copying. I would never be so presumptuous as to think that my lesson plans, real or imagined, could replace those of the teacher at the chalkface, who knows the learning needs of the pupils in his or her class. With this readership in mind, I have wherever possible translated scientific jargon into more common terms. For ease of reading, I have also deliberately omitted the scientific references from the text, and listed them in the Endnotes section towards the end of the book. The recommendations in this book are put forward as one professional educator to another.

1   Why Educational Neuroscience?

Our brains did not evolve to go to school. Yet we do all go to school as students, and some of us return as teachers. For that matter, our brains did not evolve to enable us to cope with most of the requirements of modern life. Yet we do. The human brain is composed of thousands of functional modules, mini-brains within a brain, most of which evolved in our distant pre-hominid past. It is through multiple, complex combinations of these functional modules, through a myriad of interconnections, that our brains create functional neural systems which enable us to adapt and succeed at tasks which our ancestors could not have even dreamed about. For several hundreds of years, such tasks have included formal education, both as learners and as teachers. More recently, one of the activities which some of our brains have turned to has been research into how our brains function. That's neuroscience. Within neuroscience, a central focus has been how our brains enable us to think. That's cognitive neuroscience. And within cognitive neuroscience, a particular interest is how our brains enable thinking in educational contexts. That's educational neuroscience. To be precise:

> *Educational neuroscience is cognitive neuroscience which investigates educationally inspired research questions.*

In other words, educational neuroscience is cognitive neuroscience that is relevant to, has implications for, and might lead to applications in, educational practice and policy – pedagogy and curriculum – because the neuroscience addresses an educational problem or issue. Consequently, educational neuroscience, as a research endeavour, only makes sense if the genesis of its projects lies in educational issues, concerns and problems. Without being rooted in education, neuroscientific data and interpretations are unlikely to be embraced by the education profession. Therefore, I suggest, educational neuroscience should incorporate an action research cycle wherein the original educational issue inspires a set of neuroscientific research questions, the results of which are likely to have implications and applications for educational policy and/or practice. For the latter phase, the research cycle is not complete until the putative applications have been field-tested in classrooms. Of course, the outcomes of this might lead to a revision of the articulation of the original educational issue such that a whole new raft of neuroscientific research questions arise, and another research cycle is initiated. That is, a discipline-specific method-ology for educational neuroscience needs to be established. Here are four examples.

1   Education problem: the watershed of fractions.
    • Neuroscience research: neural dissociations and connectiv-ity between concrete and symbolic representations of fract-ions.
    • Possible education application: design of more efficacious cur-ricula for symbolic fractions.
2   Education problem: the decline in second language studies in sec-ondary schools.
    • Neuroscience research: neural dissociations and connectivity between orthographic and phonemic representations of first and second languages.
    • Possible education application: design of more efficacious cur-ricula for second language acquisition in primary schools.
3   Education problem: how to optimize creative thinking in school.
    • Neuroscience research: neural correlates of fluid analogical rea-soning.
    • Possible education application: pedagogies that utilize ana-logizing to enhance creative thinking in all curriculum areas.
4   Education problem: how to optimize general academic perfor-mance.
    • Neuroscience research: neural fractionations of working mem-ory, and neural distribution of long-term memory.
    • Possible education application: redesign of assessment tasks, especially rote recall exams.

Well, that's the ideal. In practice there are any number of limitations and challenges. For one, researchers from different disciplines have their own discipline-centric worldviews, communicated through a specialist lexicon within their discipline. Genuine interdisciplinary endeavour is therefore hard work. My preferred solution here is to use education as the start-ing point. However, I recognize that it's the neuroscientists who have so far done most of the running – for the obvious reason that they are the researchers, not classroom teachers.

One of the early hopes of cognitive neuroscience in general, and edu-cational neuroscience in particular, was that the results of these investi-gations might help us to choose between the many 'black box' models of cognition and learning that fill the pages of every textbook on education – at least one per theorist, and several per chapter. As the oft-repeated quip at science conferences goes: 'A theoretical model is like a toothbrush – everyone has one, but no one wants to use anybody else's!' Yet, the plethora of cognitive models can only mean one thing – they cannot all be correct. My bet is that they each contain a glimmer of truth somewhere within, but none are 'correct' as a complete description of how the brain enables thinking and learning. And let's face it, none of those flowcharts of boxes and arrows is ever of any help, or has much meaning, when one is engaged with Year 9 on a Friday afternoon.

Apart from their pragmatic shortcomings, cognitive psychological models reflect a different level of understanding from the neural, so it is important to distinguish these levels when interpreting neuroscientific studies for classroom applications. And most of the classic cognitive learning models, such as those of Piaget, Vygotsky or Bruner, had very little neuroscientific data to inform their construction. But this difference in levels between cognitive and neuroscientific interpretations poses a paradox: the design of any cognitive neuroscientific experiment – typically, taking brain images while subjects undergo some cognitive task, perhaps matching pairs of words or doing arithmetic calculations – implies some *a priori* model of cognition. That is, to test how the brain does anything, neuroscientists must first conjecture at how this is done at a cognitive level in order to devise appropriate experimental stimuli, for example, word pairs that cognitively connect, or arithmetic sums that demonstrate stages of competence. So, we are faced with the paradoxical situation of trying to examine the brain's cognition with tests which we know do not completely reflect how the brain actually functions. It's not as extreme a situation as the A-level English class who discover in their literature paper that they have studied the wrong set text – but there are analogical similarities. This is not to say that brain imaging studies are futile – far from it. The results are usually intriguingly informative, especially if there are significant activations in those areas of the brain hypothesized to be active. But, at the same time, most neuroimaging results are open to alternative interpretations, since we do not yet know precisely what contributions each of those activated areas is making to any particular cognitive task. Furthermore, in any neuroimaging experiment, there are usually additional areas of activation beyond those hypothesized. What can they be up to one wonders?

Education neuroscientific research questions

Whenever educators and neuroscientists gather to discuss educational neuroscience research agendas, there never seems to be any shortage of potentially interesting and relevant research questions. At the National

Science Foundation 2007 neuroscience and education workshop mentioned in the Introduction, many complementary approaches and multilevel foci were noted that could be fruitful in addressing a suite of research questions. These included:

- What are the critical developmental links between precursor skills and building expertise?
- How do brain systems build up prior to the emergence of competence?
- What role do basic sensory processing, as well as cross-modal processing, play in learning?
- What are the effects of age on learning, e.g., phonological processing? Is early 'special' and, if so, how and why?
- How do social factors such as socioeconomic status (SES) and home environment make their relative contributions at different points to brain development?
- How does the brain build structured representations? Is bilingualism an informative exemplar?
- What is the nature of complex imagery in informational input and representation?
- What are the neural bases of individual differences in learning and development?
- Can neural correlates be used to measure the effectiveness of different interventions, e.g., symbolic vs. concrete, analogical vs. contextual, naive vs. conceptual?
- What are the roles in learning of components across the whole brain, e.g., amygdala, cerebellum?
- Is core knowledge as designated in national curricula neurally privileged?
- What are the neural signatures of emotional engagement which promote educational achievement?
- What, from a neuroscientific perspective, are the effects of sleep on learning?
- Is there any neural reality to so-called learning styles? And if so, does one teach to a delineated preference or try to enhance a delineated dis-preference?
- Can neuroscience account for expertise and best practice?
- Can neuroscience help explain the big-school–small-school effect whereby best practice in one fails in the other?
- Are there neural switches for establishing secure mentor–student roles? And if so, what supranormal stimuli trigger these switches?
- How do correct concepts supersede or inhibit incorrect naive concepts?

- What are the neural underpinnings of attention: its multidimensionality, informational salience, temporal dynamics in learning situations and developmental trajectories?
- Is there a neural account of attention span?
- Can neuroscience provide a better understanding of memory and knowledge?
- Can neuroscience provide a better understanding of the neural characteristics associated with reward, punishment and motivation?
- What are the roles of mirror neurons in learning by imitation?
- What could be a social neuroscience perspective on the roles of teacher and student?
- What could be a social neuroscience perspective on classroom atmosphere?
- What are the neural markers for teacher–student empathy?
- What types of school learning can be explained by Hebbian models, and which cannot?
- What types of informal learning can be explained by Hebbian models, and which cannot?
- What are the neuropharmacological substrates of working memory?
- What nutritional factors are best to support brain function for learning?
- Are there differentiable and reliable educational endophenotypes?
- Does teaching pupils neuroscience improve their learning outcomes?
- Does teaching teachers about neuroscience improve their students' learning outcomes?
- How do genetic predispositions for neural plasticity interact with learning contexts and social environments?
- What brain systems enable high-value feedback during learning?
- Are there distinct neural correlates of curricula 'tipping points', e.g., fractions in arithmetic?
- How are the brains of high-ability students different from the brains of normal students?

This quest to better understand the brain's learning systems should be particularly informed by neuroscientific accounts of non-normal development such as dyslexia and dyscalculia. Again, there are many potential areas of promising research:

- How do mechanisms of learning contribute, or not, to developmental disabilities?

- How do the brain's multiple learning systems, which operate via different rules, contribute, or not, to learning difficulties?
- How are developmental links altered in disorders of learning such as dyslexia?
- What could be the neural trade-offs for individual pupils, e.g., the mix of 'skill and drill' vs. comprehension tuition required when interventions are delivered?
- Are there specific limits to learning determined by various learning disabilities, e.g., ADHD and working memory capacity?
- Which components of global processing are unaffected by various learning disabilities?
- Are the neural dynamics of competence of children with identified learning disabilities different from those of normal children, e.g., dyslexics who have successfully learned to read?
- Can early neural markers for learning disabilities be identified?
- Can neuroscience provide biomarkers of risk for future learning difficulties?
- How can neuroscience be used to clarify developmental continuums, so that the importance of research on disabilities for understanding typical development is clear?
- What is more effective for brain development, e.g., should educators focus intervention on areas of weakness or strength (or both)? And, if so, in what combination, for which disorder?
- What are the neural effects of stress on learning?
- What neuroscientific data can be gathered to usefully inform reports of learning disabilities in school-age populations?
- What are the contributing neural factors towards resilience to environmental stress?
- What can the brain functioning of children with autism tell us about which brain systems are involved in representing the actions and intentions of others?
- Are there neural markers for children's emotional 'meltdowns'?

Phew! You can certainly rely on academics to generate long lists. But what about research suggestions from school educators? The Oxford Forum asked its teacher members to pose questions which they would like addressed by neuroscientists. Here the generic issue was: 'Many of my students are finding understanding of this or that difficult – what can neuroscience tell me to help me teach them?' Specific teacher questions were grouped under four headings:

1. Cognition of learning (attention, learning, motivation and self-esteem, memory, genetic development):
   - Is ADHD due to a lack of neural connections?

- Is there a negative influence caused by the interference from distracting factors such as noise, movement, etc.?
- What teaching strategies can improve pupils' sustained attention when surrounded by distractions?
- What, if anything, can a classroom teacher do to complement clinical treatments of those pupils with attentional problems which would be classified as developmental disorders, i.e., were a result of neurological deficits?
- What strategies can a classroom teacher employ to improve the attentional abilities of those pupils who have developed bad habits of attention?
- Can pupils keep their concentration better with an explicit understanding of the brain functions involved in keeping and losing concentration?
- Does abstract thinking develop separately within each subject?
- How do adolescent brains develop?
- Are there some developmental disorders which are specific to adolescence?
- What is the neuroscience of dyslexia?
- Why do people learn some things at some times more easily than at others, e.g., pupils in the top science set who cannot write A-level papers, but later in life write articulate research reports?
- Has neuroscience given us a handle which can help teachers select between competing neuroscientific models of learning?
- Why do some pupils learn more easily than others (in certain subjects or across all subjects)?
- Why are there such wide individual differences in perception, e.g., why do less-able pupils have difficulties in interpreting sparse diagrams?
- How is understanding an emergent property of the brain?
- How does experiential learning with external stimuli improve understanding and retention?
- Do successful adult learners make the best teachers?
- Does a pupil's own understanding of brain function influence their ability to learn?
- Can teachers enhance working memory (WM) function, e.g., through training/practice in chunking information?
- Can memory games and mind-mapping help pupils to better organize their thoughts?
- What is the influence of stress on teachers and pupils, and is it a good thing?

- Does teaching emotional literacy enhance children's personal well-being?

2. Environment of learning (sleep, nutrition including water, drugs, physical exercise, lighting, ventilation, noise):
    - Is natural light better for attention and memory?
    - Are there performance-enhancing drugs which are to be recommended?
    - Can recreational or prescription drugs have a detrimental effect?
    - Should pupils/teachers take fish oils?
    - What is the value of tranquillity/calm/reflection upon learning?
    - Can meditation techniques in the classroom improve children's attention through enhanced executive control?
    - What is the importance of good nutrition in cognitive terms?
    - Does exercise enhance cognitive ability?
    - Does this need to happen concurrently with the learning?
    - What about regular, brief, high impact exercise sessions?
    - Is the social environment in which pupils live relevant to their learning, e.g., lack of books in the home, poor role models, lack of parental support?
    - Is there evidence that lack of sleep impairs cognition?
    - Should there be a period of sleep in school? Would this be valuable for all ages?
    - Is the best time for study revision just prior to going to sleep?
    - What are the cognitive effects of drinking water for pupils?
    - Can you teach happiness?

3. Curriculum (literacy, numeracy, science, music, arts, IT/ICT):
    - What are we trying to help pupils to learn?
    - Do we value the academic pursuits above all others when we talk of learning?
    - Should the curriculum be designed around key concepts across different subjects?
    - Are targets a motivating factor or can they be demotivating?
    - Are children's brains different today because of their use of computers and IT?
    - Are there sensitive periods for the acquisition of complex grammar in first and second languages?
    - There is a website that claims that brains can be synchronized to a common frequency, which can then be utilized beneath

music to enhance performance in particular areas. Does this have any scientific credence?
- Do the CASE (Cognitive Acceleration through Science Education) materials and lessons need to be re-interpreted in the light of new neuroscientific evidence for cognitive strategies, such as analogical thinking?
- Are there differences between the brain representations of naive or folk physics, and school physics?

4. School organization (socializing, school hours, timetabling, play, coeducation, early years, gifted and talented):
- Should quieter pupils who seem to concentrate better on their own be taught separately from the more active, boisterous children?
- Is grouping pupils by age the best organization for their learning?
- Do children with learning difficulties have 'bad' bits of their brains?
- Should we teach to a disability or around it?
- How does executive control affect delayed gratification?
- Is there some neuroscience to support the 'big-school–small-school' effect?
- Are there are 'sensitive periods' in human brain development in which certain skills are learned with greater ease than at other times?
- What is the neuroscientific account of how gifted and talented pupils learn?
- How can teachers apply an understanding of gifted students' brain development to develop pedagogic strategies that could be integrated into mixed ability lessons for gifted and talented pupils who suffered lapses in attention due to being unstretched by the work from day to day?
- What motivates G&T pupils?

Maybe academics aren't the only ones to generate long lists! How much overlap, how much commonality is there between the two lists? It is such a merging of perspectives and aspirations that is contributing to the development of educational neuroscience as an interdisciplinary field of research and application. But the creation of true interdisciplinarity will require translation between the 'two languages, one lexicon' of education and neuroscience. Teachers don't need to be experts in neuroscience, but neither should they be inadvertently misled. Perhaps what is needed is a few interdisciplinary ambassadors to act as translators: a few teachers who change careers to become neuroscientists, and a few neuroscientists who take a couple of years for graduate teacher training and school classroom teaching.

An illustrative example of the need for translation arose at a meeting of the Oxford Forum, during the discussion following a presentation from a professor of pharmacology on neurochemicals, and the possibilities and dangers of smart drugs. The question was, how could drugs such as amphetamines, which usually enhance physical activity, reduce such activity in children with ADHD? The key term was 'inhibition', and its different usages in describing behaviour vs. neuronal interactions. ADHD seems to be the result of an underperforming (relatively immature) part of the brain's prefrontal cortex responsible for executive functioning, whereby the ability to inhibit off-task behaviours is inadequate. At a neuronal level, the inhibiting functionality seems itself to be inhibited. The effect of medications such as Ritalin is to strengthen or enhance this inhibitory functioning.

Similarly, the cognitive neuroscientific and educational data needed to be gathered in order to satisfactorily address many of the research questions posed above will ideally be mutually informative. In particular, longitudinal and large (non-clinical) population studies hold promise for neuroscience data to go beyond the behavioural in addressing educationally relevant questions. Certainly, educational neuroscience would benefit immensely from a large database of neuroscientific information about the typically developing brain. The problem is that no such database exists! But, it could easily be created with international cooperation. Given the thousands of MRI scanners now operating in laboratories and hospitals around the world, if each were to scan, say, 100 subjects in the age range of formal education (5 to 25 years), then combining these data could produce a database of normal brain structures with which to compare the neural effects of particular educational interventions in normal classrooms. This would require international multi-site studies using agreed protocols and multiple measures of brain structure and function, including behavioural measures and SES indicators, and so on. The very large size of the database should control for the multiple variables that we know affect educational outcomes beyond teaching and curriculum. Most education systems administer age-normed tests of literacy and numeracy, (SATS or CATS) together with international comparative tests (e.g., Trends in International Mathematics and Science Study (TIMSS)), and these ready-made large databases of standardized educational achievements could be used for standardized behavioural measures.

As an alternative means to tackling such neuro-epidemiological questions with a realistic sample of students, Czech neuroscientist Tomas Paus provocatively suggests setting up a brain scanner in a school basement.

This way, neuroscientists could image the developing brains of all students in all years as they move through their educational trajectory. Such educational population studies, Paus argues, have good prospects of producing useful information about the complex interactions between neural plasticity within neural development, and formal and incidental learning within institutional settings. To realistically capture such educational complexity, analytic models would have to be dynamic and non-linear in structure, explicitly incorporating feedback as a necessary feature of learning. Obvious ethical and logistic issues notwithstanding, the rationale for such a provocative suggestion is that at present, many of the research questions posed above cannot be addressed, the main reason being the weak mapping between individual variance in brain structure and behaviour due to the unique trajectories of individual neural development. Moreover, genetic data would have to be added to the mix, and the small contributory variance of individual alleles to the multiple genetic bases of educational cognitive behaviours currently imposes another limitation. Consequently, data from a whole-school population over, say, six years, could go a long way towards overcoming this weakness.

Limits to educational neuroscience

Before closing this chapter, we should note, however, that some commentators have argued that the education–neuroscience connection, while well meaning, is basically flawed. Leading American neuroscientist John Bruer, in an article published over ten years ago entitled 'Education and the Brain: A Bridge Too Far', argued that education cannot be directly informed by neuroscience as the former is unable to generalize from detailed specifics of neuronal processes to the behaviours observed in classrooms or with young children's learning. Descriptions of brain function at the cellular level are just too far removed from the behavioural to be of any use at school. Consequently, neuroscience, in its current state, cannot inform education. Bruer noted that experience-dependent neural plasticity is particularly sensitive to environmental complexity, and it occurs throughout the lifetime of the individual. His exemplar of an unsupportable neuroscience–education nexus is that the growth of new neurons in the brains of young animals implies critical periods of educational priming for young children. This critical stage argument proposes that some of the apparently effortless learning of very young children, particularly in learning to speak their native language, is indicative of a window of opportunity which closes with the slowing down of neuronal growth. The difficulty with this line of reasoning, Bruer points out, is that too little is known about the process to be predictive of what stage is attained at what age for any individual child. Rather, the neuroscience–education connection requires the mediation of cognitive science.

I agree that misinterpretations of the science are problematic, perhaps even potentially dangerous, and certainly counterproductive for informed considerations of educational issues. A popular example is the over-simplification of laterality studies, especially of split-brain patients, leading to programmes of left- and right-brain thinking which ignore the important caveat of this research that normally the two cerebral hemispheres are massively interconnected. The point here is that past over-simplifications of some neuroscientific findings do not *a priori* exclude an education–neuroscience nexus. Rather, this compels us to proceed with due caution, as usually exercised in the natural sciences if not in the popular media – especially when it comes to education.

Bruer's other main point was that the conceptual gap between neuroscience and education is too wide to be readily bridged, and so requires the mediation of cognitive science as a half-way point. To me this seems rather an unnecessary distinction – these two disciplines have been married as cognitive neuroscience for several decades. Nevertheless, for many experimental situations it is true that the different levels of description need to be bridged by intermediary levels. To this end, I have proposed a ladder of levels of partial variance in individual differences (Figure 1.1), with descending levels of reduction, and ascending levels of causation from education to brain structure (measurement indicators in parentheses, neuroscience acronyms to be explained later).

But there is nothing to prevent a research project skipping any number of levels depending on the relationship under investigation. For example, within the broad research question: Are there any predictive correlations between differences in brain structure and school outcomes? It is perfectly feasible to seek correlations between aspects of frontal cortical structure such as cortical thickness and educational outcomes across a designated age span (Figure 1.1, dashed arrow). And in fact, this has been done, as reported in Chapter 4. But at the same time, this need not be a one-way street from neuroscience to education. To continue with our example, despite informative psychological models of working memory, we don't fully understand how working memory is fractionated or instantiated at a neural functional level, so to complement neuroimaging investigations into the neural basis of working memory the efficacy of classroom interventions aimed to optimize working memory could be usefully informative.

My difference with Bruer's position is that connections can be made between any of the different levels on the ladder, including directly from neuronal processing to education, as with the many applications of Hebbian learning outlined in the next chapter. It depends critically on the experimental design, and the types of data that emerge. For example,

Education (grades at public and school examinations)

Learning (gain scores)

Intelligence (IQ / g-loaded tests, e.g., RPM)

Executive function (neuropsychological tests, e.g., Stroop)

Working memory (WM tests, e.g., n-back)

Frontal cortical function (fMRI with ROI in PFC)

Frontal cortical structure (MRI with DTI, VBM)

Neurophysiology of neurons, glial cells (single cell recordings)

Neuropharmacology of action potentials, synaptic processes (in vitro experiments)

Biochemistry of protein metabolism (genetic profiling)

Figure 1.1 Bridges of partial variance between education and scientific descriptions of the brain

rather than the research on critical, or sensitive, learning periods having nothing to say for curriculum design, such research could inform the timing and extent of the use of Vygotsky's Zone of Proximal Development (ZPD) as a pedagogical tool with which to base maximally challenging learning experiences in schools. Moreover, it suggests further research into whether there are critical periods for context-expectant neurological development and parallels for context-dependent neurological development. All of which underscores my argument that educators should be influencing the directions of cognitive neuroscientific research under the rubric of educational neuroscience.

However, I recognize that many educators are persuaded by the argument that the holistic level at which education is conducted is mismatched with the reductionist level at which scientific investigations are undertaken. This is hardly a new argument. Over a century ago, the father of modern psychology, William James, famously said in his *Talks to Teachers*:

> You make a great mistake ... if you think that psychology, being the science of mind's laws, is something from which you can deduce definite programmes and schemes and methods of instruction for immediate school room use.
> Psychology is a science, and teaching is an art.[1]

But James was speaking well before the development of educational psychology, pioneered by Vygotsky and Piaget, as a significant specialization within the psychological mainstream. Similarly, the early criticisms of the ambitions of educational neuroscience were made before the explosion in functional neuroimaging as the major investigative tool in cognitive neuroscience, and its consequent applications to understanding the brain bases of learning. My counterargument to James's is that more relevant and useful professional and classroom applications of educational neuroscience will become available as we gradually come to understand more about brain function through research, which answers educational questions about learning, memory, motivation, and so on.

Nevertheless, it has to be noted, despite neuroscientific and technological advances, scepticism about educational neuroscience has not completely abated, although it has become more diverse. In fact, one could note a rather curious dichotomy. On the one hand, there are those aging education academics who, after a lifetime of not understanding and disparaging all science, see no need to change their ways. On the other hand, there are the 'brain-based' enthusiasts who hope that the current fads of left–right thinking, brain gym, etc., will address the complexities and daily challenges of the mixed ability classroom. One way to portray these various perceptions of neuroscience and education can be to position

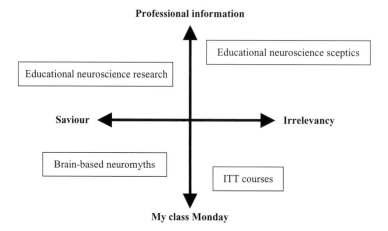

Figure 1.2 Perceptions of educational neuroscience schematic

them along each of two independent conceptual dimensions: a *salience* dimension, ranging from *saviour* to *irrelevancy*, and a *pragmatic* dimension, ranging from *professional background information to my classroom on Monday* (Figure 1.2).

Drawing these dimensions orthogonally to each other produces four quadrants. The top right quadrant, background information but practically irrelevant, represents the position of hardline sceptics. This is in contrast to the so-called brain-based schemes, mostly founded on neuro-mythologies, in the lower left quadrant representing educational neuroscience as the saving grace of education's future. Initial teacher training (ITT) or pre-service training courses have become increasingly pragmatic in recent years, at the expense, many have argued, of academic background. One might conjecture, therefore, that as ITT courses have yet to encompass educational neuroscience (although sadly in many ITT courses in the UK these neuromyths are taken uncritically as 'gospel'), that teacher training would be positioned in the lower right quadrant, possibly practical but its relevancy as yet unproven. It is my hope that in the years to come, ITT, together with teacher continuing professional development programmes, might move to a more central position in this schematic, where these tensions of theory vs. practice, background vs. lesson plan, might be better balanced. To this end, some American educators have recommended that all future doctoral studies in education should include a coursework component of educational neuroscience.

> Core courses in subjects traditional for education programs, as well as relevant interdisciplinary areas such as neuroscience ...

should be required for all entering doctoral students; these courses must be scholarly, rigorous, and intense enough to bear the burden of familiarizing students with the orienting concepts [of] the field, the culture of scientific enquiry, and the special demands of research in education.[2]

But this will come about, I suggest, only if teachers contribute to the educational neuroscience research effort by articulating educational problems and posing possible research questions, and then field-testing the resultant potential applications in their classrooms. Wouldn't we love to know more about questions such as:

- How can we tell if children are learning?
- How can we teach to optimize intelligent creativity?
- Why do individual students learn differently from each other?
- How can we minimize anxiety about school learning?
- Is there a critical period for learning a second language, or music, or physics?
- Should boys and girls be taught separately in some subjects?
- Are the brains of children today different from those of previous eras due to high levels of IT usage?

These are not matters for neuroscientists alone. As much as education can learn from neuroscience, so neuroscience can learn from education, not least by involving teachers in helping to set the educational neuroscience research agenda.

Educational neuroscience questions in a box

Ten years ago, *The Sunday Times* claimed that over 1000 schools in the UK were using 'brain-based' strategies for learning enhancement. Presumably there are more now, as indicated by Sue Pickering and Paul Howard-Jones's survey of UK teachers. This immediately suggests a preliminary programme of research:

- What is the current level of knowledge of cognitive neuroscience in the education community?
- To what extent do school teachers base any of their practice on their understanding of cognitive neuroscience?
- In particular, is there a describable folk psychology of school teachers regarding genetic heritability of intelligence and learning abilities, and genetic correlates with classroom environment?
- To what extent do university educators in teacher preparation pro- grammes incorporate cognitive neuroscience into their courses?
- To what extent do parents expect teachers to employ cognitive neuro- scientific evidence-based practice?
- To what extent do students perceive their teachers as being in or out of touch with modern developments in understanding brain function?

Presumably, a large number of schools have been embracing 'brain gym' programmes. Another line of research could be a rigorous evaluation of ex- isting interventions in schools which claim to be based on neuroscientific evidence, e.g., brain gymnastics which purport to increase cerebral blood flow. Would a psychometric analysis of a well-designed (e.g., using matched controls) quasi-experiment find the same level of benefit in school perfor- mance that anecdotal reports indicate?

2   Neuroimaging Technologies

Before going any further, we need to briefly survey current neuroimaging techniques, and while noting how informative of brain functioning these ingenious technologies can be, we must also note some of their many limitations and shortcomings. Readers who are already well acquainted with the workings of fMRI, PET, EEG and MEG could skip this section. Figure 2.1 is for reference throughout this and the following chapters.

Do teachers need to know much of the detail of how brain images are made? No. At least not for embracing educational neuroscience as a source of professional information for teaching practice. Of course, physics or mathematics teachers could use some of the detail as exemplars of application, and psychology teachers could use some of the neuroimaging findings to demonstrate brain function, in their classes. The main purpose of presenting this level of detail here is to make the important point that brain imaging is not magic, despite popular newspaper reports to the contrary. Rather, neuroimaging is a clever interdisciplinary interaction between physics, engineering, mathematics, statistics, computing, neurophysiology and psychology.

First and foremost, neuroimaging data are essentially statistical. Those coloured blobs ('technical' term for the highlighted part of a map or picture of the brain) represent areas of statistically significant different levels of neural activation compared with the activation levels of some comparative task or baseline. It is important to note that this is in the hands (mind?) of the experimenter. Change the statistical parameters and you can change the extent, number and distribution of the blobs. Statistically, histograms can serve the same function. In fact, some of the earliest neuroimaging articles did show significant activation levels as histograms – columns sticking out of the relevant regions of the brain. Of course this looked rather silly, and with colour printing, was quickly forgotten as a way of displaying data. However, the apparent ease with which brain images can be created has possibly inadvertently reinforced the silliest of the neuromyths: that we only use 10 per cent (or any other percentage) of our brain. Doing anything at all while lying in a scanner can produce abundant activations all over the brain. The real difficulty in designing an interpretable neuroimaging experiment lies in figuring out suitable control stimuli to contrast the main stimuli, in order to avoid showing that actually most of the brain is involved in any cognitive task. In the classroom

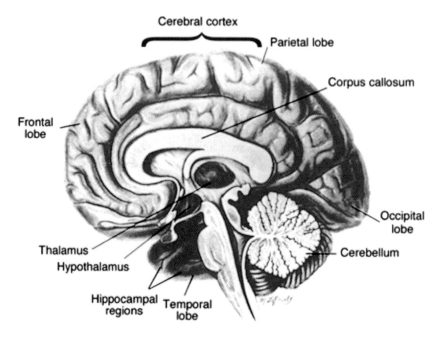

Figure 2.1 Drawing of the right hemisphere of a human brain as seen from the inside (medial surface); the front (anterior) of the brain is to the left of the diagram.
Source: Oscar-Berman, M. and Marinlovic, K. (2003) Alcoholism and the brain: an overview, *Alcohol Research & Health,* 27(2): 125–33.

it is absurd to think that only a small portion of any pupil's brain is involved in a particular activity, just because a particular area of the brain was reported in a neuroimaging experiment involving a simplified version of that classroom task.

In other words, most experiments find some neural correlates of some cognitive behaviour does not mean that the neural functioning in the areas of the brain identified in the neuroimaging study completely determine the supposed cognitive demands of the task that the subjects do in the scanner. As Nobel Laureate Charles Sherrington warned some 70 years ago: 'To suppose the [cortex] roof-brain consists of point to point centres identified each with a particular item of intelligent concrete behaviour is a scheme over-simplified and to be abandoned'.[1] That is, there are no simple mappings between brain function and cognitive behaviour. There is no *User's Manual of the Brain!* While it could be said that neuroscience is trying to write such a *User's Manual,* it should be noted that this is necessarily a bootstraps operation.

There are many different ways to make images of the brain. The suitability of any particular technique depends on several factors, not least the nature of the research question being asked, the sort of stimuli being used, the type of responses being solicited from the participants, and whether the participants are volunteers from the general population or a sample selected by some criterion of interest such as school pupils. Each neuroimaging technique has limitations in terms of the range and quality of data that its technology can produce.

Let's begin with the current favourite of television documentaries: functional magnetic resonance imaging (fMRI). This is really two neuroimaging techniques in one. Magnetic resonance imaging (MRI) shows brain structure by contrasting different types of cerebral tissue, particularly grey matter and white matter (the difference is discussed in Chapter 3), using a very strong magnetic field. The magnetic fields involved are typically 1.5 or 3.0 Tesla (T), which makes them many thousands of times stronger than the Earth's magnetic field. Consequently, MRI requires a superconducting magnet composed of tons of copper wiring in the shape of a large doughnut, cooled to very low temperatures by liquid helium to enable the superconducting currents necessary to generate the intense magnetic field. To be scanned, a subject's brain is positioned in the middle of the bore of the magnet by sliding the person into the circular hole in the middle of the doughnut (Figure 2.2).

To create brain images, MRI uses electromagnetic energy pulsed at a similar frequency to that of the waves received by your radio. The magnet bore is fitted with two concentric coils of metallic latticework: the inner (RF) coil transmits the pulsed energy input to the brain, the outer (gradient) coil collects the output signals (echoes) from the interactions between the input energy, the magnetic field and the brain tissue. These interactions involve quantum mechanical resonant energy transitions of protons in the hydrogen atoms in the water molecules in the brain tissue. The output signal of each water molecule is affected by its chemical environment. So, with a good deal of computer processing driven by some remarkably clever software programming, these myriad resonant echo signals can be combined into maps of the different tissue types, (using the mathematics of Inverse Fast Fourier Transforms to convert signals into grey-scale pixels) and hence into grey-scale images of a brain. What is especially clever about the outputs of the gradient coil is that they are spatially in 3D. This enables brain images as 2D slices to be constructed in three orthogonal orientations: sagittal, as though there was a camera looking in through the side of the brain; coronal, as though there was a camera looking in from the front of the brain; and axial, as though there was a camera in the neck looking up through the brain (Figure 2.3).

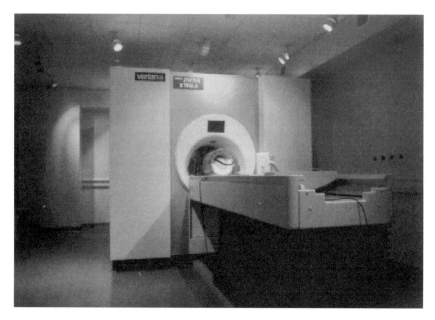

Figure 2.2 FMRI scanner, Centre for Functional Magnetic Resonance Imaging of the Brain (FMRIB), University of Oxford

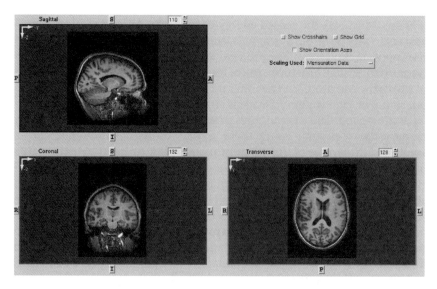

Figure 2.3 MRI scans in sagittal, coronal and axial orientations

MRI can be particularly useful for medical diagnoses of abnormalities arising from injury or disease, and is often used pre-surgically if an operation is judged to be the optimal intervention. MRI can be used in research to address questions about the variance in brain structures within a particular population such as children with learning difficulties, or changes in brain structures with development in general, for example, of children across the years of compulsory schooling.

Most brain imaging research, however, is interested in the brain in action. To image this requires functional magnetic resonance imaging (fMRI). FMRI images blood oxygen level changes in active areas of the brain using MRI with an additional response signal (a second echo). These blood oxygen level changes involve neurally induced dilations of local vasculature resulting in a dilation of concentrations of (slightly paramagnetic) deoxygenated haemoglobin, generating a blood oxygen level dependent (BOLD) response. The underlying physiology is that the brain's information processing cells, neurons, not only connect with one another (described in Chapter 3), but also connect to their nearby capillaries. Thus, the neurons can exert some control over the amount of blood oxygen they get when working particularly hard. In fact, this process has evolved to be so efficient that the concentration of blood oxygen usually overshoots the mark. Hence the BOLD signal reflects reductions in signal distortion arising from relatively enhanced neuronal activity in response to the experimental stimulus.

It cannot be emphasized enough – brains do *not* spontaneously light up; they retain their slimy brown colour. (Having said that, the new experimental technique of optogenetics enables researchers to breed genetically modified animals whose brains will selectively fluoresce in response to laser light.) To reiterate, the coloured blobs in neuroimages are statistical maps of significant data. In fMRI, these are created by colouring every voxel on a brain map in which there is a statistically significant correlation between the BOLD signal and the stimulus. A voxel is a small 3D volume of brain tissue, typically a few cubic millimetres. For example, voxels where the BOLD signal rises as the stimulus is shown might be coloured yellow–red, while voxels where the signal falls as the stimulus is shown might be coloured blue–purple in contrast. All other voxels are left uncoloured, the assumption being that activity in these bits of brain during these changes is not related to the stimulus. Isolated voxels don't count, only blobs of colour appear on the maps.

But even with rigorous statistical parameters (typically a z score of greater than 2.5, which for the non-statisticians, is like saying we'll only consider data which is in the ninty-ninth percentile of difference from baseline), for most stimuli, cortical activations appear nearly everywhere. This simply reflects the brain's massive interconnectivity. So, to try and

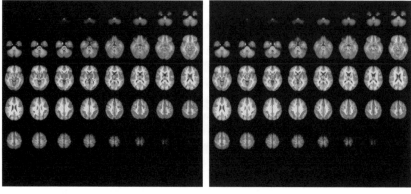

Stimulus activations   Control activations

Figure 2.4 Statistically significant fMRI activations for experimental stimulus and control

isolate those parts of the brain that might be more relevant to a particular task, a neuroimaging experimental design, as noted above, needs a control stimulus or contrast condition, the activations of which can be 'subtracted' or compared with the activations of interest (Figure 2.4). Designing a convincing and effective control stimulus often turns out to be the most difficult aspect of neuroimaging research. It is relatively easy to get someone in a scanner to see, hear, smell, touch, and so on (in Holland, couples have had sex in an MRI scanner), and perhaps more interestingly, to think, puzzle, remember, imagine. But then, for the control condition, getting your subject to, say, imagine something else while not thinking about the original requires considerable scientific creativity.

Thus fMRI entails a cycle of stimulus, neural responses, blood vasculature responses, BOLD signal detection, BOLD signal analyses, generation of imagery of blobs on standardized brains, and finally, interpretation. This last stage, it has to be said, is still very much a voyage of discovery: there is no *a priori* certainty about what any particular area of brain is contributing to any particular task. Of course, there is a vast experimental literature, and as a neuroscientific researcher you spend a great deal of time pouring over the reports, and looking at the blobs of others, to try and make sense of your data. And your report will add to that literature, and so to humanity's most fascinating albeit narcissistic enquiry to understand the workings of our own brains.

As with any investigatory technology, fMRI has implicit and explicit strengths and limitations. An important strength for participant safety and comfort is that fMRI is a non-invasive technique. Because this method of neuroimaging has no known deleterious effects (but see comments below), it can be employed for repeated measure designs (having the same subjects scanned again and again, over months or years). It also means that experiments presenting contrasting stimuli can be run for long time periods, say, an hour or more. The main drawback is that having a brain scan is not necessarily such a pleasant, relaxing experience. FMRI is noisy, physically restrictive and uncomfortable, even claustrophobic.

From the experimenter's point of view, there are limits to the BOLD response resolution which restrict the extent of fMRI data both spatially and temporally. Because vasculature changes are relatively sluggish, the BOLD relaxation time is typically between three and nine seconds. FMRI is therefore uninformative about the relevant neural temporal dynamics which typically happen in fractions of a second. The spatial resolution of fMRI data is limited by the voxel size, typically no smaller than one cubic millimetre. Whereas this is about as small as our visual system can distinguish, it is a huge volume of brain tissue at the cellular level, containing around 2.5 million neurons, interconnected with up to 1.5 billion synapses. One thing is certain, not all of these neurons will be doing the same thing in response to our stimuli. Perhaps most critically, fMRI cannot distinguish between the activations of neurons whose primary function is to excite the firing of neighbouring neurons, and neurons whose primary function is to inhibit the firing of its neighbours. The best we can do today is to make statistically significant estimates of which blobs of voxels have changes in blood flow presumably caused by the stimulated firing of a temporary majority of neurons involved in the task of interest.

For the future of neuroimaging, scanning technology needs to develop in ways that spatial resolution can be shrunk to voxels of a fraction of a cubic millimetre. This can be achieved with MRI scanners employing stronger magnets. Magnets of 7T, over twice as strong as the 3T magnets currently in widespread use, are already being trialled in some American laboratories. It has to be said, however, that subjects emerging from a 7T magnet often report that they don't feel too well. This raises the question: Are there any long-term side effects from lying inside a very strong magnetic field? The honest answer is that we don't know. Obviously none have been detected in hundreds of animal studies carried out before fMRI was deemed safe for humans. But the aetiology of dementia in humans is not well understood at present. Who knows if in 20 years' time, when some of today's neuroscientists and neuroscience experimental participants will be suffering from dementia anyway, that there might be some causal link between their disease and their neuroimaging experiences?

Another limitation to fMRI data is their generalizability, that is, how applicable are the findings from the group of people scanned in the experiment, typically around 12 to 15 in number, to the population at large? Plenty of potential subjects are excluded from fMRI studies. On medical grounds, people with neurological and other diseases, women who are or might be pregnant, people with shakes such as Parkinsonian tremors or suffering from drug withdrawal symptoms, especially from nicotine, people with poor eyesight (uncorrectable with temporary refractive lenses, as spectacles cannot be worn in the magnet – no room inside the close-fitting head mask) if responses to visual stimuli such as read instructions are required, and people with auditory sensitivity to loud and sudden noises are usually excluded. On physical grounds, people with pacemakers or any surgically implanted metals, people with metal from industrial experience such as iron filings or shrapnel from military wounds, people with facial tattoos which have used metal-based dyes and people with some metallic body piercings and unremoveable jewellery are not permitted in the magnet. Then there are experimental exclusions, especially people who are left-handed or ambidextrous. Neuroimaging is almost the exclusive province of right-handed subjects, because, as noted in Chapter 3, there is about a 95 per cent probability with extremely right-handed people that structure–function relationships will coincide sufficiently well to produce a group map of the activations of all of the participants in the study. That probability falls to 60 per cent with left-handers, some of whom will have their functional modules reverse lateralized (i.e., on the other side of their brains from where the majority of people's are located).

And they are just the *a priori* exclusions. Some people are just too big to fit comfortably inside the scanner – their shoulders are too wide or their torsos too bulky. Some subjects have to withdraw from a study because they find the experience too claustrophobic or uncomfortable, and literally hit the panic button. And compared with the age distribution of the general population at large, those who do participate in neuroimaging studies fit the Goldilocks criteria: not too old and not too young.

Perhaps not surprisingly then, the standard modern map of the human brain, the Montreal Neurological Institute (MNI) Atlas was made from the average (co-registration) of 305 extremely right-handed subjects, of whom 239 were male (male brains being usually more lateralized than female brains, even within the right-handed population), with an average age of 23 years 4 months (ranging from 19 years to 27 years), being the age range of the opportunity sample afforded by the student population on campus at the University of Montreal where the atlas was compiled. If you happen not to be a right-handed man in his mid-twenties, do you feel somewhat excluded? And as a much older right-handed male who can recall what I got up to as a student in my mid-twenties, the thought that this brain is the standard used to interpret the brain structure and function of all humans is, to put it mildly, rather alarming.

And it should be noted *en passant* that there is more to MRI than imaging. Voxel-based morphometry (VBM) uses high resolution MRI to compare cell density in the various (white and grey matter) tissues of the brain. These data are then combined to give regional or whole brain estimates of tissue density which can then be correlated with some psychological, demographic or behavioural measure of interest. For example, in a VBM study of intelligence led by Californian neurologist Richard Haier, it was found that grey matter volumes (about 6%) which correlated with IQ are distributed throughout the brain. Most are found in the frontal lobes, but many are also found in the parietal lobes for older subjects, and in the temporal lobes for younger subjects.

Another MRI-based technique is diffusion weighted MRI or diffusion tensor imaging (DTI). DTI is an MRI technique in which the directions of movement of the water molecules in various white matter tracts are compared. Significant directional biases (fractional anisotropy) are indicative of a more robust functional interconnectivity of those tracts. DTI enables the construction of connectivity maps in the brain. The importance of this will be elaborated on in Chapter 3, but for now it is worth noting that the functional specialization of regions of brain is largely due to the particular connectivity that region makes with its neighbouring and more distal regions. In other words, brain function is determined by interconnectivity, and DTI can help image this.

An important aspect of the interconnection story is the overlapping roles of the brain's other chemicals: neurotransmitters such as serotonin and dopamine, and hormones such as testosterone and oestrogen. Attempted regulation of these neurochemicals is a major plank in the modern medical repertoire. Magnetic resonance spectroscopy (MRS) uses the underlying physics of MRI to measure concentrations of some of these chemicals in the brain. MRS data can only be applied to the whole brain, and not all neurochemicals give a signal in the range detectable by current equipment. Nevertheless, MRS can be an informative tool in medical diagnosis, and in some experimental studies where a particular neurochemical is hypothesized to play a role in a particular aspect of cognition, for example, dopamine in decision making.

On a historical note, MRI was originally known as nuclear magnetic resonance (NMR) – not nuclear as in power or bombs but as in the nuclei of atoms. The name changed after PR sensibilities prevailed. The development of the physics of NMR/MRI as a technique to advance the quest to penetrate the internal structure of our material world has been recognized as being of such importance that its pioneering researchers have been awarded at least five Nobel prizes over the past 60 years: Rabi (1944) for discovering NMR; Purcell and Bloch (1952) for detection of the re-emission of resonant radiation; Ernst (1991) for developing NMR spectroscopy for use in medical diagnosis; Wuthrich (2002) for using NMR to identify the structure of large biomolecules such as proteins; and Sir Peter Mansfield, University of Nottingham (2003), for the development of MRI of whole biological structures.

That is more than enough about fMRI. The following reviews of other neuroimaging technologies are comparatively brief, as the above principles of neuroimaging generally apply.

Positron emission tomography (PET) images metabolism in active areas of the brain using emissions of a radioactive tracer injected into the blood. The radioactive tracer is usually an unstable isotope of oxygen within molecules of glucose. Radioactive glucose, as does ordinary glucose, crosses the blood–brain barrier and diffuses throughout the brain where it is metabolized and consequently emits radiation in the form of positrons (anti-matter electrons emitted by the nuclei of the oxygen isotopes). Positrons interact with nearby electrons to produce gamma radiation which is detected by a radiation counter surrounding the brain (see Chapter 9). In those areas of the brain more involved in responding to the experimental stimuli, the metabolic rate increases relative to baseline. Thus the rate of radioactive decay of positrons in those areas also increases relative to the rate in the rest of the brain.

As a neuroimaging technique, PET has its strengths and limitations. Because the half-life of the radiation is short (minutes) for obvious safety reasons, the presentation of experimental stimuli is restricted to block design over a short time period. That is, PET is more restrictive than fMRI for experimental design. And, whereas fMRI can be repeated with the same subjects, for example, to investigate the neural correlates of learning over a period of time, repeated subject designs are not conducted with PET – again for safety reasons. However, a big practical advantage of PET over fMRI is that PET is silent. Studies of music cognition or auditory sensitivity can produce better data within with the noisy environment of an MRI scanner. At the conceptual level, the PET surrogate variable of raised glucose metabolism is in a sense more directly associated with enhanced neural activity than the fMRI surrogate variable of increased blood flow. PET imaging of neuronal-associated glucose metabolism is in that sense more direct with fewer assumptions. For this reason, among others, PET is often the neuroimaging technique of choice for medical diagnosis.

As good as fMRI and PET are as techniques of locating where in the brain stimuli associated neural activations occur, they are relatively blunt instruments for understanding the temporal dynamics of neural activity – how brain functions change over time. That task is achieved with electroencephalography (EEG) and magnetoencephalography (MEG). EEG and MEG can provide synchronized temporal data on the time course of neural activity to complement the spatial mappings of fMRI and PET.

EEG records the electrical field of the neural activity generated by the cortex. These data are recorded by sensitive electrodes on the scalp (temporarily glued in place or, more conveniently, in a cap that fits over

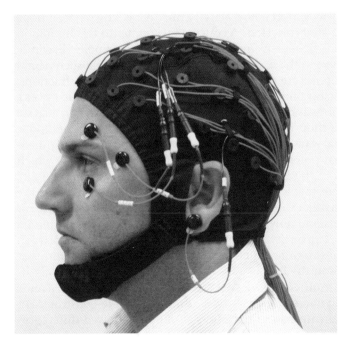

Figure 2.5 EEG cap (courtesy Jonah Oliver)

the head) (Figure 2.5). Because EEG is a passive technique, it is suitable
for use with young children, even babies, with EEG caps scaled down
to fit. The whole electroencephalogram signal is a complex waveform
(which sounds like white noise or static if played through an audio am-
plifier). Consequently, EEG recordings are usually categorized into different frequency bands (the Greek letters indicating order of discovery, not
frequency range, which is given in Hertz (Hz) = number of cycles per
second). Delta waves (<4 Hz) are seen in deep sleep. Theta waves (4–
8 Hz) are associated with drowsiness, daydreams, lucid dreaming, light
sleep and the pre-conscious state just upon waking, and just before falling
asleep. Alpha waves (8–12 Hz) are associated with a relaxed, alert state
of consciousness. Beta waves (>12 Hz) are associated with active, busy or
anxious thinking, and active concentration and attention. Gamma waves
(25–100 Hz) are associated with higher mental activity, including perception, problem solving, fear and consciousness.

A general limitation of EEG is that the signals, being recorded through
the scalp, are weak and distorted by the skull. Moreover, the signals generated by the cortex are further distorted by the electric fields generated
by parts of the brain beneath the cortex. That is, the extra-scalp electrical

field is a result of widespread neural activity, and that is why the technique is insensitive to spatial correlates. A conceptual counter to this limitation is to regard the EEG signal as being generated by electric dipoles (like little television antennas) in the brain. It must be emphasized that such neural electric current dipoles are not real – they are mathematical abstractions. The underlying assumption is that the electrical currents recorded over a patch of active cortex is due to the activity of a group of adjacent, aligned neurons, and that these can be modelled as an equivalent current dipole.

There are several ways in which neuroscientists can use EEG experimentally. Event-related potentials (ERP) are a particular form of EEG which measure changes in the EEG response to experimental stimuli. The ERP waveforms of interest typically occur 100, 300 or 400 milliseconds after the stimulus onset. In other words, ERP data are very temporally sensitive. For example, to understand how the brains of babies function when listening to speech sounds, University of Cambridge neuroscientist Usha Goswami found that the most significant changes in the babies' ERP waveforms at various electrodes in the babies' EEG caps occurred 300 milliseconds after hearing their mothers speak. Another way of analysing EEG data is by spatial mapping across all electrodes using the dipole construct. For example, American neuroscientist Michael O'Boyle showed differences in the production of alpha waves in right and left hemispheres between mathematically gifted boys and girls when engaged in a chimeric faces task (more of which in Chapter 8). A third approach is to use the whole complex EEG signal and to analyse it with non-linear dynamics (or, more popularly, chaos theory mathematics) and reduce it to a single dimension (such as the Haursdorff dimension). For example, a group led by American neuroscientist Walter Freeman did this with the EEG of the olfactory bulb of rabbits to investigate learning about new odours (more of which in Chapter 3). Of course, the ideal neuroscientific study would be to have both good spatial and temporal data, and following pioneering work by Greek neuroscientist Nikos Logothetis, many neuroscience imaging laboratories now combine ERP and fMRI data by using non-metallic EEG electrodes in the MRI scanner.

MEG is the measurement of the magnetic fields naturally present outside the head due to electrical activity in the brain. Like EEG, the technique is completely non-invasive and harmless. The magnetic fields generated by the brain's electrical activity are thousands of times smaller than the Earth's magnetic field, so MEG systems have to be situated within a magnetically shielded room. These tiny magnetic fields produced by brain activity can be measured using superconducting quantum interference devices (SQUIDs). To reduce interference from surrounding thermal fluctuations, the SQUIDs operate at very cold superconducting temperatures. Sensors are therefore placed in a large dewar containing liquid helium,

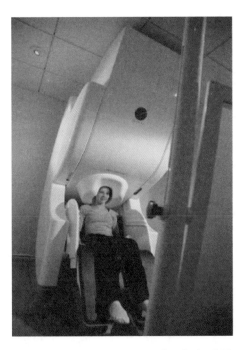

Figure 2.6 MEG scanner, the Oxford Neurodevelopmental
Magnetoencephalography (MEG) Centre

which looks like a very large hair dryer (Figure 2.6). MEG is especially applicable to the study of children because subject preparation is minimal, the scanner is silent, subjects can sit upright, their face is not covered by the detector array, they can be accompanied by a parent in the shielded room if necessary, measurements are easy and fast to perform, and data analysis is robust to some head movement during experimental tasks.

There are strengths and limitations to MEG. Compared with EEG, while spatial resolution is not significantly better, there is less blurring of signals by the skull and scalp with MEG. As with EEG, MEG data are interpreted by the construct of hypothetical dipoles. But unlike EEG, MEG can detect synchronized neural activity which does not produce a net increase in signal strength. MEG data can be displayed as movies of spreading and contracting activations over the cortical surface. For example, Morten Kringelbach and colleagues at the University of Oxford have used MEG to construct such a movie to portray the changing involvement of various brain regions in the first half-second of visual word recognition.

What all of these major brain-imaging techniques have in common is the use of surrogate variables to measure neural activity. Of course, it would be ideal to directly measure what the neurons are actually doing at the time, but there is no way to do this with humans. In some animal studies, recordings are made directly from neurons, but only from a few of these cells at a time, not the millions involved in any act of cognition. So, neuroscientists use surrogate variables of physiological changes which are believed (assumed, hoped) to be directly (and proportionately) associated (correlated) with the neuronal activity. In PET, this is glucose metabolism measured by radioactive decay of an injected tracer isotope. In fMRI it is decrease in deoxygenated haemoglobin due to increased blood flow through the capillaries surrounding the active neurons. In EEG and MEG the surrogate variable is the hypothetical electric dipole. The images of these variables are the familiar coloured blobs. The selection of these surrogate variables is based on the most up-to-date scientific understanding of brain physiology to hand, but since science is about changing our understanding, new surrogate variables will undoubtedly replace these in the future.

An important consequence of using surrogate variables, however, is that the hypotheses that can be tested are necessarily correlational, not causal. This point is often overlooked in the popular media: neuroscientists most often claim to have found a neural correlate of some act of cognition, not its cause. For example, John Duncan at the University of Cambridge found neural correlates in the bilateral (both sides) frontal cortex of subjects performing difficult spatial and verbal items from a standardized IQ test. Duncan was not claiming that these frontal areas of the brain caused subjects to be able to solve these problems, just that these brain areas are somehow involved.

But although most neuroimaging data only inform us about correlations between levels of neural activation and behaviour, neuropsychological analyses of neural lesions or trauma, for over a century before the invention of modern neuroimaging, have supported conjectures of neural causation. Perhaps the most famous is that of the French neurosurgeon Paul Broca, who in 1861 found in a postmortem examination of a patient who had lost his ability to speak following a stroke that the damage was focused in the left frontal cortex. This left frontal region is now known as Broca's Area and was originally thought to be the brain's speech centre. Today the exact function of this region in supporting speech is not so clear (more of which in Chapter 7). Clearly there are many advantages in examining the dysfunctions of patients with brain damage, and the Russian neuropsychologist Alexander Luria did much to advance this field with his diagnoses of stroke patients during the twentieth century. But, a limitation to this approach is that it is essentially opportunistic. The location and extent of lesions are obviously uncontrolled, and due to the distribution of major vasculature tracts, some areas of brain are affected more frequently than others, while other areas are generally

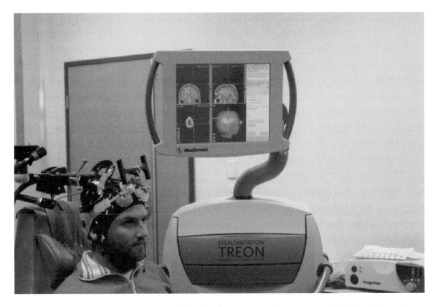

Figure 2.7 TMS apparatus, School of Human Movement, University of Queensland (courtesy Jonah Oliver)

spared. Furthermore, the brain's remarkable plasticity in recovery can limit interpretation of lesion data if not tested immediately after the injury (which is hardly a good time for the patient).

An experimental technique that does enable causal hypotheses to be tested is transcranial magnetic stimulation (TMS). TMS temporarily disables a small area of brain to test its necessity for an aspect of behaviour. TMS is based on the laws of electromagnetic induction: a current passing through a coil of wire (in this case, as a figure of eight) generates a magnetic field perpendicular to the current direction in the coil (Figure 2.7). A rapid change of this magnetic field elicits in turn a transient electric field, which if placed on the scalp scrambles the electrical activity of neurons of the cortex beneath, which may interfere with the activity of interest. Commercially available stimulators offer the possibility to generate peak magnetic fields up to 2.5 T, with frequencies up to 30 Hz. In order to precisely localize the area stimulated by TMS, the target area is first imaged with high resolution MRI. Then, by using frameless stereotaxy the investigator can position the TMS coil over the scalp so that the peak of electric field is localized on the desired area. In sum, TMS induces a very localized temporary brain lesion.

Is TMS safe? Single pulse TMS has no reported harmful side effects, although repetitive (multipulse) TMS has been known to induce epileptic seizures in susceptible individuals. At an international workshop held in 1996, safety guidelines were established for the parameters of repetitive TMS which have been universally accepted by the scientific community. Since then no cases of seizure have been reported. As with fMRI, many potential subjects have to be excluded on safety grounds. People with pacemakers, aneurysm clips, prosthetic valves, intracranial metal prostheses, pregnant women and young children are all excluded from research studies. TMS has also been used in medical treatment, where repetitive TMS has been used with patients suffering from clinical depression.

As with all techniques of studying the brain, TMS has its strengths and limitations. Its main strength is that by interfering with the normal functioning of a brain area, TMS enables experimental inferences to be made about a causal link between this brain area and behaviour. Also, because of the limited duration of the interference it induces, TMS can be used to investigate when a brain area is making its critical contribution to behaviour. A limitation is that since the magnetic field decreases rapidly (as the inverse square of the distance), only the most external parts of the brain can be targeted with TMS.

There are yet other neuroimaging techniques coming into wider use. Of these, near optical infra red (NOIR) and the new nuclear magnetic resonance mobile universal surface explorer (NMR-MOUSE) hold promise for applications in educational rather than just laboratory settings (see Chapter 10).

In sum, there are several general limitations of neuroimaging. First, because of the brain's massive functional interconnectivity, mappings from structure to function are not simple or one to one. Consequently, there are no unambiguous neural correlates of learning difficulties, learning styles, and so on. Second, the functional data are as good as the surrogate measures of brain activation employed. Third, activation maps are statistical, and are usually group maps where the considerable individual differences in brain structure and function are averaged. Fourth, the brain is structurally very complex: brain function is essentially nonlinear. In other words, understanding how our brains actually function is a very tough problem. Nevertheless, despite these limitations and caveats, whenever I am having an fMRI scan, as uncomfortable and restrictive as that is, I feel tremendously privileged to be alive at this point in history when for the first time I can see a picture of my own brain.

3　Learning and Memory

The question which this chapter attempts to address is this: How does our brain enable us to learn and remember? A neuroscientific account of learning and memory involves delving into the cellular level of the brain's operation in order to consider the functioning of neurons, the brain's billions of interconnected information processing cells. Thus the opening question can be rewritten: Which dynamic processes in the vast network of neuronal functioning enable learning? The key construct in answering this question is adaptive plasticity, the capacity of the brain to change at a neurophysiological level in response to changes in the cognitive environment. Or to recast the question more prosaically: What alters in the brain in order for us to learn (anything new)?

The brain contains an estimated ten billion neurons, the main information processing cells, together with even more glial support cells, notably the astrocytes which provide nutrition to the neurons. Neurons are characterized by having many branches forking off their cell body. Most of these branches are dendrites which receive incoming information from other neurons. One main branch is the axon which sends information to other neurons. Interneuronal connections are made via synapses, a small space between an axon and a dendrite of another neuron. Communication is initiated by an axon discharging an (electrochemical) action potential which stimulates the release of neurotransmitters. These neurochemicals diffuse across the synaptic gap to be taken up by receptors which stimulate the dendrite, and possibly stimulate another action potential. If sufficient dendrites are stimulated more or less simultaneously then that neuron will generate an action potential in its axon. In such a way, information is passed on around a neuronal circuit or neuronal group. As neurons typically have tens of thousands of dendrites, the total number of synapses in an adult brain is estimated at around 100 000 billion. So, the often-cited 'fact' that the human brain is the most complex structure in the universe might have some basis – not that anyone is able to tour the entire universe to check.

However, as noted in the preceding chapter on neuroimaging technologies, the main thrust of cognitive neuroscience research has been the delineation and analysis of functional modules in the brain. How does this neuronal level of description fit with the constructs of brain modules and neural systems? Actually quite well. Neurophysiological evidence suggests that the units of brain function are neuronal groups, with neurons more strongly connected locally than distally. However, as neuroscientists well recognize, modularity begs the question of intermodule synchronization, or binding. For example, although separate areas of the dominant hemisphere may be crucial for reading and speaking, synchronized communication between these areas must also be a fundamental aspect of brain functioning, or reading a piece of written text aloud would not be possible. The means by which intermodular binding is accomplished is one area of neuroscientific puzzlement, and therefore research. Presumably temporary functional connections are selected via inhibitory processes as much as excitatory. But however managed, intermodular binding is but one example of the ubiquitous neurophysiological characteristic of neuronal interconnectedness.

Individual brains

One prediction we can make from such extensive complexity is that, although all healthy brains develop along well-described courses, there are many sources of difference between individual brains. Noble Laureate Gerald Edelman lists eight main areas of neural developmental difference:

1   Developmental primary processes, e.g., cell division, adhesion, differentiation and death.
2   Cell morphology, e.g., shape and size, dendritic and axonic aborizations.
3   Neuronal connection patterns, e.g., number of inputs and outputs, connection order with other neurons.
4   Cytoarchitectonics, e.g., cell density, thickness of cortical layers, layout of columns.
5   Neurotransmitters, both spatial (some cells and not others) and temporal (some times and not others) variance.
6   Dynamic responses, e.g., synaptic electrochemistry, synaptic reinforcement, neuronal metabolism.
7   Neuronal transport, e.g., ion channel efficacy.
8   Interactions with glia.

What all of these neurobiological terms mean in detail needn't detain us – the important point is that it is a long list of sources of individual difference. And, moreover, the fact that these morphogenic molecular and cellular processes are mostly non-linear, chaotic in the mathematical sense, means that their outcomes cannot be precisely predicted. To emphasize this, we can say without fear of contradiction that no two human brains are, have ever been or ever will be, identical. This applies to identical

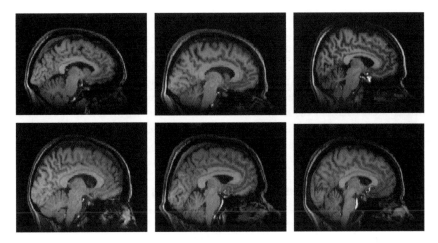

Figure 3.1 Six MRIs – sagittal orientation ~2–3 mm off the midline left hemisphere (courtesy Peter Hansen)

twins, who are not identical people, and for that matter, to any possible human clones. Politicians who are quick to condemn cloning experiments should note that it is impossible to replicate exactly the brains of Hitler, Einstein or of any other individual from the past. For a classroom teacher, this simply underlines that uniqueness of each child in his/her charge. To illustrate this point, note the individual differences in the contours of the six adult brains whose MRI scans are shown in Figure 3.1. Whereas each brain has the same basic configuration, just as faces usually have two eyes above one nose and one mouth, the details of brain structure are also similar in overall form but recognizably individual.

Do these individual differences in brain structure affect cognitive functioning? Well, yes, although in the absence of any obvious pathology, at our present state of knowledge, it is usually not possible to predict exactly what these cognitive differences are outside of a specific experiment. In the study which produced the images in Figure 3.1, the individuals whose brains are shown were all healthy and of above average IQ. One had German as her first language. Can you tell who? Obviously not. Television crime dramas to the contrary, the days of using neuroimaging alone for educational assessment and diagnosis seem a long way off. Which is not to say that individual fMRI data could not complement other behavioural and cognitive diagnoses of educational disability.

The images in Figure 3.1 illustrate this point. While our unidentified participant grew up learning to speak German, the other five participants grew up learning to speak English. To return to our main question: What changed in their brains to enable all this learning? When we learn, what changes in our brains so that later we can recall an item of knowledge or perform a rehearsed behaviour? The most widely accepted model of how the brain learns and remembers was first proposed in the 1940s by a Canadian high school English teacher turned neuroscientist, Donald Hebb. One can imagine him standing at the front of his classes, expounding the virtues of Chaucer or Shakespeare, while wondering what is going on between the ears of his pupils. Haven't we all wondered this at some time or other while teaching? 'This lesson is going well, and I seem to have their attention, but am I getting through to their brains?'

Hebb's model of learning through synaptic plasticity

A distinguishing feature of brain tissue, in contrast to all other body tissue, is that the neurons are each connected to tens of thousands of others at their synaptic junctions. Hebb's insight was that, since other body organs don't behave as the brain does, it must be synaptic processes that enable learning. Hebb proposed that repeated coincident firings of the particular synapses involved in 'processing' the response to a particular stimulus results in a permanent physiological change. In terms of neuronal functioning, this change may be manifested as either a stronger excitatory or stronger inhibitory signal. In other words, an item of learning can be instantiated in the brain through the biochemical processes that convey information across the synapses which become more efficient with repetition. 'Neurons that fire together, wire together' has become the catch phrase for the brain's adaptive plasticity.

The power of Hebb's model is that it can explain how functional modules in the brain can learn. Neuronal groups, which can often be found as cellular columns in the cortex, are responsible for processing particular types of information, for example, a specific edge orientation in visual cortex or a specific sound frequency in auditory cortex. Intermodular neuronal circuits involve feedforward and feedback pathways between the various neuronal groups. These synchronized neural pathways can themselves 'learn' via Hebbian rules by becoming more efficient in response to repeated coincident stimulation of the synapses along the route.

It was over 50 years ago when Donald Hebb first proposed his model of how the brain learns and lays down memories through the reinforcement of synaptic function following repetition. At that time, Hebb had no means of testing his conjecture. In recent years, his insight has been substantiated by several neuroscientists who have earned Nobel prizes for their successes. But Hebb's account can explain the results of many neuroscientific experiments. An early confirmation of Hebb's model can be seen in the results of a 1970s American study led by neuroscientist Walter

Freeman into the non-linear dynamics of brainwaves. The researchers needed a brain which had a large area dedicated to just one main purpose; they chose a rabbit's brain because rabbits can be very single-minded at doing what rabbits do best – sniffing and detecting odours – and a rabbit has a large olfactory lobe in the front of its brain dedicated to enabling that behaviour. The experimental design was quite straightforward – give the rabbit something new to smell and record the EEG signal of its olfactory lobe. Then give the rabbit something familiar to smell and repeat the EEG recording. Differences in the EEG signal, then, should be indicative of the learning required for an odour to become familiar. Comparing EEG signals turns out not to be so straightforward – a plot of the signal across all frequencies appears random or chaotic, like white noise or static. But these researchers were able to analyse these EEG signals by employing mathematical techniques from non-linear dynamics (chaos theory). They showed that the EEG signals had a non-linear structure which could be quantified as a dimensionality of its complexity (Haursdorff dimension (H)). The EEG response to a novel odour immediately after sniffing it produced a high complexity (around $H = 8$), consistent with the rabbit directing significant neural resources into the identification or categorization of the new odour. After all, it might indicate something good to eat or a potential mate, in which case not a moment to lose. Or, it could indicate a life-threatening predator, a fox or a dog so, again, not a moment to lose. What about the EEG response complexity of the familiar odour? Immediately after sniffing this odour the complexity fell to a lower value (around $H = 2$), indicating that less neural resource was required to identify a well-learnt smell, consistent with Hebb's prediction that learning is enabled through more efficacious interneuronal processing. However, after a second or two, the value of the complexity then rose to the pre-sniffing 'resting' value which, it's important to note, was not zero, but quite high (around $H = 6$). So long as we are alive, our brains are never at rest. Healthy neurons, even if not being stimulated for intense activity, still fire at random, in preparation for action. Our brains evolved as sentinels to enable us to cope with not knowing what's going to happen next – a critical survival strategy in a random and often unpredictable world.

Teaching certainly involves coping with not knowing what's going to happen next – take a class of excitable young 5-year-olds, or another group of surly 15-year-old adolescents. All of the best lesson planning cannot pre-empt the behaviour of the child who, unbeknownst to you, is having an 'off' day. Successfully coping with the unexpected is what provides teaching its satisfaction and, obviously, its stress. Moreover, in certain circumstances, non-linear brain states will be hypersensitive to fluctuations in conditions – the much maligned butterfly effect of chaos theory. A dropped ruler, an uncontrolled fart or a slip of the tongue made while answering a teacher's question, and a class can dissolve into laughter or erratic behaviour. In other circumstances, however, cognitive outputs can be highly predictable and linear. The lowering of complexity with familiar stimuli is what we experience as the automaticity of true learning, the proverbial not forgetting how to ride a bicycle, perhaps most impressively seen with chess masters playing blindfold.

Further research has both realized a better understanding of the neurochemistry of synaptic processes and at the same time delineated limitations to the applicability of the Hebbian model. This has raised further questions about learning as a brain function. For starters, not all learning is Hebbian. Many events have such salience or emotional potency – especially events that are frightening – that we do not need repetition for learning. In the hectic urban environment in which most of us live, we have probably all experienced something like the following scenario. You are about to step off the pavement to cross a road when a blue van comes speeding 'out of nowhere' and nearly runs you over. From then on, whenever you see a blue van, even if it is parked, your heart will pound a little faster. Or imagine you are walking along a path near the edge of a cliff, and suddenly the ground beneath your feet begins to crumble, and you have to grab on to a nearby bush, or companion, to prevent yourself going over the edge. For the rest of your life, whenever walking in similar conditions, you will be very wary. A cognitive capacity for learning from a single life-threatening event so as not to have to suffer a repetition with, in all probability, a fatal outcome, has obvious positive survival value. We can readily construct an evolutionary story along these lines to illustrate the adaptive value of one-shot aversive learning. This theme is a focus of Chapter 6 on the importance of emotion for learning and motivation. For now, let's note that non-Hebbian learning is not restricted to negative experiences – significant positive events can also result in one-off learning: remember that surprise birthday party or that magic evening with one's partner/lover?

But for learning in school, highly significant one-off events are rather the exception than the rule. In times long gone, the threat of corporal punishment did engender a degree of fear-invoked learning, especially, it seems, in the Catholic boys' schools of certain teaching orders, the products of which can still recite Latin catechisms word perfectly some 50 years on. Today, thankfully, there are few educators who advocate a return to that Dickensian stereotype of pedagogy, although there are more than a few who argue that the ritual of public, competitive examinations has much the same fear-invoking effect. However, none of these aversive impositions, historic or contemporary, can do away with the necessity of repetition for most school learning. But that in turn raises a question about adaptive plasticity for which, it is important to note, cognitive

neuroscience does not know the answer: Are there thresholds of stimulation for permanent learning? Certainly the considerable range of variables contributing to individual neurological differences would suggest
that there are individual learning thresholds, a suggestion which supports
teachers' common knowledge that some students 'get it' much quicker
and more readily than others.

Moreover, before considering the implications for curriculum and pedagogy, it's worth noting that not all Hebbian learning takes place at school,
college or university. Another way to regard Hebbian learning is as a means
by which our brains represent repeated regularities in our mental, cultural
and physical environments. Clearly, many of the drivers for doing this are
genetic. All healthy infants learn to grasp, walk and speak in their mother
tongue(s). Hebbian learning in early development is nicely illustrated by
babies babbling. Through fluctuations of their larynxes, young babies can
babble with every different sound that a human is able to make. In doing this, babies are not, as sometimes claimed, universal linguists: their
laryngal outputs are random. However, by as early as 6 to 8 months of
age, their repertoire of babbling sounds has become constrained to the
phonemes of the parents' mother tongue(s) and accent(s). Plots of the frequency profiles or formants of vowel sounds match those of the parents
in relationship to one another, except that the baby's profiles are all located within a higher frequency range – hence 'motherese' is spoken at a
deliberately higher than usual frequency, especially by fathers. This also
raises an interesting question for music education of whether singing can
be effectively taught to young pupils by men whose voices are naturally
pitched an octave lower?

The phenomenon of babies learning to babble in their mother tongue
is also a good example of the effects of synaptic pruning. Seemingly paradoxical, it is the progressive loss of synapses as a central feature of early
neural development which is necessary for the development of specialized
cognitive abilities and general intelligence. From birth, neurons rapidly
continue to synapse on to other neurons for the first two years or so. Estimates suggest that a 2-year-old child has at least 40 per cent more neurons than an adult, and hence a prodigious relative excess of synapses.
However, although they have more neurons and synapses than adults,
2-year-olds are not more intelligent. Two-year-olds do not rule the world,
despite what their parents might think at times. The reason is that much
of this neuronal surplus has not been affected by any stimuli; many of
the potential neuronal circuits have not had their synaptic processes reinforced in a Hebbian manner through repetition. In other words, much
of this neuronal surplus at 24 months is not used to represent any behaviour or knowledge of the world. This, incidentally, is why we don't
have memories of our birth and our first months out of the womb. As

we grow, we reinforce huge numbers of neuronal circuits to create our mental representation of our world and our place in it. But the neuronal circuits that are unused wither away. That is, neurogenesis, the growth of neurons in an infant brain, is mediated by a selective pruning of this less differentiated surplus to reach the relatively more differentiated neuronal complexity of maturer brains. It is this neural 'sculpting' that creates our unique set of memories and worldviews that contribute to our individual personalities.

The process of synaptic generation and pruning continues in a much more restricted manner throughout the lifespan, with a special burst in the frontal regions of the cortex in adolescence. But there is a specific implication for education that arises directly from babies babbling the phonemes of that baby's mother tongue. Due to an absence of repetition, the non-mother tongue phonemes are not learnt as part of the child's vocal repertoire. This is why, as adults, we usually speak foreign languages with an accent. Moreover, as American language scientist Pat Kuhl has shown, our ability to learn second languages, as opposed to most other subjects, declines with age. Musical abilities often show a similar age relation. At least, this is true for learning through an immersion pedagogy. It is not the case that learning a second language is impossible after childhood, it is just that for such learning to be effective the curriculum requires 'top–down' lessons in grammar, spelling and other structural aspects of the target language. This ability of young brains to assimilate languages via informal learning is an example of a sensitive, but not critical, period for learning. Sensitive, but not critical, does suggest that second language learning might be better moved out of the secondary school curriculum and into the junior primary, or even early childhood syllabi, assuming of course that the teachers concerned have the appropriate professional development to effectively assume second language teaching. But sensitive, not critical, does not support hot-housing, or a regime of Latin flash cards before breakfast. Infant hot-housing is another example of running too fast and loose with the science. Neuroscientist Bill Greenough famously showed that the brain development of rats was denser and more connected if they were brought up in a stimulating environment – treadmills to run on, places to hide in, and so on – compared with rats confined to a laboratory wire cage. The conclusion of the scientists was, since rats in the wild enjoy a rich and varied environment, an understimulating upbringing can limit neural development in the young. But this does not mean Latin flash cards before breakfast. The 'natural' environment of most children in Western societies is, if anything, over-stimulating. This is why hot-housing has only been shown to improve cognition in socially deprived children, and then only as a means of catching up to age norms.

All early developing, fundamental life-essential abilities – grasping, walking, talking, and so on – require repetition to learn, and to attain the high levels of competence that most children enjoy. Three significant issues arise from this observation. The first, as noted in Chapter 1, is that school learning relies on appropriating brain functions which originally evolved for other purposes. Much of school learning, especially literacy and numeracy, does not enjoy similar genetic drivers as walking and talking. Many parents of children beginning school get distressed when their child, who learned to walk and talk so easily at home, does not learn so readily in the classroom. It has to be emphasized that learning to read is *not* as easy for many children as learning to walk and talk. A popular educational philosophy of the 1970s, with roots in the writings of Rousseau, was that all learning, including school learning, should be 'natural'. As well intentioned as this approach was, one unfortunate outcome was the unrealizable expectation of some teachers and parents that all school learning should come easily or, in extreme cases, be abandoned. Schools and teachers were unreasonably castigated when this did not happen. That said, it is certainly the case that for some gifted children, academic learning is accomplished as easily as walking and talking. However, for some other children most school learning is a struggle. Consistently, research into early language processing suggests that there might be some underlying relationships between a child's facility in learning to talk and learning to read, and even learning to walk and learning to read (Chapter 7).

The second issue arising from early childhood Hebbian learning is that of the role of context. No stimulus is an island, so to speak. Every stimulus is seen/heard/tasted/smelt along with an uncountable, myriad associated stimuli. How does the brain 'know' what, out of all of this, is being repeated? Consider a young infant learning to walk. The first few unaided toddles might be in a park during a family picnic. The next might be at grandma's, to where the infant has been whisked in order to demonstrate this landmark achievement. And the next, to parental surprise, occurs in the local supermarket – each instance involving a different walking surface (grass, carpet, tiles), different objects to avoid (gardens, furniture, shoppers), and so on. How does the brain extract the essence of walking from all of these particular instances where the actual instances of walking are necessarily adjusted on each occasion to suit the different circumstances? This question intrigued American neuropsychologists Esther Thelen and Helen Smith. These two researchers decided to study how infants learn to walk. In doing this, human newborns are different from most of their animal counterparts in that they cannot independently locomote from birth. How we've marvelled while viewing many a David Attenborough wildlife documentary at the birth of a gnu, or zebra, when, after a good shake and a lick from its mother, the newborn foal trots off with the herd. Meanwhile, your human baby just lies in its crib. Yet, stand your baby on your tummy, and you can feel its push-down reflex. There is walking potential, it's just that the relative weight of the top-heavy head and torso are too much of a burden for the fledgling legs. It usually takes over 12 months for the leg muscles to 'catch up'. But, thought Thelen and Smith, what would happen if this body weight could be supported – could walking be learned earlier than 'schedule'? To find out, baby 'volunteers' were placed in water baths and on treadmills to support their weight, and encouraged to walk. Videotapes of the motion of reflector spots on the leg joints captured the behavioural aspects of the babies' learning. Thelen and Smith used non-linear dynamics to show how walking emerged as the default form of locomotion, but along with other forms of locomotion such as skipping, hopping, jumping, and so on which we delight in using in dance and sport. As to the motivating question of how context affects repetition learning, they insightfully concluded that:

The global order and the local variability are the same thing; they are inexorably tied together in a way that confers a special status on context . . . it is through repeated here-and-now experiences that the global order is developed.[1]

But, just how does the brain tie together local variability (e.g., instances of walking in different settings, instances of speaking in different conversations) to develop a global order (e.g., the ability to walk anywhere, the ability to speak for any purpose)? This is currently another of the great unknowns of brain functioning. Presumably attentional processes play a major part. We know that gaining a pupil's attention is necessary for them to learn (Chapter 4). But from a neuroscientific perspective, this just begs the question. Solving this enigma should be worthy of a Nobel prize. Regardless of such accolades, given that the essence of school learning is the acquisition of transferable life skills (global order) from multiple instances of subject-related tasks (local variability), understanding how our brains might accomplish this could be of profound significance for many aspects of formal education, not least curriculum design and normative assessment. Educational psychologists have noted for many years that not all school learning is context-free. A common example in senior high school mathematics and science is seen when students who can balance algebraic equations cannot apply this skill to chemical equations, or where equations of motion can be solved in physics class but not in a calculus lesson. The Hebbian model of learning predicts that coincident reinforced stimulation of associated neuronal circuits could result in context-dependent learning. While this is to some extent unavoidable, it can mitigate against transference of learning from one subject area to another.

Perhaps the most important implication for education of a Hebbian account of adaptive plasticity is that Hebb's model strongly supports what teachers have long known: that repetition is necessary for effective and reliable learning. This in turn has implications for curriculum design. In contrast to the usual lock-step linear progression curriculum, a spiral curriculum better incorporates Hebb's principle of reinforcement. A spiral curriculum offers more opportunities for the necessary repetition for learning by presenting similar concepts in new and increasingly complex contexts – the global concept emerging from the many instances of the local, as described by Thelen and Smith. But this, in turn, suggests that in curriculum design, depth should preside over breadth, with core knowledge having priority. An over-crowded curriculum mitigates against high general levels of basic skills, and frustrates permanent change in children's naive concepts. Of course, the possibility of an over-crowded curriculum is a political issue, especially, as is increasingly common, whenever school education is seen as the solution to some perceived social problem.

Another implication of a Hebbian account of learning addresses one of the disappointments with teaching that I experience. Despite my best efforts to provide stimulating lessons in which the content is presented with careful clarification, never do all of my students produce test papers which are 100 per cent correct. My students say that they enjoy the lessons, but still don't always 'get it' completely. Why not, I wonder? Why don't all school matriculants, say, get full marks in all of their examination papers following so much intense and specialized teaching? Leaving aside the myriad obvious personal and social factors for a moment, why does formal education seem at times so frustratingly inefficient?

Interestingly, the Hebbian model of neural plasticity not only can account for inefficiencies in learning, but can also explain why 'erroneous' learning is so hard to eliminate or counteract. A potential downside to the brain's ubiquitous neural plasticity is that what gets reinforced tends to stay learnt, only attenuating slowly with non-use. This has been nicely demonstrated with a European fMRI study on learning to juggle. A group of university students with no previous experience at juggling were recruited as subjects. They were given MRI scans to record their neural structures as an experimental baseline. Half of the group were then taught to juggle over a 3-month period, after which all subjects were rescanned. VBM analyses revealed significant increases in the grey matter density of posterior brain areas involved in visual motion perception and anticipation of the jugglers, but not in the control group. The group difference was still present in follow-up scans after a further 3 months of no juggling, although the measure for the jugglers had decreased somewhat. In other words, what is well learnt stays learnt, but diminishes without use. What is particularly interesting about this study from the neuroscience perspective is that the neural plasticity here is not just functional but involves a structural change. Studies of neuronal processes under the microscope suggest that there are several candidate processes that could be involved in such a structural change, one possibly involving growth of new dendrites (branches) between neurons. And moving out of the lab, a study from 1993 found a positive relationship between years spent at school and the density of dendrites in Wernike's Area, a part of the temporal lobe involved in the comprehension of language. Education really does involve changing children's, and teachers', brains.

Brain structural changes in response to learning were actually first observed with musicians, where, for example, violinists had enhanced areas of the part of their motor cortices which represented their left hands (compared with their right hands) which are used for the intricate fingering required for violin playing. Music teachers know full well that what a student practises is what that student plays, regardless of its musical correctness. Those brain circuits in the motor cortex which get reinforced to produce an automatic sequence of finger and other body movements may be quite neurally distal in the brain of a music novice from any musical 'censor' located in the frontal cortex. That is, the binding between these modules has not been reinforced, hence the importance of performing new pieces slowly and carefully, and learning the technically difficult passages with much patient repetition, before attempting the piece up to speed. But if the music student, with characteristic impatience, has practised an error – perhaps a mistimed phrase or an over-looked accidental – then a comment from the music teacher during the lesson will probably be insufficient to prevent the student playing the learned error in a public or examination performance. To avoid such a calamity, the student actually needs to repractice the piece slowly and correctly in order to establish an alternate neuronal circuit with, hopefully, greater selective salience, so that it, and not the previous, will drive the critical performance.

Similarly in other subject areas, where students have practised an erroneous concept, the feedback that we as teachers traditionally provide – the ticks and crosses on a maths paper, the underlinings and comments in the margins of an essay – might be completely inadequate to establish new reinforced neuronal circuits in the brains of our students with which they can more saliently represent the corrected version.

A corollary to this is that concepts learned in childhood can be very resilient to change later in school. This has been well researched with children's naive science concepts, e.g., the belief that the moon's phases are due to its changing shape. It is easy to imagine the neurally reinforcing effect of a child's favourite bedtime story book about the Man in the Moon, illustrated with engaging full-page colour drawings of a sickle-shaped yellow moon with the old bearded man, sitting on the pointy end, dangling a fishing pole (but to catch what, I wonder?). The storybook, being a favourite, is read every night for several years. Now contrast the comparatively minimal reinforcing effect of a one-off science lesson about the moon's phases, which might not have had much attention paid to it on a hot, Friday afternoon. No doubt this example is apocryphal, but it captures what in reality is a more nuanced phenomenon. Much of science is non-intuitive: Newton's laws of motion are a prime example. Our childhoods spent pushing toy cars around provide plenty of reinforcement of Aristotelian notions of impressed force, so much so that when asked questions about everyday motion, university physics majors exiting their exams on Newton answered in Aristotelian terms, not Newtonian. The proportion of adults in the UK and the USA who hold naive science constructs from their childhood, and who thus seem immune from the effects of school science, can be as high as 80 per cent depending on the issue. The myth that early humans lived contemporaneously with dinosaurs, ignoring a 65 million year difference, is particularly popular. This may be of little importance for science concepts which do not impact directly on daily life, but ignoring Newton's laws of motion when driving can lead to tragic consequences.

The implication for education arising from all of the forgoing is that teacher feedback is crucial. Therefore, I argue, more out-of-class time should be provided for teachers to provide relearning opportunities for students to establish new but more salient reinforced neural pathways. This suggestion, if fully implemented, would obviously affect timetabling and teacher–pupil ratios, and so has considerable resource implications. Interestingly, one-to-one teaching with immediate and detailed feedback is the Oxbridge tutorial model, and more generally relevant, is the model for doctoral supervision – both settings where high quality educational outcomes are expected and usually achieved.

Another prediction of a Hebbian reinforcement model of learning is that specificity is facilitated by objective-oriented or context-facilitated activity. This is based on the assumption that learning is more efficient if the same synapses of the same neuronal circuits are stimulated for each learning experience. Distractions, wild guesses, misleading concepts, and so on are all threats to learning efficiency. A distraction, for example, will likely affect another neural circuit than the one required for learning the item of content or skill at hand. This supports what teachers have long known, that, among other things, clear learning objectives need to be set at each stage of learning in the classroom. There is neuroscientific evidence to support this educational maxim. An American fMRI study investigated complex reasoning in Euclidean geometric proof. Here 15 young adults attempted to provide proofs for the equality of length for pairs of sides in triangular figures. The knowledge required was the Euclidean properties of triangles. The experimental design not only varied the degree of difficulty but had the relevant sides highlighted in colour in half the figures. The results showed a beneficial interaction effect for the colour highlighting, suggesting that proficient problem-solvers integrate problem givens and diagram information to support their logical inferences. The areas of the brain which were the most responsive were the left parietal and right pre-frontal cortices, the same areas involved in arithmetic and algebraic problem solving. The implication for teaching geometric proof is that highlighting the objects of the proof in the diagram might help maintain focused attention, especially for learners.

To take this one step further, so that Hebbian reinforcement can be well focused during the initial stages of learning a new topic, I suggest that answers or exemplars should be provided as student learning targets – distinct from pedagogic targets such as preferred method. For example, in a new topic in secondary mathematics, say, simultaneous equations, the teacher or the text book should provide solutions to the initial problem sets as learning targets, rather than let students get wrong answers, since wrong answers will also reinforce neuronal group connections just as well as right answers. This would be the equivalent in music of playing through a new piece very slowly and carefully in order to begin with an accurate rendition lest initial errors be learned through repeated mistakes while practising.

All that said, I must stress that I am not advocating a return to exclusive drill and practice. Rather, I just want to emphasize the necessity of clear relationships of learning targets within learning contexts. A spiral curriculum is designed around contextual variety. With young children, for example, a period of free or directed play may be the most efficacious strategy for generating a repertoire of relationships with the learning material prior to introducing anything so formal as a learning target.

Memory

Any discussion of learning necessarily involves a consideration of memory, a phenomenon of long-standing interest in cognitive neuroscience, and obviously of central concern (albeit implicitly) to teachers. Practically all formal assessment in education is based on veridical recall from memory; cramming for examinations is the bane of most students' (and many teachers') lives. By Hebb's model, memories are instantiated in the brain by circuits of neurons with reinforced synapses. Cognitive neuroscience distinguishes between working memory, incorporating short-term memory, and long-term memory incorporating semantic and episodic memory systems. There is some evidence that whether an item is retained in long-term memory, or vanishes from our mental grasp after a few seconds in short-term memory, is a function of the time it is kept or continually reintroduced into working memory to be reinforced as per Hebb. When the voltage at a reinforced synapse is higher for a few seconds this is sufficient to enable short-term memory. But the protein activity necessary to make the reinforcement permanent requires neuronal axon activity to last over a longer time in order to form a long-term memory.

Unsurprisingly then, Hebbian biochemical processes are the focus of much neuroscientific research directed towards understanding how memories decline with age and dementia. For several decades, Edinburgh neuroscientist Richard Morris has been leading this endeavour with his insightful research into the memory systems of rats swimming in a water maze. A water maze is simply a large tub of water in which there is a rat-sized platform submerged below the surface and out of sight. Rats love to swim, but like all swimmers, they also appreciate a rest. So, first placed in the tub, a rat will swim around until it finds the platform. Then, after a delay, when the rat is put back into the tub it will swim to the platform fairly directly: it has remembered where the platform is. The first question was: How? Two hypotheses were suggested: by dead reckoning or by using visual cues from the laboratory room. To test the former hypothesis, researchers varied the entry position of the rat into the tub. To test the latter hypothesis, researchers surrounded the water maze with curtains. It turns out that both strategies are used. The second research question was: What part(s) of the brain are involved in the remembering? The answer is the hippocampus, a small subcortical organ attached to the medial (inside) part of each temporal lobe. Prevent parts of its hippocampus from functioning properly, and a rat can no longer remember where the platform is.

These results show that the hippocampus is critically involved in forming memories, which raises the question: How does the hippocampus enable memory? The dense neural interconnections between the hippocampus and its surrounding cortex could indicate that the hippocampus encodes relational properties within memory, for example, relative rather than absolute position. It is the higher order relational properties which are encoded. For example, neuronal circuits in the hippocampus might correlate relevant inputs from different parts of the brain across sensory modalities, such as using place circuits with inputs of colour or odour. There is evidence that the hippocampus models salient perceptual and behavioural features of the task to be remembered. Consequently, the hippocampus might act as a pattern matcher, associating similar new patterns with those already in memory, and updating memory with novel patterns. That is, much of long-term memory would be laid down by relationship more than specificity but then be available in specific relevant instances. Driving a car under momentary changes in traffic conditions would be an example. The evolutionary origins of such a memory process presumably would lie in the advantage conferred on animals who can transfer performance skills to new contexts, a critical behaviour for hunting, gathering and nesting. In sum, we remember the gist of things, and fill in the detail as required.

As New York neurologist Matthew Shapiro summarizes, the hippocampus teaches the cortex. The hippocampus responds to rapidly changing here-and-now features by interleaving them with prior knowledge to create our ever-changing long-term memories. This is demonstrated in patients who suffer from amnesia as a result of an injury to their hippocampus; they are unable to undertake further learning, but their long-term memory is intact. It may also be that the hippocampus is a comparator, and only new information is sent on to the cortex. This account of the role of the hippocampus in memory highlights the dependency of children's classroom responses on their prior learning. Remembering as reconstruction is a function of post-event experiences. Thus, every post-event assessment is implicitly an assessment of post-event experiences, which include masking, distraction, dilution, contradiction, and so on. It may be helpful, then, to test for base-rate recall immediately after a new learning event in class.

We could note some other relevant individual differences here. Lower-achieving students seem to have greater compartmentalization of memory storage, that is, less remembering at a relational level. Consequently, greater mental resources are allocated to the local level of the task at hand, for example, calculation, rather than to a more global or metacognitive level of task-monitoring, for example, estimation, evaluating the reasonableness of the answer or checking the correctness of algorithm. This creates a vicious circle where 'basic' skills remain non-automatic, yet cannot be readily self-corrected. In contrast, better students seem to have less *a priori* memory compartmentalization, and rely more on metaphor and analogy, as we'll see in Chapter 5. Consequently, as matter of principle, all curricula should encourage pupils' metaphorical thinking to promote relational memory encoding.

To this end, it could be conjectured that the major convergence zones in the cortex which project and receive interconnections to and from the hippocampus could instantiate the various conventional school subject areas, the somewhat separate neural circuitry being selected through Hebbian reinforcement in response to particular educational and social conventions of categorizing 'reality'. Each zone would display relative closure for content, semantics, affect and preferred perceptual modality, as English educational philosopher Paul Hirst suggested in the 1950s with 'forms' and 'fields'. Although this would be largely driven by social conventions, e.g., music as a distinct subject area, it is somewhat idiosyncratic. Take for example, music history which is certainly socially specific as seen with Australian aboriginal song lines where music, history and geography (at least) are united. The relative strength of convergence zones could explain individual differences in subject preferences: child A with a stronger reinforced history convergence zone would prefer, and achieve better, in history, whereas child B with stronger reinforced mathematics convergence zone would prefer, and achieve better, in mathematics. But, if memory is relational, then zones featuring similar relational properties may be similarly preferred, for example, mathematics and music, given similar sufficiency of priming. In any case, the relative efficacies of cross-modal or intersubject reinforcement could be tested through school assessment across rather than within subject areas such as ratios in mathematics, physics, visual arts and music could be assessed together. It should be noted that what is proposed here is highly speculative.

That animals have a part of their brains specialized for spatial memory makes good evolutionary sense. Finding your way home after a day's hunting or foraging, and remembering the location and route to the water hole, and the annual fruiting trees, obviously have high adaptive survival value. What about in human animals? In a much reported recent neuroimaging study, London neuroscientists looked at the hippocampus of men whose visual-spatial memory was legendary in scope and accuracy – London taxi drivers. Compared with London bus drivers as control subjects, the posterior hippocampus was larger in the taxi drivers – another example of brain structure accommodating specific learning. But, the taxi drivers' anterior hippocampus was smaller. That is, there was less area dedicated to remembering other things. So, no free lunch.

A central role for the hippocampus in visual-spatial memory, however, is far from the end of the story. A suite of questions follows. How do the stimuli get into the hippocampus to form the memory? The hippocampus receives a massive number of neural projections via the entorhinal (inside) cortex from all of the sensory input areas of the brain. Does this mean that all memories are stored in the hippocampus? Surely there is insufficient room in the hippocampus for all of our memories? At a conference a few years ago I heard an Oxford neuroscientist suggest that as an order of accuracy estimate, assuming a circuit of around 10,000 neurons to a memory, the hippocampus could contain around 50,000 memories. Does 50,000 seem too small a number for a lifetime's recollections, or does this suggest that memories are not actually stored in the hippocampus? The research to date is persuasive about the hippocampus being critical for visual-spatial memories, but is agnostic about other types of memory. However, many cognitive psychologists believe that memories are organized in a kind of quasi-spatial mind map, so a speculative suggestion is that the hippocampus enables memories to be located within some kind of mental space. But if memories are not stored in the hippocampus, then where are they stored, and how do they get there? Neuroimaging studies of people recalling vivid memories, including such fantastic events as being abducted by aliens, show activations in the temporal cortex. And the hippocampus also sends out massive numbers of projections to all parts of the cortex, especially to its neighbouring temporal cortex. This presents a problem for the Hebbian model, since if the hippocampus is a memory gateway, then the location of memories might be elsewhere in the brain from the neuronal circuits which were first reinforced.

Do we remember everything we experience, but just don't recall every-thing? Leaving aside the ontological problem of whether there can be an unrecalled memory, the psychological consensus is that in order to re-member as many important things as we can, we have to ignore much that passes through our perceptual filter. The Russian neuropsychologist Alexander Luria wrote a book, *Mind of a Mnemonist*, about a famous case of his who seemingly remembered every detail of his life, but tragically was quite dysfunctional as a result. Moreover, memory is affected by contem-poraneous situational and contextual cues, including feelings and various perceptual stimuli. This has obvious educational implications for the de-gree of sharedness of classroom experience of students and teachers. A common example of this occurs when revisiting one's childhood envi-ronment as an adult – the backyard never seems as large now as it did then. This raises a whole cascade of related memory questions. Why do some memories persist, and others degrade over time? As we saw with the jugglers, an absence of reinforcing repetition results in a reduction of supporting neural structure over time. Do memories have an emotional component? Very often they do, as we'll see in Chapter 4.

Are memories veridical, or at least accurate? The slightly disturbing answer here is, no. A wealth of psychological studies have shown how the recall of an event is variable, selective and idiosyncratic, between in-dividuals and even by the same person. Eye-witness testimony in court is notoriously unreliable. Are memories fixed and unchangeable? Again, the answer is, no. The best description of memory recall is memory re-construction, with subsequent 'restorage' involving the making of a new memory. The reason is that the neuronal circuits used to instantiate a particular memory, call it A, might have some overlapping neuronal path-ways with the circuits used to instantiate another but similar memory, say, B. Repetition of B through several recalls will change the synaptic func-tioning around the B circuit, including those parts of the circuit in com-mon with the circuit for memory A. Consequently, recalling B will at the same time, inadvertently change the reinforcement pattern for memory A, and so change its representation in the brain. Evidence for this comes again from Freeman's study of rabbit olfaction, where the map of the EEG signals of particular odours changed over months of sniffing other odours. In sum, remembering requires reconstruction; memory is affected by ex-periences which have occurred since the recalled event. As Julian Barnes puts it in his 1998 novel *England, England*, memory is 'a remembrance of a remembrance of a remembrance . . .' Furthermore, that remembrances are objectively unreliable is not apparent to the individual rememberer. An-other personal example comes from a 30-year high school reunion, where one 'old boy' prepared a Trivial Pursuit game of the highlights of our leav-ing year. But instead of providing the hilarious recalls he anticipated, it all fell flat, because none of us shared his memories of what had actually happened. We were all very confident that our version of that past was correct, but our individual memories had diverged, due to the dynamic nature of all of our other life experiences over those 30 years. All this highlights the dependency of children's classroom responses on their prior-to-class learning, and, equally importantly, the dependency of children's classroom responses on their subsequent-in-class learning, however relevant or otherwise. This could affect perceptual discrimination in educational design. Simple cartoon renderings, so frequent in school texts and board sketches, may not relate particularly well to children's remembrances of the 'real thing'. Perhaps more importantly, a post-event assessment such as a term test is implicitly an assessment of post-event experiences during the term, which, as noted above, include masking, distraction, dilution, contradiction, and so on. Explicitly, however, most school assessment is based on pupils' replication of a veridical ideal. Should it be?

Another feature of memory recall with possible pedagogical relevance is the finite time that remembering takes. The time course of the spread of some neural activations has recently been seen with the aid of radioactive tracers. Previously, this has been measured with the P300, an ERP trace which typically peaks around 300 milliseconds (ms), but can last up to 1000 ms (i.e., 1 second) after the onset of a perceptual discrimination task requiring reference to mentally 'stored' information. The latency of the P300 is a function of the difficulty of the task, for example, the degree of degeneracy of an image to be recognized, and of the nature of the task. For this reason free recall (e.g., 'What can you tell me about the First Fleet to Australia?') can sometimes take much longer than primed recall (e.g., 'Where did the First Fleet first land in Australia?') if there is a particular answer that the teacher has in mind. Hence the trap which practice teachers often fall into of inadvertently having their students play the game of 'guess what's in the teacher's head'. But the main implication of the finite time required to reconstruct a memory is support for teachers' pedagogic knowledge about the timing – to allow wait-time before soliciting answers, sometimes described as encouraging a reflective rather than an impulsive cognitive style. One of the interesting observations American education researchers observed in Japanese mathematics classrooms as part of the TIMSS research was that Japanese teachers employed deliberate wait-times of at least 300 ms. As we'll see in Chapter 8, mental arithmetic involves feedforward and feedback circuits between the bilateral parietal, pre-frontal, pre-motor and motor cortices as well as the hippocampus. It takes time for answers to be generated, not least because number facts have to be remembered. It is interesting to note that successful remedial early maths programmes, such as *Maths Recovery* (Australia/US) and *Count Me In Too* (USA), use deliberate teacher wait-time as an essential aspect of their pedagogy.

Although this chapter has presented a very brief skim over a vast topic, and assuming that the Hebbian account of learning can be reconciled with the role of the hippocampus as a memory gateway, we can note a few more implications of learning and memory research for education. The first, as noted above, is that a spiral curriculum could benefit learners by present-ing similar concepts in new and increasingly complex contexts. A spiral curriculum better matches the dynamic nature of memory whereby indi-vidual memories change over time with experience and repeated recall. Interestingly, some medical schools in the UK use a spiral curriculum for the education of tomorrow's doctors. For example, at the University of Exeter, first year medical students study human development from con-ception to death, and then repeat this format in their second year but in greater depth, and so on. It goes without saying that we all want our doctor to have had the best education.

As we've seen, no two brains are ever the same, and this is obviously true in terms of personal memories. In fact, this is true of all of our brain functioning. Each cognitive or motor behaviour is the result of a cas-cade of inputs from neural circuits in many parts of the brain, most lo-cal but some distal, with subsequent outputs providing inputs for other neural circuits. In other words, every instance of thinking changes our neural environment. Consequently, human behaviour in response to a directed stimulus is impossible to completely predict, let alone the out-comes of 'spontaneous' intentionality. This is a commonplace observation with classroom behaviour, especially in response to discipline implemen-tations. Does this mean that all learning is completely idiosyncratic? No. However, whereas generic neural processes are necessarily idiosyncratic in their application, the underpinning neurological functioning *can* produce similar behaviours across individuals in response to the same stimulus. As French neuroscientist Jean-Pierre Changeux argues: 'Different learning inputs may produce *different* connective organisations and neuronal func-tioning abilities but the same behavioural capacity.'[2] The implication here is that since brain development of learning is driven by life experiences, rather than chronological age *per se*, individual pupil's learning needs seem best addressed by having them engage in appropriate curriculum for their stage of learning readiness, largely independent of their birthday. Thus, school organization of school should be based on vertical curricula with mixed-age classes and independent learning plans, rather than the present age-based lock-step progression (more about this in Chapter 10).

And, as we noted at the beginning of this section, there is the issue of educational assessment being predominately dependent on assumed veridical recall. Given the dynamic nature of memory, that remember-ing involves a process of reconstruction rather than an act of retrieval, one cannot but wonder if there might be a better way of evaluating the educational achievements of our students. It is interesting to observe that in response to public concern about grade inflation of school-leaving examination results, universities in the UK are increasingly turning to cognitive aptitude tests to determine competitive entrance, as is the case in the USA.

And then there is the issue of forgetting. Evolutionary psychologists point out the adaptive benefits of forgetting, in a similar manner to psychoanalysts who point out the benefits of suppression. There may even be social advantages to not learning too fast. Certainly some academically gifted children suffer bullying and, ironically, teacher discrimination, because of their abilities to learn quickly. To most teachers' despair, however, many of our students seem to suffer from the opposite problem. From a research perspective, a better understanding of memory, and forgetting, could be of considerable potential benefit for educational assessment.

Chapter 3 has focused on the cognitive neuroscience of learning and memory as the fundamental cognitive attributes of success at school. Learning is a physiological and measurable change in the brain in response to some stimulus. In educational settings, most of these changes involve enhancing the functioning of the synapses – the neuronal interfaces – through repetition. Such plasticity is ubiquitous in the brain. Interestingly, whereas the cortex is highly plastic, plasticity is a feature of many sub-cortical systems including the amygdala, basal ganglia, cerebellum, hippocampus and even the spinal cord. But, because of individual differences in brain physiology, and that these neural mediations are sensitively time-dependent, the inherent problem in a large classroom is the significant improbability that all students can become tuned into the same cognitive state in the same window of only a few milliseconds.

Educational neuroscience questions in a box

How does children's play help reinforce learning and consolidate memory? Children obviously cannot run around and play while lying still inside a scanner. So teachers' observations of children at play should provide crucial data to address this important question. Two technological developments might bring the lab closer to the playground. The first uses virtual reality to provide a limited in-scanner playground for a mental experience of play, and virtual reality has been used as a stimulus for many fMRI studies. The second uses inexpensive wireless head-set scanners (Chapter 10) which could be used in out-of-lab settings such as playgrounds.

4   Working Memory and Intelligence

This chapter focuses on working memory. Working memory has been identified as the central cognitive construct underpinning academic success. Chapter 4 will review the various ways in which working memory processes influence educational endeavours, including: how working memory enables creative thinking through fluid analogizing; the importance of attention to support working memory functioning; the contrast in thinking abilities between social and symbolic problems; and working memory capacity and cerebral interconnectivity as neural determinants of general intelligence and academic giftedness.

To this end, neuroscientists recognize multiple neural systems in the brain such as, in arithmetic where computation and estimation seem to involve separate but overlapping systems. Each of these neural systems involves interconnectivity between many of the functional modules which comprise our cognition. As an example of overlapping neural systems, the Wason card selection task, illustrated in Figure 4.1, has for years been a classic example of the imponderable way the brain undertakes logical thinking.

Figure 4.1 shows four cards. Each card has a letter on one side and a number on the other. The task is to verify or refute the rule, 'If a card has a vowel on one side, then it has an even number on the other side', by turning over as few cards as possible. If you haven't seen this problem before, then please stop reading and try to solve it. The correct response with an explanation is in the Endnotes for Chapter 4. You might be pleased to learn that about 80 per cent of people turn over the E and the 4. If you are in this majority then you won't be pleased to learn that this is wrong.

Figure 4.1 The Wason card selection problem

Now, change the problem setting. Imagine that you are the warden of a university residential college, and one of your onerous duties is to check up on under-age drinking. One night you walk into the college bar, where you see:

1   Someone drinking beer.
2   Someone drinking Coke.
3   Someone 21 years old.
4   Someone 16 years old.

Your challenge here is to verify or refute the assertion that if someone is drinking beer, they must be over 18. The analogue of 'turning over a card' is either 'checking someone's age' (if only their beverage of choice is known), or 'checking someone's drink' (if only their age is known). Who do you check? Easy isn't it – person 1 (age) and person 4 (drink). In this case, over 90 per cent of people get it correct. So here's the puzzle: the four cards of the original problem can be 'mapped' on to the four people in the bar. That is, the logic of the two problems is identical – they are actually two versions of the very same problem. So, why do we get it wrong in the abstract? Many suggestions have been advanced, including that it's often simpler to process positive evidence than negative evidence, or that people are primed to think about even numbers due to their explicit mention in the problem statement. But then why does the familiar social setting of a student bar make the problem seem so trivial? My suggestion is that we are seeing two overlapping but different neural systems in play. Both systems contribute to logical reasoning, but one draws on a relatively impoverished setting of symbols, while the other has a far richer repertoire of worldly experience. The latter system involves more inputs, particularly from long-term memory.

As we'll consider in this chapter, the central role of the brain's executive function, including working memory, is to coordinate such intercommunication between functional modules, including long-term memory. The neural systems involved mostly operate unconsciously, which could explain why the solution to a thorny problem often appears in the morning after a good night's sleep. Individual neurophysiological differences that effect the efficiency of information flow within and between systems, therefore, could account for individual differences in academic performance at various times and contexts. In short, because each brain is unique and uniquely organized, all brains are not equally good at everything. The cascading effect of a hierarchical curriculum at school could exacerbate such differences through positive feedback cycles. As we'll discuss in Chapter 6, learning is strongly mediated by emotion-related processing which strengthens or weakens motivation in that subject.

Working memory

As teachers, we want our students to be more cognitively active than to merely regurgitate knowledge (except possibly at exam time); we want our students to be intelligent and creative, and to enjoy their school-work as a result. And, as we've noted, teaching can be a most intelligent and creative profession. From a neuroscience perspective, just how our brains enable original and creative thinking is a big question. Every day we do things we've never done exactly the same way before, and have conversations we've never had before. How do our brains do this? The answer involves working memory as the central cognitive construct underpinning general intelligence and creative thinking. So, what exactly is working memory? Unhelpfully, that will depend on which researcher you ask. For some, working memory is synonymous with short-term memory, the mental buffer in which we store telephone numbers for a few seconds while we dial. The temporal transience of short-term memory is all too embarrassing at a party when we forget the name of someone we've been introduced to only a few minutes earlier. Noting individual differences in people's abilities for such remembering, psychologists have investigated the concept of working memory capacity, often with tests such as the digit span (repeating a list of random digits), and reverse digit span (repeating the list backwards). Most people have an upper limit of around seven digits, leading to a popular misconception that our working memory capacity is 7 ± 2 items. However, it turns out that this was just another example of a scientific inhouse joke that 'got out' but was not 'got'. In a 1950s conference paper, psychologist Arthur Millar noticed that the number 7 had appeared by coincidence a couple of times, so added this as the tongue-in-cheek confirming third.

The psychological reality is that our short-term working memory capacity is only three or four items. We remember longer lists such as telephone numbers by chunking – grouping two or three numbers into single rememberable items. We could note that our limited working memory capacity for how much information can be considered simultaneously three or four separate things at most – could be a bottleneck for academic performance. However, conceptual chunking can reduce working memory load and thus enable more information to be processed. Fortunately, in a Hebbian manner, chunking improves with experience and training, such as with phonics in reading. Moreover, as the chunks become familiar, they can be combined into meta-chunks, and so on, so that we do not have to be constrained by our basic working memory capacity. A more prosaic strategy of course is to write notes to oneself – hence the value of Post-Its for jotting down things to be remembered to save having to keep rehearsing them in working memory.

A good example of chunking in teaching is seen with lesson plans. A practising or newly graduated teacher will (and should) write out a very detailed lesson plan, sometimes with minute-by-minute self-instructions. In contrast, an experienced teacher might jot down a few key words, if that. However, it would be a big mistake for the novice teacher to think that the experienced mentor teacher was not fully prepared. Those key words, often not even committed to paper, are meta-chunks of extended detail of how the lesson will unfold. An implicit objective of effective teaching, then, is to assist pupils to meta-chunk – to combine conceptually distinct information into chunks for long-term memory. To this end, an American study demonstrated that semantic-based chunking task had a stronger relation to working memory capacity than non-semantic chunking. But intriguingly, the ability for semantic chunking did not relate to general cognitive ability measures, suggesting that such a pedagogic strategy could benefit most children. This in turn raises questions about the educational plasticity of working memory. UK psychologist Sue Gathercole points out that poor working memory can manifest a range of classroom behaviours beyond poor academic performance, including difficulties in following instructions, holding back in group activities, being easily distracted, losing the place, and appearing to be inattentive.

FMRI research into individual differences in working memory capacity typically uses a scanner-compatible version of the digit span, the n-back test. In this test you might be shown a series of pictures, at around one per second. The 1-back version is easy – press the response button if the picture you are seeing now is identical to the one you saw previously, that is, one back. The 2-back test is more challenging: here you have to respond if the picture you are currently looking at is the same as the picture you saw before the previous one. And the specifics of this task is continually changing as each picture has to be remembered for comparison two pictures later, as well as being compared with the picture you remember seeing two pictures ago. Thus the 2-back test dramatically increases working memory load. The 3-back test has the same format, but with two intervening pictures. The 3-back is very challenging: almost no one is successful at the 4-back. But how valid is the n-back test as a probe of working memory capacity? Clearly more is demanded of the brain than simply remembering a few items, since the intervening pictures have to be remembered but temporally ignored at each decision point. And as working memory load increases, so does the amount of brain activation correlated with the load demands. Thus, neuroscience research shows that temporary storage of information is an epiphenomenon, an outcome of what working memory is really all about. In fact, the tag 'memory' could even be misleading – the emphasis is very much on 'working'. The reason for this emphasis is that working memory is a central feature of executive functioning in the brain.

Executive functioning, often referred to in the past as 'cognitive control', enables metacognition, the basis of education's decades-long preoccupation with process over product. Executive functioning also incorporates a range of other cognitive tasks important for education, including planning and maintaining task-relevant attention.

This is captured by the dynamic workspace account of French cognitive neuroscientists Stanislas Dehaene and Jean-Pierre Changeux, which involves the selective combination of information from sensory inputs and long-term memory. In the previous chapters we noted that, because interconnectivity was the brain's organizational *modus operandi*, the specialist functioning of the various regions throughout the brain developed through increasingly filtered inputs and outputs to and from other interconnected modules. This account of functional development raises a potential dilemma. On the one hand, to produce adaptive behaviour much of this inter-module information flow must be synchronized, coordinated or controlled in some way. On the other hand, there is no means for the brain to achieve this beyond the development of input and output connectivity. This is the central feature of the French dynamic workspace model. To control its information processing, the brain can be conceptualized as having, alongside specialized processors, a distributed neural system or 'workspace': 'with long-distance connectivity that can potentially interconnect multiple specialised brain areas in a co-ordinated, though variable manner'.[1] Importantly, this dynamic workspace provides a common 'communication protocol' which allows communication between modular systems that do not directly interconnect. Furthermore, such intense mobilization of neural resources gives rise to the subjective phenomenon of conscious effort. In this model, working memory is essentially the workspace. So for many neuroscientists, working memory is not just a temporary store, but is rather, in a sense, what the brain essentially does.

This dynamic account of working memory raises two important questions. The first is: Where in the brain do we find interconnections with most of the rest of the brain? That is, where do we find modules whose inputs and outputs determine its executive function? The second question is: If memory capacity is an outcome, then what sort of work does working memory actually do? There is consistent neuroimaging evidence to answer the first question: FMRI studies have shown that the functional neural correlates of working memory lie in the frontal cortex. Other areas seem to be involved in supporting working memory, depending on the demands of the particular test, but regardless of the task, bilateral frontal activations are reliably seen when subjects use their working memories inside an fMRI scanner. This makes sense neuroanatomically. Frontal cortical areas are strongly interconnected with most other parts of the brain, especially the parietal and temporal lobes, but also with all of the sensory and motor areas, as well as the subcortical organs of the basal ganglia and limbic system, and the 'second brain' at the rear, the cerebellum. Thus the frontal cortex has the necessary inputs and outputs to develop as the brain's executive cognitive control functional module. Consistently, structural neuroimaging studies have revealed individual differences in frontal cortical structures which correlate positively with differences in working memory capacity.

As an illustration of how the brain might distribute the necessary cognitive processing among its functional modules or neural systems, there are several neuroimaging studies which provide evidence for the pivotal role of frontal functioning in higher-order thinking and working memory. In particular, there is evidence that the left upper frontal cortex is used to retrieve rule-based knowledge, that the middle frontal cortex is involved in changes of executive functioning required to learn new rules. The front part of the frontal cortex is involved with resolving subgoals, the left lower frontal cortex is specifically involved in relational integration of task complexity, and that the right upper frontal cortex and the adjacent middle frontal areas process distant associations that may be useful in creative thought and problem solving.

There is also consistent neuroimaging evidence to address the second question, what is working memory working at? The short answer is: selective attention. Neuroscientist Edward Vogel offers two metaphors for how the working memory system works. The first is a computer metaphor: working memory as a spam filter keeping irrelevant (and potentially harmful) information from getting on to your hard drive. The second is a social metaphor: working memory as a nightclub bouncer, admitting those on the guest list, while keeping out the wannabes. The neuroscience evidence for the working memory system that enables this selective attentional or filtering function highlights the role of the basal ganglia, interconnected to the frontal cortex. While working memory areas in the frontal cortex maintain current task goals, the basal ganglia control the inward flow of information into working memory. The role of selecting task relevancy for the basal ganglia is consistent with other evidence for its role in generic decision making, for example, selecting which particular motor movements we need at a particular moment in a dance routine, and suppressing those potential movements that we don't need at the time. Consistently, earlier fMRI studies of the neural correlates of working memory load vs. working memory maintenance found that such task separation produced separation of activated areas in the frontal cortex, the lower and upper frontal cortex respectively. However, the extent of the activation of these frontal areas was correlated, indicative of an underlying function of which selective attention would fit the bill.

So, do individual differences in attentional abilities explain the individual differences in working memory capacity we observe in classrooms? Well, yes and no. On the one hand, the American group who failed to find a relationship between general cognitive ability and semantic chunking, did find a relationship between high-level working memory capacity and top–down, but not bottom–up, attention-control tasks. They suggest that individuals with higher working memory capacity can better ignore irrelevant distractions and withhold habitual responses than do those with lower working memory capacity. The famous Stroop task of neuropsychologists provides a reliable measure of this individual cognitive difference. In the original version, the task was to read colour words such as 'red' or 'yellow' written in other colours such as blue or green. More recent versions involved the words 'small' and 'large' written in large and small font sizes, e.g., small and large. And it hardly needs elaborating that a student whose mental scope is primarily celebrity gossip, personal blogs and YouTube party clips has a working memory 'bouncer' with quite a different guest list to that of the teacher's. On the other hand, correlations between working memory capacity and parietal cortex activations seem to suggest that parietal functioning contributes to working memory systems in determining capacity limits for new information before, and possibly after, chunking. Perhaps at this stage, when there is clearly so much more to learn about working memory, we would do best to conclude with working memory expert Nelson Cowan that both storage capacity and filtering efficiency affect an individual's working memory ability. In sum then, working memory is the cognitive construct of the neural process of combining information from the perceptual here and now with information from long-term memory, under attentional selection for what is relevant to the task at hand. Different memory systems – short-term, long-term, working, spatial, rote, and so on – receive and process information in different ways, and are processed through distinct, though sometimes overlapping, neural systems.

Attention

Focusing on working memory as the most relevant memory system for everyday classroom activities, we want to know if our educational mediations can help construct better mental spam filters, or more perceptive mental bouncers. The key process is attention. Of course as teachers we have always recognized the necessity for our students to pay attention. However, maintaining children's attention in the classroom is a real challenge (pardon the obvious), not least because attention refers to several quite different brain functions.

At the most basic level, attention as a function of the brain stem determines cortical tone – sleeping (deeply or lightly) or awake (drowsy or alert). It is dispiriting to find a student asleep in one's class, but with adolescents, there could be a good reason given their particular circadian rhythms (Chapter 10).

Then there is orienting attention. As noted above, the frontal areas of the brain are very well connected to the sensory areas, and so can direct the visual, auditory, olfactory and motor systems to 'pay attention' to particular stimuli rather than others. Hence the importance for ITT students during practice lessons to vary their voice inflection, to use engaging visual aids, to break the lesson up with hands-on activities, and so on, in order to engage the attention of their pupils. When doing this it can be worth bearing in mind the perceptual limits to the various human sensory systems. We hear a range of sounds only between certain frequencies, and this range deteriorates with age. We see with a limited range of the electromagnetic spectrum – visible light. As primates, our visual systems are usually our most salient – around 75 per cent of all information entering our brains comes through our visual system. Our visual system evolved to enable us to move around the physically complex world of jungle and savannah. What we do with most of our visual information is to create mental spatial maps of our world. These can be physical maps, for example, which child is sitting in which desk in the classroom, but also conceptual spatial maps, as in which group of children is likely to be disruptive, who can be called on to run an errand, and so on. Even congenitally blind people use their auditory and tactile inputs to construct spatial maps of their world – in the same areas of the brain as sighted people. Similarly, blind people process Braille, not in the kinaesthetic areas of their brains, but in those parts of their visual cortices that sighted people use to learn written language. This is a good illustration of the interconnectedness of the various sensory areas of the brain: vision with hearing, vision with touch, touch with smell, and so on. As science journalist C. Kayser puts it, the brain sees with its ears and touch, and hears with its eyes. Another illustration comes from people who, after acquiring a cochlear implant, find that they are suddenly much more dependent on the visual aspects of speech to conduct a conversation. But we don't need to limit our considerations to sensory deficits. Our everyday sensory processes are neurally interconnected. Eating does not engage just taste, but smell, tactile (inside the mouth), auditory and visual sensations.

Evidence for the neural bases of cross-modal binding, as it is known, comes from fMRI studies of listening to speech while looking at videos of the speaker with the lips in and out of synch with the voice, much as we sometimes experience on the evening news with a live feed from a reporter at a remote location. The fMRI results show that simultaneously seeing and hearing the same information works better than first just see-ing and then hearing it. This is a legacy of our evolutionary past. Imagine you are a primate ancestor many aeons ago making your way 'home' on dusk. You hear the snap of a twig breaking behind you. Quickly you turn around to synchronize your vision with the sound. It could be dinner, or worse. Cross-modal binding clearly has critical survival value, attested by the fact that we descendants are here to speculate about its importance. As Nobel Laureate Sir Charles Sherrington noted over 70 years ago.

'The naive observer would have expected evolution in its course to have supplied us with more various sense organs for ampler perception of the world . . . Not new senses but better liaison between the old senses is what the developing nervous system has in this respect stood for.[2]

And we exploit this in classrooms every day. For example, in early years education, a teacher pointing to the words of the story as she reads them out aloud is based on coincident bimodal information processing, espe-cially sight and sound. In later years, the learning of a second language, and the practice of it, requires the coordinated use of visual, auditory and kinaesthetic modalities.

That said, our evolutionary legacy is not all necessarily positive. Our an-cestors' jungle environment was characterized by irregular fractal shapes and surfaces, and mostly slow moving entities. It is perhaps not surprising, then, that we can fool our visual system with graphic illusions such as the Necker Cube, or fast changing images – the basis of the film and television industries. The point for pedagogy is that an illustrative 2D sketch on a board, or in a textbook, simplified for ease of comprehension, might actu-ally be more difficult for many children to make sense of than seeing the real thing. Fortunately, these days we can readily bring pictures of the real thing into the classroom. One of the many reasons that David Attenbor-ough's wildlife documentaries command our attention is the measured pace of the changes of image. There is time for the brain to coordinate and then process the information that is coming from the picture and Attenborough's measured voice-over.

However, it is most important to note that while paying attention is necessary for learning, it is not the same thing as learning. Confusing the two is the mistake made by the promulgators of visual auditory kinaes-thetic (VAK) learning styles. The VAK proponents claim that all children have a dominant learning style (V, A or K), and therefore will profit from being taught according to whether they are visual, auditory or kinaes-thetic learners. Why not olfaction, I've often wondered? Why no smelling learners? The implicit assumption in VAK is that the information gained through one sensory modality is processed in the brain independently from information gained through the other sensory modalities, and this is learned independently. All this is false. In fact, we don't even create sensory perception in our sensory cortices. Whereas the sensory areas of the brain create neural representations of the sensory stimuli, it is actually in the working memory areas of the frontal lobes that we create the sense of perceptual experience from the combination of the sensory information with long-term memory. Consequently, an exclusive pedagogic focus on one sensory modality at a time is impossible given the brain's natural interconnectivity. A simple demonstration of this is seen when 6-year-olds are asked which of two groups of dots is the larger, the groups being too large for direct counting. So long as the number of dots in the groups are not too close, young children, and adults, can do this reliably. But what happens when one group of dots is replaced by an equal number of sounds played too rapidly for counting? There is no difference in the accuracy of the responses. Substituting a V vs. A for a V vs. V version of the task makes no difference. Little wonder that American education researchers Kratzig and Arbuthnott conclude from a study into the learning outcomes of VAK that: 'focusing on learning styles as defined by sensory modalities may be a wasted effort'.[3]

I have met many teachers who, having VAK foisted on them by gullible headteachers, observe how their children are never constant in their V-, A- or K-ness. The reason is that sensory responses are a variable depending on the type of lesson – we want out students to be appropriately but differently stimulated in music, art and technics lessons. As several commentators have stated, VAK trivializes the complexity of learning and, in doing so, threatens the professionality of educators. Fortunately for their students, many teachers have not been taken in by the VAK ideology. Rather, and perhaps ironically, VAK has become, in the hands of these practitioners, not a method of restrictive teaching but a reminder of the benefits of explicit mixed modality pedagogy, as recommended in all pre-service and ITT courses.

So, for teachers to optimize students' attention in the classroom, to develop attentional control, a three-pronged approach is needed for the alerting, orienting and executive levels of attention. By executive attention I mean the top–down task-specific focus of the brain's executive functioning. A good example of the interaction of orienting and executive attention, mentioned in Chapter 3 and elaborated on in Chapter 8, comes from an fMRI study into Euclidean geometric proof. While lying in the scanner, subjects had to try and prove the equality of sides in pairs of similar or congruent triangles. One of the experimental conditions was the triangle sides in the question were highlighted in colour. The results showed a beneficial interaction effect for the highlighting. The areas of the brain which were the most active were those involved in working memory – the frontal and parietal cortices. Similarly, I advocate providing the answers to the initial sets of problems in any new mathematics topic so that students have their attention directed towards the relevant goal. When teaching matriculation physics many years ago I was struck by how often students, especially the weaker ones, were overwhelmed when faced with a long verbal problem. The relevant area of physics, much less what formula or solving approach was being solicited by the problem, seemed stubbornly opaque. But, highlight the key words in the text, and the appropriate solving strategy then seemed to leap out of the page. Later, while researching the information processing abilities of musical prodigies, I found that they were particularly good at the Stroop test, suggesting that their prodigious rate of learning music could be attributed to their high levels of attention to the relevant musical information. In general, then, explicitly highlighting target concepts would seem to be of benefit to all students, but especially those with more limited working memory capacities. Such a deliberative approach is possibly even more important whenever attentional functions are compromised, as with Attention Deficit Hyperactivity Disorder (ADHD) (Chapter 6).

Intelligence

ADHD is a failure of parts of the cognitive control system. Unless sympathetically and effectively treated, a condition such as ADHD has a marked negative effect on school performance. But the fact that many children with ADHD can score within the normal range on IQ tests, some even in the high band, illustrates that there is more to intelligence than selective attention, the key neural process of working memory. Neither executive functioning nor working memory, then, are synonymous with general intelligence. But neuropathologies aside, there is a strong correlation between measures of working memory capacity and measures of intelligence. Neuroimaging studies led by John Duncan at the University of Cambridge show bilateral frontal activations on difficult IQ test items from both spatial and verbal subtests. Furthermore, meta-analyses of other neuroimaging studies show that frontal areas on both sides of the brain are involved in a great range of general high intelligence tasks, including reasoning, memorization and linguistic expression. These results suggest that the neurons in these areas of the frontal cortices are task adaptive.

> [T]hroughout much of the prefrontal cortex . . . the response properties of single neurons are highly adaptable . . . Any given cell has the potential to be driven by many different kinds of input – perhaps through the dense interconnections that exist within the prefrontal cortex. In a particular task context, many cells become tuned to code information that is specifically relevant to this task.

In this sense, the prefrontal cortex acts as a global workspace or working memory.[4]

That is, consistent with the working memory metaphors of the bouncer and the spam filter, these frontal neurons can retrieve data from long-term memory or engage in logical inference, categorize new information or monitor the progress of a task, depending on current demand. Moreover, as described in the dynamic workplace model, adaptive frontal functioning can maintain task commitment through the persistent activation of relevant inputs from other brain areas. Once again we see how complex brain function can arise from neural interconnectivity.

Consequently, there are common brain functions for all acts of intelligence, especially those involved in school learning. Beyond the working memory systems involving the frontal cortex and basal ganglia, these interconnected brain functions include: long-term memory involving the hippocampus and other cortical areas (Chapter 3); emotional mediation generated in the limbic subcortex (Chapter 5); sequencing of symbolic representation in the fusiform gyrus and temporal lobes (Chapters 7 and 8); conceptual interrelationships involving the parietal lobe (Chapters 7 and 8); and conceptual and motor rehearsal in the cerebellum (Chapter 10). Importantly, these neural contributions to general intelligence are necessary for all school subjects, and all other aspects of cognition. But, to extrapolate from Sherrington's warning in Chapter 1 about brain mapping, there are no individual modules in the brain which correspond directly to the school curriculum. Cerebral interconnectivity is necessary regardless of the lesson, from science to cookery to IT to art to maths to music to geography to history to Chinese as a second language.

So, before we go any further, my definition of general intelligence is:

Intelligence is context-appropriate cognitive activity involving abstraction, reasoning, learning and memory.

In short, pretty much everything involved in thinking. General intelligence, however, has had a rather bad press in educational circles, and not just over the past couple of decades. Most theorists who examine intelligence come to the conclusion that it is not a unitary construct. Most popularly, intelligence has usually been regarded as having two dimensions, and every couple of decades throughout the twentieth century these have been reconceptualized: education + reproduction by Spearman in the 1920s; convergent + divergent by Guilford in the 1940s; fluid + crystallized by Cattell in the 1960s; and analytic + creative + practical by Sternberg in the 1980s. Clearly there are many ways to cut this enigmatic cake. However, none of theses accounts had the benefit of neuroimaging studies. The twentieth century also saw the proliferation of batteries of intelligence tests. Most of these have subtests whose remit assumes a basic dichotomy of spatial and verbal information processing. There are some notable exceptions, particularly the simultaneous–successive approach of the Russian neuropsychologist Luria. In the West, spatial and verbal have been popularly regarded as basic modes of cognition. Certainly this dichotomy is the basis of the most widely cited pre-neuroimaging model of working memory by UK psychologist Alan Baddley. Baddley saw working memory as having separate semantic and spatial buffers, combined through a central executive. And as we've noted earlier, of course there are separate neural systems to represent and process verbal and spatial information. Otherwise, at the risk of over-stating the obvious, how could we tell the difference?

But the fact that our brains operate with separate neural systems does not necessarily mean that our cognitive repertoire is best described by postulating separate intelligences. The best-known, and probably the greatest splitter of intelligence is Howard Gardner with his model of multiple intelligences (MI). Gardner originally divided human cognition into seven intelligences: logic-mathematics, verbal, interpersonal, spatial, music, movement and intrapersonal, although more recently this set has been expanded to eleven and a half. It should be noted that such a division is not original; Plato, some 2500 years earlier, stated that the ideal curriculum should be composed of six subjects: logic, rhetoric, arithmetic, geometry-astronomy, music and dance-physical. For aspiring philosopher-kings, meditation was also recommended. With a couple of updates of terminology, Gardner's MI is Plato's curriculum. But as worthy as such a curriculum might be, does this imply that our brains process the specialized information of these subject areas completely separately from each other? No. Each school subject area requires working memory to coordinate the sensory information processing, memory recall, language articulation, computation, and so on. In other words, there are not multiple intelligences so much as multiple applications of general intelligence to various endeavours. The mistake with MI as a model, as anticipated by Sherrington's point quoted in Chapter 1, is that the way that the brain goes about its multiple functions does not map on to how we see such functional divisions from the outside, or even introspectively from the inside. This is elaborated in a recent critique of MI by educational psychologist Lynn Waterhouse:

> The human brain is unlikely to function via Gardner's multiple intelligences. Taken together the evidence for the intercorrelations of subskills of IQ measures, the evidence for a shared set of genes associated with mathematics, reading, and g, and the evidence for shared and overlapping 'what is it?' and 'where is it?' neural

processing pathways, and shared neural pathways for language, music, motor skills, and emotions suggest that it is unlikely that each of Gardner's intelligences could operate 'via a different set of neural mechanisms' [as Gardner claims].[5]

It would seem, then, that deliberate attempts to restrict intelligence within classrooms according to MI theory will not promote children's learning. It has to be said, in Gardner's defence, that his MI model has often been misinterpreted in its enthusiastic application to the classroom, especially in the implication that with more intelligences to go round, every child should come up trumps by being highly intelligent in at least one of them. As well intentioned as this might be, the more sober reality is that cognitive abilities tend to be correlated within an individual; hence, the increasing numbers of teachers' reports about not observing any long-term impact of applying MI theory in their classrooms.

To elaborate, there are two different types of evidence which suggest that there is a general cognitive ability underpinning all of these possible dimensions of intelligence. The first is statistical. In the 1990s, psychometrician John Carroll conducted a large meta-study of thousands of other research reports of individual differences in a vast range of cognitive measures. He found that to a modest but significant degree these various measures all correlated. In sum, there were groups of similar types of ability which suggested that intelligence could have fairly narrow application. For example, manipulating symbols is necessary for in reading and arithmetic. And these were underpinned by broader cognitive characteristics such as spatial and verbal information processing. But, finally, these few broad characteristics were underpinned by one general intelligence factor. Carroll, of course, was not the first researcher to find evidence for a general intelligence factor – usually denoted by the letter g. That idea had been around at least since Binet devised the first IQ test in 1904. The long-standing pre-neuroimaging question was: What neurophysiological attribute or process in the brain could account for general intelligence?

Researchers in the 1960s, noting that measures of g are inversely correlated with reaction times and inspection times, suggested that the neurobiology of intelligence involved nerve conduction speeds. Interestingly, studies of peripheral nerve conduction speeds – along the arm, as there was no means of testing this in the brain at the time – supported this hypothesis. Consequently, a simple way to assess the relative IQs of a class is through the 'drop the ruler' test. The quicker the ruler is caught indicates both a faster reaction and a briefer inspection time. And now that neural conduction speeds can be investigated in the brain, at least to a limited extent, there are two competing accounts. Both models agree that neural speed is a function of neural density, often measured by cortical thickness. One line of evidence suggests that thinner is faster, presumably because there is a lower impedance from less neural tissue being 'in the way'. The counterevidence is that thicker is faster, presumably because there are more parallel neural pathways available to conduct the message.

However, as important as neural conduction speed is, the answer to the question of a neurobiological substrate for g is that, due to the brain's extensive interconnectedness, there is no g-spot! Several extensive reviews of the relevant research reports have concluded that general intelligence is enabled in the brain through a frontal-parietal system or dynamic workspace which embraces and synchronizes multiple functions throughout the brain. Individual differences in g, then, arise partly from individual differences in the brain's executive coordination of these various functions, which in turn depends on the capacity of working memory.

A consideration of the origins of such individual differences highlights the feedback loops inherent in cognitive development. Very briefly, how the brain grows the cognitive machinery it needs to succeed at necessary cognitive tasks ultimately involves gene expression, which can be switched on or off by neural and social environmental stimuli (epigenesis). This includes school learning which both reflects and contributes to individual cognitive differences. Since school learning requires the integration of multiple neural systems in the brain, any asynchronies in neural development such as relatively delayed integration of some cognitive areas together with delayed or precocious hormonal development, which in turn might effect the maturity of the brain's executive functioning, could delay or accelerate learning in particular subject areas. In other words, we should expect to find that there are large individual differences in subject-specific abilities, as we do.

Gifted and talented pupils

One group of students who are interestingly different from a neuroscience perspective are the academically gifted and talented, also variously labelled 'able' or 'of high intelligence'. The natural variation we observe in all living things, attributed to their genes, predicts that there will be children who, through no fault of their own, adapt to school work better or worse than the majority do. As Canadian educational psychologist Françoys Gagné points out when distinguishing giftedness as potential, from talent as actualization that no child is gifted or particularly intelligent at birth. But presumably gifted children have a greater number of 'advantageous' alleles for the proteins that enable the neuronal growth and interconnection necessary for the precocious development of intelligence.

Consequently, my definition of giftedness is pragmatic.

A gifted pupil is one who can benefit from a gifted education programme.

Fly the flag and see who salutes. So long as there is no penalty for trying something harder, one never knows which unassuming pupil might realize untapped potential by rising to the challenge of a faster-paced, above-age curriculum. My definition is deliberately circular, but I prefer to label programmes rather than pupils. However, most of the rest of the world prefers otherwise, and will call pupils 'gifted' if their IQ score exceeds some cut-off. Although high IQ measures are bandied about in the media with talk of child geniuses, it's worth reflecting that an IQ as high as 130 is actually quite extreme. As IQ is a ratio of mental to chronological age, a 10-year-old with an IQ of 130 has a theoretical mental age of 13, in other words, is thinking like a junior high school student while still in the 5th Grade primary. But such children, assuming that their distribution in the general population follows the ideal bell curve, are by definition, rare. An IQ of 130 is found in about one child in 200, in other words, one pupil in a small primary school, a handful in a large secondary school. So, parenthetically, despite the hopes raised from some misinterpretations of MI theory, not all children are gifted by definition.

What these gifted children have in common is a high working memory capacity. Neuroimaging evidence shows that the neurobiology of giftedness is characterized by high-level frontal cortical functioning within a bilateral frontal-parietal network. This network enables a more efficacious intermodular information processing, which in turn supports a suite of high-level cognitive abilities including a relatively enhanced executive capability – hence, a more efficacious working memory. My research into the information-processing abilities of young gifted musicians showed that it was their superior use of executive strategies as mediated by the frontal cortex that contributed most towards their remarkable abilities. Highly adaptive cognitive control (a top quality spam filter, or perspicacious bouncer, depending on your metaphor) of gifted pupils can account for the characteristic predilection for top–down perspectives. This has been described as:

> a finely tuned capacity for activating (or inhibiting) the very brain regions known to play (not play) specialized roles in the performance of a given task ... That is, precocious individuals are especially facile at knowing [sic] what steps to take in solving a given intellectual problem.[6]

For example, many gifted students demonstrate creative mathematical thinking: their highly task-adaptive frontal functioning can compare and contrast putative ideas to generate candidate solutions to the mathematical problem at hand. This was illustrated in an information-processing study which operationalized Vygotsky's zone of proximal development (ZPD) in elementary school children undertaking mathematical pattern problems. Canadian educationist Lannie Kanevsky and I found that the gifted children sought top–down, meta-level hints and suggestions from their teacher rather than item-specific suggestions which were preferred by their peers.

Evidence for the neurobiological characteristics of high intelligence comes in various forms. Consistent with the interpretation of high IQ scores as meaning that these children can think like older children do, there is evidence that gifted children are precocious in their intellectual development. In an EEG study which compared the brain waves of gifted 12-year-olds from the Iowa Study of Mathematically Precocious Youth with college students, the researchers found no differences between the two groups in the EEG data from their frontal lobes, suggesting that the frontal lobes of the young gifted adolescents seemed to be operating with the equivalent maturity of university students some five years older. Earlier evidence that the brains of gifted people were physiologically different from their age-peers came from a postmortem study performed 20 years ago in Soviet Russia. Correlating the results of the brain autopsies with IQ measures held on file, the researchers found that, across the age span, the cortical thickness and density of both the neurons and glial cells were more than double in the frontal cortices of the high IQ people compared with those of people with average IQs. Fortunately these days we don't have to wait until our gifted subjects are deceased to examine their brains. Further evidence that the brains of gifted children are structurally different from those of same-age peers comes from an American six-year longitudinal MRI study of cortical development in 300 children and adolescents, in which the rate of change in the growth of the frontal cortex was closely related to the children's measures of IQ. Interestingly, the frontal cortices of the high IQ group were thinner when the children were young, but then grew rapidly so that when the gifted children reached adolescence, their frontal cortices were significantly thicker than average. A third study using VBM, by Richard Haier's group in California, links these two investigations: most of the 6 per cent of grey matter volumes distributed throughout the brain which correlated with IQ was found in the frontal cortex.

Complementary evidence that gifted children demonstrate rapid information processing is rather indirect by comparison, relying instead on evidence for greater interconnectivity in gifted brains. That is, denser neural connections enabling rapid information processing can in turn can account for the superior performance of gifted children on tests of intelligence. As noted above, high intelligence is therefore supported by a frontal-parietal (-basal ganglia) system, which exercises adaptive control over relevant inputs from and outputs to other brain areas. Direct evidence to test this conclusion was found in a Korean fMRI study which compared gifted and age-matched adolescents on high-*g* and low-*g* loaded IQ test items. In this replication of Duncan's Cambridge PET study, the gifted group showed increased activation in bilateral frontal cortical regions when engaged on the high-*g* loaded tasks as well as stronger activations in their posterior parietal cortices, regions involved in forming conceptual interrelationships. The researchers concluded that when doing high-*g* loaded items, the frontal-parietal network might be driven from the posterior parietal area. Consistently, an Australian fMRI study of mathematically gifted male adolescents led by neuropsychologist Michael O'Boyle showed bilateral activation of the parietal lobes and the frontal cortex. O'Boyle and his colleagues concluded that: 'the parietal lobes, [and] frontal cortex ... are critical parts of an all-purpose information processing network, one that is relied upon by individuals who are intellectually gifted, irrespective of the nature of their exceptional abilities'.[7]

Importantly, as a variety of psychophysical experiments have shown, enhanced bilaterality seems to be a neurobiological characteristic of gifted individuals. How this supports academic high achievement is demonstrated in a Chinese ERP study of gifted and non-gifted school children involved in a visual search task, where the superior performance of the gifted suggested that these children had better spatially and temporally coordinated neural networks. Moreover, it has been recently suggested that enhanced functioning of the cerebellum in mental rehearsal might be another neurobiological characteristic of giftedness.

By these accounts, then, it is clear why enhanced working memory capacity, as supported by efficacious frontal functioning and structure, is a hallmark of intellectual giftedness, enabling gifted people to achieve high levels of creative intelligence through task adaptation and selectivity, as well as to score well in IQ tests. What are some of the educational implications for teaching gifted children? The first is that, despite the structural and functional brain differences discussed above, the basic functioning of a gifted brain when learning is the same as for all brains, as described in Chapter 3. Thus it is an unfortunate edu-myth that gifted students can teach themselves. They can't. With appropriate teaching, most of these children can become outstandingly capable and enthusiastic students, but like any children, they need adult guidance and encouragement along with appropriate intellectual challenges. Consequently, specific implications for the pedagogy and curriculum for gifted education programmes include:

- setting tasks with high working memory demands, e.g., tasks with multiple components which require extensive information selection;
- reducing the quantity of small tasks, e.g., repetitive basic examples;
- using challenge tests to evaluate prior knowledge (gifted children, like all children, learn extensively outside of school);
- designing assessment tasks with the higher-order Bloom's taxonomies of analysis and synthesis;
- using above-age learning materials;
- offering lessons on topics beyond the regular curriculum.

Longitudinal studies of gifted education in Australia have shown that the most effective school organization to accomplish such a differentiated curriculum is to group gifted children with other gifted children, regardless of age. Whether or not to segregate gifted children from the mainstream is the subject of heated debate in schools. Although many studies suggest that the losses outweigh the gains, one American study led by Lynn Fuchs compared the mathematical problem-solving performances of homogenous and heterogeneous ability pairs of primary school students. Analysis of videotapes showed that homogeneous ability pairs interacted more collaboratively and were more productive than the heterogenous ability pairs. Interestingly, both high-ability and normal-ability subjects preferred homogeneous ability pairings: the high-ability children because they could get on with it at their faster pace; the normal-ability children because they felt less intimidated when working with peers of like mind. They found working with higher-ability children restricted their problem-solving performance.

This sounds like commonsense. We all relate and work best with like-minded peers. How many friends do we have who are also educators! An interesting finding from genetic research is that IQs of spouses/partners are much more similar (on average about 0.4) than other attributes such as personality (0.1) or height and weight (0.2). It seems that we can intuitively judge the intelligence of others. (How our brains make such intuitive judgements is taken up in Chapter 7.) Similarly, gifted pupils seek out other gifted people in their school, be they older students or teachers. Out of school, subject mentors such as retirees from the local community can be popular. Interestingly, a longitudinal study by Australian educationist Miraca Gross showed that gifted students whose regular daily school classroom experience was an accelerated or dedicated gifted programme did better than other gifted students in their after-school adult life, especially those aspects concerned with establishing mature social relationships.

But however we respond to gifted children, or to those with learning difficulties, individual differences are a fact of life, especially in the classroom, as well as in the neuroimaging lab. Recall from Chapter 1 that the reason we need to image at least 15 people in an fMRI study is to average out all of those individual structural differences between our participants' brains. The fMRI studies reviewed above revealed different developmental trajectories in the brains of children of different abilities. This explains the considerable variance in cognitive abilities and prior knowledge observable at school entry, and why that spread of abilities increases with every subsequent school year. In early years education, cognitive control abilities as an indicator of working memory maturity are actually a better predictor of school readiness than entry-level mathematics or reading achievements.

Sex differences

The difference that teachers are most interested in, however, judging by the frequency of questions asked at conferences, is, perhaps unsurprisingly, about sex: Are girls' brains different from boys' brains? The best answer with the evidence to date is: Mostly no, but in many important respects, definitely yes – both structurally and functionally. This is, of course, how it is with all of human anatomy and physiology. Evolutionary adaptation has determined that where hominid ancestors of either sex responded to their environment in much the same manner, the same relevant biology of both sexes was selected for. But where the adaptive responses for each sex were different, as with reproduction (in very distant non-primate ancestors), or hunting and child rearing (with more recent primate ancestors), the biology was selected for those differences. The basic human body plan is the same – head at one end, feet at the other – but there are many noticeable sex differences – apart from the obvious, men are, on average, taller and heavier. As a result, men, on average, have larger heads and larger brains. The important caveat here is 'on average': obviously there are plenty of women who are larger than plenty of men, and so have larger brains.

Dare I ask: Does (brain) size matter? The answer is: It depends on how size is measured. Throughout the animal kingdom, most of what brains do is keep bodies going, so unsurprisingly, bigger animals tend to have bigger brains. Elephants and whales have bigger brains than humans, but that does not make them more intelligent. A better measure of brain size is the ratio of brain volume to total body volume. With this ratio measure, humans have a much larger brain than seems necessary to run their medium-sized bodies – much larger than the brains of cats and dogs, twice as large as the brains of chimpanzees (our closest genetic relatives), and considerably larger than the brains of elephants and dolphins. And, with this ratio measure, the brains of men and women are equal in size.

But that does not answer the question: Does size have any relationship with intelligence? The answer here is: Yes, sort of. There is a positive correlation between adult head circumference and IQ of a little over 0.3. To the extent that head circumference is proportional to the internal volume available for the brain to fill – the thickness of the skull is also a factor – this correlation implies that brain total volume would explain about 10 per cent of the variance in IQ. But the most differentiating feature of the human brain compared with all other animals, including chimpanzees, is the size of the human cortex, especially in the frontal lobes. A rat cortex is smaller than your thumb nail. A chimp cortex is about the size of a small pocket handkerchief. The human cortex *in situ*, as can be readily seen in Figure 3.1 in the previous chapter, is very convoluted. The folds of the cortical hills (gyri) and valleys (sulci) form a fractal contoured surface, which allows a maximum surface area to fit inside a fixed volume. Imagine taking your least favourite pupil, splitting his skull open, shaving off his cortex and ironing it out flat. Surprisingly, perhaps, his cortex as a 3 mm thick sheet would cover the top of a card table, nearly 80 per cent of a square metre. Is any of this relevant to education? Not directly, although it is interesting to reflect on how much spatial navigation a rat can manage on a thumbnail's worth of cortex, or how birds, with even smaller brains, can accomplish their high speed 3D spatial processing. What it all does underscore is that brain function rather than structure is the more relevant aspect for educational neuroscientific research.

That said, returning to the previous question of sex differences, there are a couple of broad sex-linked structural differences that could result in sex-based differences in cognition that apply in the classroom. Females, in general, have a more robust corpus callosum than men. The corpus callosum is the thick bundle of white matter fibres that is the main connection tract between the two hemispheres. The corpus callosum is the brain's superhighway of interconnected information flow. In females, the corpus callosum has more fibres, which project to more sites in each hemisphere. Such a structural advantage is not inconsistent with the stereotype of women having a cognitive advantage for multitasking, or of having an advantage in articulating emotional thoughts into speech. Males, on the other hand, have greater variance in the structure of their parietal lobes, which are more often denser or thicker than those of women. Parts of the parietal cortex, as we've seen earlier in this chapter, make important contributions to working memory, but the main purpose of the parietal cortex seems to be spatial processing, especially navigation and tracking moving objects. This structural advantage, it could be noted, is not inconsistent with the stereotype of male fixation with sports involving a moving ball. But more seriously, as we'll see in Chapter 8, spatial processing in the parietal cortex is a consistent neural correlate with all areas of mathematical thinking. Einstein, as the postmortem study of his brain famously revealed, had particularly enlarged parietal lobes.

This is not to say that school girls cannot achieve in mathematics as highly as boys do – clearly they do. But it does raise the question of whether the mathematical thinking of girls and boys might be different. Interestingly, in many high schools in Australia, senior students have voted for single-sex classes in mathematics and science. In support of the idea that girls and boys might think differently while doing maths, the Iowa study of mathematically gifted youth found differences in brain activation when comparing the EEG patterns of the gifted boys with the equally gifted girls. The researchers speculated that mathematically gifted boys might have a different way of thinking mathematically from mathematically gifted girls, as well as from non-mathematically gifted boys. The notion of sex differences in mathematics ability, while controversial in some circles, might be expected, given the different hormonal make-up of adolescent boys and girls. Furthermore, it seems that differential prenatal exposure to testosterone is significant too, as one of several neurotaxic agents affecting how neurons grow out of neural stem cells and migrate to form the cortex, particularly affects parietal development. These dynamic developmental processes influence underlying brain organization, specifically by enhancing the development of the non-dominant (usually the right) cerebral hemisphere while concomitantly slowing the maturation of the dominant (usually the left) cerebral hemisphere. O'Boyle's neuroimaging and psychophysical studies of mathematically gifted boys consistently show that the right cerebral hemisphere plays a major role in successful high-level mathematics performance, possibly by supporting the creative dimension (discussed in Chapter 8). Because males and females differ in testosterone levels, it might follow that on average, male and female brains differ in terms of a predisposed affinity for mathematics. Such an account could explain the consistent ratio of about ten males to one female in university departments of mathematics, physics, computing and engineering, despite decades of campaigning to encourage girls to take up mathematically based careers. Of course, many readers will strongly disagree that this has anything to do with sex hormones.

Genetics of intelligence

The brain is a complex of dynamic systems, the plasticity of which is changed by daily experience across the lifespan. At the most reductionist level of the explanatory hierarchy (Figure 1.1, Chapter 1), this involves epigenesis – the expression of genetically encoded programmes triggered by environmental stimuli. How genetic expression is related to variance in intelligence is typically researched through studies which compare the abilities of identical with fraternal twins. Monozygotic (MZ; identical) twins share 100 per cent of their genes (alleles) due to zygote division postfertilization, whereas dyzygotic (DZ; fraternal) twins share 50 per cent of their genes (alleles) because two zygotes were fertilized, the same as for other biological siblings. Strictly speaking, practically all humans share 100 per cent of their genes – that's what makes us human, and not something else. It's variants of these genes – alleles – that underpin our individual differences. The logic of these twin studies is that since the MZ twins have 50 per cent more shared genetic material than the DZ twins, wherever the intra-twin pair correlations on some cognitive or behavioural ability are significantly higher for the MZ twins, it can be concluded that the source of the individual differences in that ability is genetic. A statistical comparison of the intra-twin correlations generates a percentage measure of the genetic heritability.

Leading this international research effort is London-based behavioural geneticist Robert Plomin. One important study by his group into the genetic contribution of high general intelligence involved twin babies. Of course you can't give a baby a normal IQ test, but there is a baby version, the Bailey Scale, which can measure infant mental and motor development, such as reaching and grasping, for babies as young as 2 months. A comparison of MZ to DZ correlations of the top 10 per cent of the Bailey Scale scores showed that heritability for high cognitive abilities was zero at 14 months, but rose to 64 per cent at 36 months. One conclusion from this and similar studies is that heritability is dependent on task difficulty, with performance on more complex tasks having a higher heritability than less difficult tasks. This has implications for understanding the learning needs of gifted children (considered earlier in this chapter).

But the most challenging result from this study is that the heritable genetic contribution increases with age. This, it has to be said, runs counter to the usual assumption made in education that since babies seem to operate on automatic, their genes must be predominantly in control, whereas with older children in school, non-genetic environmental influences such as family should be more important. The evidence from the Plomin group and many other genetic studies suggests the opposite. But recall the discussion of the development of infant intelligence in the first 24 months from

Chapter 3. At a neural level, it is synaptogenesis – the growth, reinforcement and selective pruning of synapses – that determines early cognitive development. All of these neurobiological processes are epigenetic. The more they become important in shaping the emerging individual cognition, so the more heritable genetics contributes to that outcome. Another way of looking at this is to say that while learning obviously improves skill level, at the same time it also increases genetic influence by reducing random environmental effects. That is, learning enables us to reach our genetically mediated ceilings. Epigenesis is therefore an important contribution to behaviour at all ages, but increases to greater levels of stability with older children. This explains the results of adoptive twin studies where adoptees become more like their biological parents than their adopting parents as they grow older. With another suite of genetically driven behaviours emerging with adolescence, and then in adulthood, no wonder we become more like our parents with age, and especially after we ourselves have become parents.

Closer to educational concerns, other studies of the Plomin group with MZ and DZ adolescent twins have shown that one of the many genetically mediated behaviours of that age is a preference for certain styles of classroom organization. I often found it interesting in school staffroom gossip about individual students how one teacher's pet was another's nightmare, or vice versa. This was always put down to a clash of personalities, but Plomin's research suggests it has more to do with the approach we as teachers take to promote learning in our classes. In other words, a student might enjoy our class because of how they learn in it, without especially liking us as a person. And to overstate the obvious, students are not passive in class, but rather are active agents who contribute to the class dynamics and the classroom atmosphere. In other words, students will try and change their classroom organizational environment to suit their genetically driven preference for that particular style of classroom organization. Leaving aside the fact that in a class of 30, these individual student agendas cannot possibly all be compatible, much less with the teacher's approach, the situation is an illustrative example of how genetic effects contribute to the environment. As Figure 1.1, Chapter 1 indicated, it's a two-way arrow of cause and effect between all of the layers, including the genes. It's probably not too far-fetched to comment on the extent to which a newborn baby, simply by being a baby, determines his or her environment. The newborn's home now has a newly painted room full of baby clothes and toys, the car is kitted out with baby carriage and other safety features, and the kitchen cluttered with bottles and sterilization equipment. And then there's the baby's control over adult behaviour: one lusty howl in the wee small hours has the parents awake, comforting, feeding and so on, while grandmother will willingly travel halfway around the world to coo and cuddle. So, the baby's physical and behavioural environment changes to suit the baby – just as classroom organizational environments and teacher behaviour can change to accommodate the learning needs of the students.

Genetic determinants of intelligence are not simply manifest as the passive responses of a child to his or her home or classroom learning environment, but also include reactive (by parent or teacher) and active (by the student) determinants of learning environments in and out of schools. With school-age children, a child's genetic contribution to his or her reading ability may be activated not just by the class reading programme, or parents' books at home, but also by the recommendations for further reading made by the teacher in response to the child's observed interest in or questions about a particular genre or author, and by proactive behaviours of the child such as joining and borrowing from the school or community library. Growing up in a house full of books may have little effect if none of the books is read. Alternatively, by active exploitation of the town library, a child with a high-level genetic predisposition for reading could become an early prolific reader in a house of philistines, as portrayed in Roal Dahl's *Matilda*. Which is not to suggest that fiction can substitute for the tragic reality of children whose 'genetic aspirations' are insufficiently robust to overcome the inertia of an intransigent or hostile learning environment.

Learning, then, is an epigenetic constructive process, and as we saw in Chapter 3, usually dependent on repetition. This process of reinforcement leads to neural systems which build themselves up prior to the emergence of competence. This could explain why performance abilities seem to progress through plateaus rather than along a continuum. The human brain learns best when facts and skills are embedded in contexts that are, in some way, familiar to the learner. Perhaps this is one of many reasons why there is no one gene for intelligence. Plomin's group, among others, have searched for genetic correlates with IQ, and while these exist, each gene only explains less than 1 per cent of the IQ score variance. But this is hardly surprising; if intelligence is an emergent property of what the brain does, then most if not all brain processes will contribute in small but synchronistic ways to cognitive measures such as IQ. So strictly speaking, there are no genes for intelligence, just genes for the protein synthesis underpinning neural developmental processes, such as neuron and glial cell metabolism; the growth of neuronal projections; interlaminar neuronal migration; synaptic neurotransmitter secretion and uptake; and axon myelination. These are the sorts of processes which enable the development of the neural systems by which our brains enable us to be intelligent. Such a 'gene's eye' view of intelligence can explain why IQ scores are predictive of academic performance. As IQ is a ratio measure of the development of intelligence relative to that of a matched population, IQ scores capture, to some degree, the interaction of mental maturity with contextual learning.

IQ scores as a measure of social evolution

An intriguing example of the development of context-mediated neural systems is known as the Flynn effect. New Zealand philosopher James Flynn first brought to the world's attention the fact that during the past century, average IQ scores have been increasing at a rate of about three points per decade. This is true of every country that administers IQ tests. So, was your grandmother stupid? In Chapter 5 we shall take up the common teacher criticism of IQ tests, that they do not capture all that there is about a child's intelligence. But, for now, let's acknowledge that differences in IQ scores do reflect certain differences in children's intelligence, and are predictive of academic success. It is true that older people tend to have lower scores on IQ tests than younger people, and this outcome was once interpreted as meaning that intelligence diminishes with age. However, this age effect only occurs when older people take modern IQ tests that have been rewritten and renormed in the intervening decades since they were children. If older people's IQ is evaluated with tests calibrated for the period during which they grew up, then, barring dementia, an old person scores as well as a young one. Granny can now put down that rolling pin, she's doing just fine.

How then are we to explain the Flynn effect? Are we getting better educated? One might expect that the Flynn effect would be stronger for those IQ subtests which emphasize culture or education. However, the opposite is truer: the increase in average scores is most striking for IQ subtests which measure the ability to recognize abstract, non-verbal patterns. In contrast, subtests emphasizing traditional school knowledge show much less progress and, in the USA, scores on some of these have actually declined. This means that something more profound than mere accumulation of data is happening inside people's brains. The search for possible contributing factors has been vexing. Longer schooling cannot explain the effect; since the 1960s the time spent in school for most children has remained the same, whereas during that period the IQ scores of those children have been steadily rising. Stimulation by the media, and in particular by television, may be another factor, but this cannot explain progress before the advent of television in the 1950s. Improved health and nutrition seemed likely to contribute, but this could only apply to children who have been severely malnourished. What about the home environment? Don't parents nowadays tend to pay much more attention to their children, thus stimulating their cognitive development? But then again, both parents usually work these days, and spend more hours away from the home doing that. Attempts to find a satisfactory explanation for the Flynn effect just produced a puzzling set of paradoxes. It seems absurd to believe that each generation is significantly more intelligent than the generation of their parents.

The answer came from focusing on the abstract pattern recognition subtests which contributed to the largest gains in overall IQ scores. What has improved is not general intelligence itself but an abstract problem-solving ability in response to the ever-accelerating production of science-based technological innovations, exacerbated in recent times with computers and information technology. Unsurprisingly, I am writing this book using word processing software on a laptop computer. In contrast, my undergraduate physics thesis was hand-written and sent to a typist. The minimal computing for that thesis was entered on to punch cards to be undertaken by a machine which filled an entire air-conditioned basement, with a RAM many thousands of times smaller than that of the solid state memory stick which I'm using to store a backup copy of this text. Today, I purchased a home information pack, not in a shop but over the Internet, not with cash but with my credit card. Later tonight I'll set the DVD recorder to tape a programme broadcast over a digital television channel. I'll be using the satellite navigation system, not a map book, in my car to find my way to a hotel for a conference, where I expect to deal with a whole set of unfamiliar digital room devices from the door lock to the climate control. In our daily lives we are immersed in IT. How do we manage? In our brains, such a technologically driven abstract problem-solving ability is enabled by specialized neural systems which have developed to cope with these task demands. Most likely, these systems involve the functioning of the parietal cortices. Parietal functioning, as we've seen, makes important contributions to working memory, and mathematical thinking, through an evolved specialism for spatial organization. A side benefit is that we can perform better on IQ subtests which tap into this ability. Look at the popularity of Sudoku.

But, more relevantly for school education, there seems to be an age effect, described as 'digital natives' and 'digital immigrants'. The younger generations who have grown up immersed in an IT culture with personal computers and other digital devices are the natives; we older people, coping as well as we do (while boring the young with stories of large computers with limited RAM and punch cards) are the outsiders, the digital immigrants. The archetypical contrast used to be that a parent needed to ask their 8-year-old to programme the videorecorder. Now, while we can manage the videorecorder, the 8-year-old is visiting an online virtual reality in Second Life, or 'twittering' in their blog about the latest Augmented

Reality download on their iPod. Many teachers report that the usual generation gap seems exacerbated these days with this digital divide. Oxford neuropharmacologist Susan Greenfield is concerned about the potential effects on the brains of the current generation of children, or at least those who are IT enthusiasts. As we saw in Chapter 3, what is repeated is what is learned, often regardless of its merit. Greenfield hypothesizes that the neural systems developed from excessive IT usage will reflect those particular task demands, with fast responses but insufficient personal engagement, and lacking a capacity for in-depth analysis. As a research question, it clearly needs input from teachers about the behaviour of today's pupils.

Educational neuroscience questions in a box

1   Could education improve working memory?
    Given that we don't fully understand how working memory within executive functioning is fractionated or instantiated at a neural level, could teachers and cognitive neuroscientists join forces to research pedagogies to optimize working memory functioning in the classroom, including:
    - short-term memory capacity;
    - accessing appropriate long-term memory store;
    - making creative connections;
    - delaying closure;
    - evaluating relevance?

2   Conjectures about possible genetic correlates with predispositions to learning and thus manipulations by the child of the school learning environment could be tested with twin studies in classrooms. Such research could investigate subject preference. Is there evidence for a genetic preference for English or maths? Many teachers say there is. Pupils' rates of learning could be another focus for investigation. Evidence for reactive and active genetic correlates should be evident in schools through teacher selection for special activities and student volunteerism respectively.

5 Creativity and Imagination

While one of the joys of teaching comes from the achievement of good exam results from one's students, it is their insights, humour, original solutions to difficult problems, interesting questions and challenging arguments that provide teaching's intrinsic rewards. How does the brain generate such apparently spontaneous creativity? The main themes for Chapter 5 are how the brain enables creativity through cerebral interconnectivity and how the brain employs neural systems for imagination. Together, these generate suggestions for promoting creative thinking in the classroom.

The previous chapter focused on working memory as a cognitive-level description of how our brains enable us to think and be intelligent. The key idea is that brain function can be described in terms of task-specific neural systems which the brain uses to respond to different types of cognitive demand. Neural systems are a useful way of conceptualizing the coordinated flow of information around the brain's myriad functional modules. Executive processing mediates the emergence of these various neural systems, and the adaptive functioning of working memory selects the most appropriate system for the cognitive task at hand. Neuroimaging research has shown that the same brain modules are involved in many different cognitive abilities – spatial, verbal, language, logic, mathematics, memory. This commonality of brain functions provides a neural explanation for general intelligence over a multiple intelligences interpretation.

In the dynamic workspace model of brain functioning of Dehaene and his colleagues, adaptive functioning continually assesses the relative importance of these inputs such that, from time to time, a thought becomes conscious – it literally comes to mind. How often when we're in the midst of doing one thing a thought concerning something completely different suddenly 'pops' into our consciousness. It's as though it were waiting in our unconscious for its turn in our mental queue, and now the more urgent matters have been dealt with, it can take priority. You've rushed to get to school early one morning for the pre-assembly staff meeting. During the principal's report, you suddenly have the thought: Did I turn the gas off on the cooker? Now you cannot possibly concentrate on the principal's new discipline policy – you'll have to phone your neighbour to have her check. Your working memory filter has changed its selection criteria, and a whole new set of neural systems, involving some anxiety, are now prioritized. The students in our classes are no different. Once their immediate priority of getting to the timetabled lesson in the designated room at the correct time has been met, then other matters can assume mental prominence; hence the challenge of maintaining the attention of the whole class for the whole lesson.

In fact, the example of your sudden thought in the staff meeting is typical of our thinking most of our waking life. We're forever challenged with new situations which require an adaptive response – the conversations with family, colleagues and strangers we've never had before, the answers to pupils' questions which we've never had to elaborate in quite that way before, the reports we've never written before, the books we've never read before. To live we must continually be cognitively creative. Our working memories enable us to do this by joining up the appropriate sensory inputs with a myriad disparate but relevant memories necessary to hold that conversation, to provide an answer to that child's question, to write that report. So an interesting question for neuroscience research is, how do our brains enable that to occur.

Fluid analogizing

The approach which I, together with colleagues in Oxford, have used to address this question is to take a cognitive model which captures that creative process and then undertake fMRI studies into the associated neural correlates. The hope is that the results could be applied to the design of curricula to promote creative thinking in the classroom. The cognitive model of creative thinking is based on analogizing: not analogies in the strict sense used in IQ testing, for example, black is to white as night is to . . . ?, but fluid analogizing, where there is not one correct, but several plausible, responses. The concept was developed by artificial intelligence (AI) researchers Melainie Mitchell and Douglas Hofstadter. They were interested in creating AI programs that could embrace conceptual slippage as a way of representing the inherent ambiguity of real-world contexts. As an illustrative example, consider geographical fluid analogies involving cities. What is the London of the USA? Most people answer New York, for obvious reasons, but not if you're a UK politician, when Washington, DC, is your equivalent across the pond. Similarly, a film maker might answer Los Angeles, while a toponymist could point to London, Kentucky. The point is that none of these responses is wrong. It is this attribute which I think captures some of the flavour of creative thinking that we aim to foster in our students. Mitchell and Hofstadter took the idea further with recursion. What is the London of New York? (Soho?) What is the New York of London? (Soho?) What is the London of London? The last sounds like a silly question, until you have a visitor from Australia who is in London for a few days and wants to see the essential sights. In all major cities, tour operators have addressed this very question for some years, with open-top bus or boat tours, and the like. As an example in fiction, Julian Barnes based his novel *England, England* on a fictional extrapolation to the answer to this recursive question. To save tourists from the hardships of travelling on England's crowded and deteriorating roads, an enterprising entrepreneur builds replicas of all of the major tourist attractions – Stonehenge, Anne Hathaway's cottage, Buckingham Palace complete with the royal family, etc. – in one place, on the Isle of Wight. Mitchell and Hofstadter defined creativity in terms of recursion, which is rather different from the sorts of conceptualizations in the arts education literature: 'Full-scale creativity consists in having a keen sense for what is interesting, following it recursively, applying it at the meta-level, and modifying it accordingly.'[1]

The point behind all of the forgoing is that the *modus operandi* of creativity is analogizing. Historically, the most enduring conceptualization of human intelligence is that it is essentially analogical. As William James wrote over a century ago: 'A native talent for perceiving analogies is . . . the leading fact in genius of every order.'[2] That is, the essence of intelligent behaviour lies in making insightful metaphors or analogies. Evidence that analogical thinking is a fundamental cognitive process comes from studies of the conceptual development of young children by Cambridge educational neuroscientist Usha Goswami; emerging intelligence is characteristically analogical. Insightful analogy making is necessary for success in a wide range of educational endeavours, including pattern recognition, composition of musical variations, producing and appreciating humour, translation between languages, poetry, classroom exercises and much of everyday speech. Certainly the use of analogies is prominent in the work of more able students. And in philosophy, it could be noted, Bertrand Russell argued that the essence of reality lies in relationships rather than in objects.

But most importantly in education, a characteristic of good teachers is their ability to create appropriate analogies for explanation and clarification. That is, effective pedagogy entails fluid analogizing to deal with the imprecise categorical relationships of the real world. As Hofstadter elaborates: 'Categories are quintessentially fluid entities; they adapt to a set of incoming stimuli and try to align themselves with it. The process of inexact matching between prior categories and new things being perceived . . . is analogy-making par excellence.'[3] That is, analogizing as a basic pedagogic process is not exact analogizing, but fluid analogizing. Consequently, it is the judicious (albeit often instinctive) employment of fluid rather than exact analogies that enables effective categorization and thus the assimilation of new knowledge. To investigate the neural basis of fluid analogizing, however, a more constrained format was required for the lab than real-world knowledge such as cities. Mitchell and Hofstadter, facing a similar constraint with their AI program, pioneered a formalization of fluid analogizing which involved implicit transformation rules applied to pairs of letter strings. The task, given the first transformation pair, was to complete the second in an analogous way. As a simple example, to **abc** → **abd, ijk** → **?** most people respond '**ijl**' (increase the last letter by one), although '**ijd**' (change the last letter to 'd') and other responses are possible. However, examples can be made arbitrarily more complex, such as **abc** → **abd, iijjkk** → **?** or **a** → **ab, z** → **?** each of which have a number of plausible responses. An example and brief discussion of research into different human responses is provided in the Endnotes for this chapter. Such variance in human fluid analogizing suggested that these letter strings could serve as suitable stimuli for neuroimaging investigations into the neural correlates of fluid analogizing. Our results revealed significant neural activations for difficult fluid analogies in bilateral areas of the frontal cortices, with more activation in the left side for our right-handed participants. Interestingly, in previous neuroimaging studies, these same frontal areas had been associated with inductive reasoning tasks involving syllogisms, and with linguistic creativity.

Moreover, the strength of the activations in two areas in the left frontal cortex were strongly correlated with measures of verbal IQ as determined by the National Adult Reading Test (NART). This seemed a provocative result given that verbal IQ is a measure of crystallized as opposed to fluid intelligence. However, NART scores correlated strongly with the neural physiological response of undertaking fluid analogy tasks. Our interpretation was that since the NART requires implicit knowledge of irregularly pronounced English words (e.g., aisle, yacht, cello, timbre, quiche, rhyme, trait, syncope), fluid thinking with letters is enhanced by a knowledge of real-world letter combinations. In other words, and stretching the interpretation beyond these data, creative thinking builds on embedded knowledge, the knowledge that you don't know you know. This can be simply illustrated by asking the pupils in class to create in their minds a pink unicorn. That's easy: everyone has a conception of pink, and we've all seen pictures of unicorns in storybooks, and more recently, galloping around on screen in the Harry Potter movies. Now ask your class to mentally create a pink potteroo. Unless your class is located in outback Australia, it is unlikely they'll have much success.

One obvious limitation to our study was that it employed only letter string fluid analogies. So, our second fMRI study used numeric and geometric fluid analogies as well. We also included a set of non-fluid analogy tasks using the same stimuli. Again, the patterns of neural activations included bilateral frontal and parietal areas, with considerable overlap in activations associated with the letter, number and geometric analogy strings. The absence of differences between the three stimulus types in their frontal-parietal activations supports the claim that fluid analogizing is a generic cognitive process. Given the similar pattern of frontal-parietal neural activations for fluid analogizing and working memory, it seems reasonable to suggest that fluid analogizing is a cogent cognitive-level description of the brain's integration mechanisms, ranging from assimilation of the new to recognition of the old, through associated representations from long-term memory. For the present it could be speculated that, as a neural mechanism, fluid analogizing is enabled through neural signal match–mismatch articulations between the brain's myriad functional modules. Such speculation is not too far removed from the proposed function of the dynamic workspace in providing a communication protocol which facilitates the flow of information between the brain's many specialist functional modules, many of which do not directly interconnect. Thus fluid analogizing as a basic process of creative thinking within this dynamic workspace model can be conceptualized as describing how a distributed neural system of specialized processors with long-distance connectivity can interact in a coordinated yet flexible manner. Such neural synchronization of possible interrelationships would result in the creation of a suite of temporary solutions in working memory that provide the content for creative thinking.

To attempt to tie this in with education, in our second study we measured participant's IQ scores with a test more widely used in educational psychology – the Raven's Advanced Progressive Matrices (RAPM). An example of the style of a RAPM question is given in Figure 5.1.

Although the RAPM is described as a test of fluid thinking, each item requires one correct answer. We found that the RAPM IQ scores correlated with frontal activations of the non-fluid analogy tasks. This might sound like a rather esoteric research finding, but it actually has significant implications for education. It implies that IQ is a good predictor of academic success in those areas which do not necessarily require outstanding levels of creativity or fluid thinking. In other words, fluidity of thought is not well captured by conventional measures of intelligence such as the RAPM or other IQ tests. This of course has been a long-standing criticism of such instruments in education. Sternberg and others have pointed out that conventional IQ scores do not predict success in the 'real' world very well. Could it be that in real-word problem solving, success is more reliant on a combination of expertise (appropriate long-term memory retrieval), ability to transfer (fluid analogizing in application) and innovation (fluid analogizing in imagination)? Consistently, Clancy Blair in a wide-ranging review argues that the neural development of general

Which answer fits in the missing space to complete
the pattern?

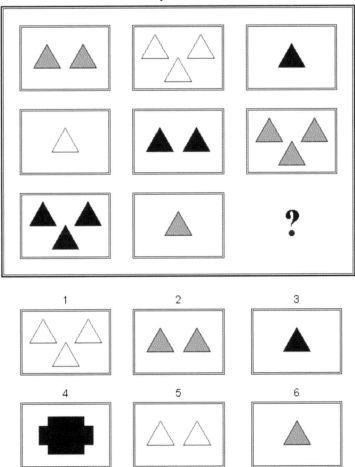

Figure 5.1 Example of a Raven's Matrices-type question

intelligence and fluid cognition in the infant brain embark on separate trajectories, albeit both elicit frontal activations with neuroimaging, because both neural systems require working memory. As a consequence, since fluid analogizing might underpin creativity through the adaptive re-organization and restructuring of novel information, there seems to be a good case for explicitly promoting fluid analogical thinking in the classroom.

Creative intelligence

At a cognitive level of explanation, creative thinking involves combining fluid analogical relationships between disparate concepts within working memory in response to current task demands. At a brain function level, creative thinking would not be possible without our extensive neural interconnectivity. With the hope of developing pedagogical strategies for improved creative thinking in learning environments, and to illustrate the integration of the various cognitive and neural characteristics which contribute to creative intelligence, I created a neuropsychological model which features the role of the dynamic workspace encapsulating working memory within which contextual, perceptual and experiential knowledge is recruited by means of fluid analogizing. Creative people optimize the products of fluid analogizing through enhanced selective attention, including the ability to move between focused and broadened states of attention, and prioritizing relational properties over surface features. The variety of information considered is enhanced by delaying closure and not inhibiting initially irrelevant thoughts. Of course, not all possible solutions or insights are necessarily creative; creativity requires the output to be externally judged as both original and functional.

Like any black box model, Figure 5.2 can be understood by following the arrows. Both external and internal contexts are critical for creatively intelligent outcomes. External context includes extrinsic goals and problems. Internal context arises from tasks that require the internal representation, maintenance and updating of information. Working memory keeps contextual information accessible to influence creative processing. Attentional processes determine the temporary activation of appropriate informational circuits, and thus provide access to the information content of those functional modules when required. Possible interrelationships between problem and context are explored by fluid analogizing.

Recent studies have found a significant relationship between the various indicators of creativity and the ability to inhibit the formulation of an association between a meaningful and a meaningless stimulus. This situation is reversed for a pairing of meaningful stimuli. However, creative individuals are actually slower at drawing final conclusions about information they perceive in the environment. In other words, creative individuals tend to keep an open mind, not readily closing down alternative possibilities to solving a problem while keeping open other possible solutions which in turn could lead toward creative insights. Deliberately delaying closure when problem solving, then, could be one means to enhance creativity in the classroom. However, to keep alternative solutions trajectories online when already an apparent solution is evident within the dynamic workspace requires certain personality traits. Patience and a determination

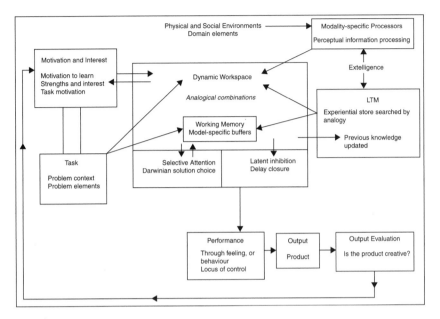

Figure 5.2 A neuropsychological model of creative intelligence (Geake and Dodson, 2005)

to better the already existing solution would seem to be two obvious qualities. So, more creatively intelligent students hold online rather than reject *a priori* a greater number of creative insights or solutions which also requires such students to be characteristically highly task-motivated. Thus a large working memory capacity is critical for high-level creative intelligence because it enables the relative salience of putative solutions to be re-assessed rather than lost. The robustness of neural processing in general is also important, since the efficacy of information transfer (how much or how little information is lost when transferring from one brain module to another), and informational gain (how the salience of particular information is enhanced or reduced on transfer from one brain module to another) determine what particular items of information are available for working memory to consider. The greater the ability to manage large amounts of information in working memory, the larger the number of potential solutions possible. The deeper the knowledge base, the deeper and more prolific these creative possibilities are likely to be. This enables the self-selection of creative ideas. 'Practically all creative individuals say that one advantage they have over their peers is that they can tell when their own ideas are bad, and that they can immediately forget the bad ideas without investing too much energy in them.'[4] Even after self-selection, however, not all possible solutions are deemed to be creative. As noted above, this requires the product or behaviour to be deemed useful and original. Such a judgement can come from the child's perspective, in that it is useful and original for them, or from external peers. Thus, if the route to enhancing creative intelligence lies in fluid analogical thinking, then in the classroom students could be explicitly encouraged to explore how any concept or piece of knowledge is like another, and what insights these possible analogical relationships might afford. Such student insights need to be explicitly evaluated and selected for their usefulness or plausibility. In this way, teaching to maximize a student's creative intelligence through the challenge of high quality creative output could also be a means to optimize working memory function.

There is a considerable literature on pedagogies for teaching creativity, most of which include three elements which reflect working memory function: (1) sensible, insightful and broad perception of existing, available and open data, as well as information searched for and acquired openly and purposefully; (2) solution-orientated but highly flexible processing and utilization of unusual associations and new combinations of information with the help of data from one's own broad and comprehensive knowledge bases (experiences) and/or with imagined elements; (3) synthesizing, structuring and composing these data, elements and structures into a new solution-gestalt. Most authors emphasize the need to highlight the interconnectedness of knowledge, and thus to reward students who make spontaneous interconnections, or use innovative selection criteria, especially concerning ideas that the learners care about, are interested in and about which they have prior knowledge. The challenge for this prescription, however, is that most pupils are attracted to the surface features of analogies. An approach to address this challenge might be at a meta-cognitive level, where students could monitor their use of fluid analogizing to explore new relationships between familiar concepts, or to speculate in the case of less familiar links. They could also monitor their ability not to discard outlier thoughts too early, and to value the feedback received from offering their putative solutions and suggestions to the critical scrutiny of other students in the class.

My argument, in sum, is that fluid analogizing is a universal cognitive trait, and therefore used by all children to greater or lesser effect in the classroom. And given that gifted pupils are attracted to deep structures and relationships, you might expect to see evidence for extensive use of fluid analogizing in the cognitive behaviours of gifted pupils. To this end, in describing the cognitive characteristics of giftedness, education psychologist Barbara Clark notes the close relationship between intelligence and creativity in gifted children. Such characteristics include: an ability to generate original ideas; persistent goal-directedness; a heightened capacity for seeing unusual and diverse relationships; early use of metaphors and analogies; ability to delay closure; and an evaluative approach toward self and others. These characteristics can be accounted for by assuming that gifted pupils have a large working memory capacity supported by a precocious propensity for fluid analogizing. For example, the cognitive processes required of musically gifted children involved in creative improvisation, which include planned musical analyses, compositional variation, delayed inhibition before selection and performance critique, are similar to those displayed by mathematically gifted students in arriving at parsimonious but aesthetically elegant solutions to difficult problems. In both cases, proficiency at fluid analogizing can explain how these processes are seamlessly and unconsciously enabled in the brain.

Imagination

But however creative thinking is managed in the brain, its central subjective experience involves imagination. Imagination as a mental experience embraces many different neural phenomena, as demonstrated by a raft of neuroimaging studies. Not surprisingly, there is no one 'module' for imagination, or even a series of modules for the various forms of imagination. Rather, imaginative processes are highly distributed activities which recruit many different brain areas and neural systems, as described by the dynamic workspace model. For example, forms of imagination involving anticipation, mindedness and counterfactual thinking rely on components such as the cingulate cortex, the lower parts of the frontal cortex, the cerebellum and the orbitofrontal cortex (the bottom part over the eyes).

Nevertheless, there are some common operating principles which underpin the manifestation of different forms of imagination. One is that when we imagine something which we've previously perceived or done, the areas of brain involved in the imagining are much the same as those involved in the perception (with the important exception that imagined movements do not activate the primary motor cortex). For example, a PET study of verbal creation found activations in the left parietal-temporal cortex, an area of the brain associated with using word knowledge in speech. We can't be verbally creative with words that we don't know, James Joyce notwithstanding. To generalize, memory recall has been described as a form of imagining the future. Another principle is that when we imagine something without an external referent, we still utilize memories, including past perceptions. In other words, we create an imagined mental world from our embedded knowledge. For example, the characters which our students create in their fiction will embrace our students' often unconscious experience of persons they have encountered, perhaps best evidenced by the typical introspection of adolescent storywriting. In fact, neuroscientific evidence indicates that the brain conjures up such fictional persona as if they had external referents, perhaps explaining a common report of authors who claim that their characters 'take over' their novel, with the author now a kind of amanuensis for their own imagination.

It has to be said that most neuroimaging studies have not deliberately sought evidence for the neural correlates of imagination as such. In fact, many neuroimaging studies have regarded subjects' imagination as experimental noise, in other words, off-task thinking. Nevertheless, neuroscientific evidence has been sought for the neural correlates of at least six overlapping aspects of imagination, including: prediction through anticipation; perceptual, sensory and motor imagery including pain; pretence; mindedness and empathy; counterfactual thinking including delusion; and creativity. In seeking such evidence, there is a necessary distinction between imagination as a mental product and imagination as a mental process. In the first sense, imagination is a cognitive state stimulated by other cognitive states whether these arise internally or in response to external stimuli. But, imagination can also be the process which creates mental experiences and, moreover, can manipulate them for planning, scheming or any act of creative thinking. Such processing can involve imaginative insights or leaps of imagination – the proverbial 'Aha' experience. As further described in Chapter 8, an American team of neuroscientists led by Jung-Beeman used both fMRI and EEG to study the 'Aha' experience on solving a mathematical problem. The fMRI data showed right temporal involvement with insightful problem solving. The EEG recordings revealed a burst of high-frequency neural signals in the same area beginning 0.3 seconds prior to the insightful solution. Previous studies have shown the right temporal cortex area to be associated with making connections between distantly related concepts. This study suggests that insight occurs when the separate neural systems representing the distantly related concepts are suddenly joined, creating a new system in which previously distinct concepts are now conceptually connected.

The simplest studies of imagination compare the neural activations in the visual cortex arising from seeing a particular object and then visualizing that same object with the eyes closed. Whereas the same areas in the visual cortex are activated in both conditions, the overlap is not 100 per cent. However, the overlap of associated neural correlates in the frontal and parietal regions are more pronounced, suggesting that cognitive control processes might function comparably in both imagery and perception, whereas at least some sensory processes may be engaged differently with imagination. Of course, in most normal situations we can distinguish between perception and imagination, and use the relationship to advantage in visual art classes. However, experiments with inattentional blindness show how easily the brain can be deceived, and pathologies such as schizophrenia are characterized by symptoms involving an inability to distinguish between internally and externally generated auditory and visual imagery.

Perhaps the form of imagination most applicable to education is prediction – the mental representation of possible future events or experiences. Most discipline regimes are based on the assumption that students can predict the consequences of continuing with some behaviour which has been deemed unacceptable. In the brain, predictions are performed by the cerebellum which, as a functional module for mental rehearsal of possible action, can also predict higher cognitive and emotional functions. However, the cerebellum is best known for its involvement in predicting the motor sequences we use every day, and which are obviously critical in sport, dance and musical performance. Mental rehearsal of motor sequences has become a central feature of sports psychology and coaching: athletes, notably gymnasts and high-divers, not to mention goal kickers in rugby, now spend a lengthy period of inwardly focused attention immediately pre-performance. Several fMRI and TMS studies have examined the relationships between the neural correlates of imagined mental rehearsal and execution of simple and complex motor tasks. Interestingly, the network involved in motor performance involving the motor and parietal cortices, and the cerebellum, was more active during mental rehearsal of the complex task. It seems that a musician or athlete can improve their performance skill by appropriate imagination. Moreover, motor task imagery also activated some parts of the lower frontal cortex inside Broca's Area, a region known to be involved in speech production. This finding could be interpreted as evidence for a human analogue of the mirror neurons found in non-human primates (described in Chapter 6). In turn, this could suggest that imagination is not exclusive to human cognition, in other words, that the higher mammals, including monkeys and apes, dogs and cats, all enjoy an imaginative life.

Another common form of mental rehearsal is observed with professional musicians whose performances, particularly solo roles such as playing concerti, are often from memory. A research team of neuroscientists and music cognitive scientists compared brainwave activations of professional and amateur violinists during actual and imagined performance of the first 16 bars of Mozart's violin concerto in G major (KV216). Compared with the amateur violinists the professional musicians showed higher activity in the auditory cortex and sensorimotor cortex, among a suite of areas, but only during execution and not during imagination. The researchers interpreted these findings as evidence that in professional musicians: 'a higher economy of motor areas frees resources for increased connectivity between the finger sequences and auditory as well as somatosensory loops, which may account for the superior musical performance'.[5] That is, the motor and auditory neural systems of professional musicians only became co-activated in real performance situations. The issue of imagined musical performance is taken up in Chapter 9.

Finally, a brief mention of the imaginative life of young children. One of the often reported regrets of growing up is that one no longer can believe in products of imagination which feature conscious or unconscious pretence: imbuing entities or events with imaginary properties, or even fantastical phenomena such as a childhood belief in fairies. Nevertheless, from a neuroscientific perspective, young children make poor subjects for brain scanning studies. Religious experience falls into this category of imagination, and several neuroimaging studies have sought associated neural correlates in adults. One investigation employed PET to measure the relationship between serotonin receptor density and self-ratings on a personality scale measuring religious behaviour and attitudes. The authors concluded that: 'the serotonin system may serve as a biological basis for spiritual experiences [and] ... that the several-fold variability in [serotonin] receptor density may explain why people vary greatly in spiritual zeal'.[6] Another PET study of the neural correlates of religious delusions in psychiatric patients found high levels of activation in the left temporal cortex, a site for 'storing' long-term memories. Interestingly, similar activations in the temporal cortex have been associated with false memories of alien abduction. Whereas it is beyond the remit of this book to pursue this area in more depth, it has to be noted in passing that issues of fundamental religious belief – faith schools, religious dress – do impact on education policy, and those fundamental beliefs of students' such as creationism, which contradict scientific accounts of reality, are becoming an increasing source of conflict in the classroom. The point of raising this issue is that such beliefs, if well embedded in long-term memory through years of social repetition resulting in Hebbian reinforcement, are unlikely to be reconciled in school science lessons.

Educational neuroscience questions in a box

The design and interpretation of scientific experimentation in general require considerable imagination. Thinking up a tractable research question with measurable variables is not easy. Nor is canvassing every possible alternative interpretation when analysing the results. The following chapters outline the neural underpinnings of literacy and numeracy, and of the arts. Chapter 8 mentions fMRI research showing the thinking processes of an experienced artist. What about other school curricula, especially the sciences: physics, chemistry, biology and geology, and their combination in environmental science? Could an fMRI study compare the brain activations of an experienced scientist tackling a scientific problem to see if there are interpretable differences from the activations of a non-scientist? We know from research using talk-aloud protocols that physicists solve physics problems differently from beginner students. Presumably there are neural correlates to match these differences in cognition. Perhaps these findings could be insightful for teaching difficult subjects like physics?

6 Socializing, Emotion and Motivation

This chapter considers social and emotional behaviours as brain characteristics – what on the surface might be regarded as non-cognitive aspects of brain function which are nevertheless important in education. There are close connections between how the brain enables these characteristics and those of intelligence and creativity. The main focus of Chapter 6 is on how the unconscious outputs from our subcortical emotional brain determine much of our students' behaviour, and misbehaviour. Importantly, the brain has separate neural systems for processing rewards and punishments, and this in turn has implications for how we help our students become positively motivated towards learning.

Mirror neurons and socializing

In the previous chapter, the section on imagination as a component of creative thinking introduced mirror neurons as a critical neural correlate of our capacity to envisage the mental states of others, in other words, our ability to put ourselves in other people's shoes. While we usually invest more of our emotional energy in relationships – obviously true for our adolescent students – our relationships with other people are also determined by our predilection for sympathetic imagination. Thus mirror neurons contribute to our capacity for effective socializing.

The recent discovery of mirror neurons in the brains of macaque monkeys and their implications for human brain evolution has been heralded as one of the most important findings of neuroscience in the last decade. Mirror neurons were discovered serendipitously as many important discoveries in science were made (e.g., X-rays, penicillin). The researchers in this Italian neuroscience lab were trying to understand how neurons in the motor cortex of macaque monkeys determine action. Very thin electrodes were placed in some of these motor neurons so that their action potentials could be recorded. A typical experiment was to offer a monkey a piece of food and see which neurons fired when the monkey reached out to take it. One day the audio recorder of one monkey was accidentally left on, so the lab attendant was surprised when it sounded while the attendant was feeding a neighbouring monkey. The food was some distance from the first monkey, so it did not reach for it – monkeys are far too smart to waste energy on a literally fruitless task. The point is that these neurons fired in the brain of a monkey who was not actually performing the motor action at the time, but observing it. These neurons were named mirror neurons since they are active when the monkeys perform certain tasks, but they also fire when the monkeys watch someone else perform the same task such as reaching for a peanut. At least, it seemed that these neurons fired in response to seeing the other monkey reach for the food. This assumption could be tested scientifically. It turned out that while there was mirror neuron activity from hearing peanuts being grabbed in the dark, there was no activity in response to observing another monkey reaching but without any objective. The important conclusion is that the most critical aspect of the task is its inferred intention.

Of course this story would not be of great general interest were it not for the predicted discovery of mirror neurons in the human brain. In an fMRI scanner, there are areas of brain which activate in response to seeing a video of a hand reaching and grasping a cup of coffee, but do not activate in response to seeing a cup of coffee just sitting there, or to seeing an arm moving and fingers grasping at thin air. It is action with intention that is mirrored in the brain of the observer. Interestingly, the homologue in the human brain of the areas of the monkey brain that contain mirror neurons for action is Broca's Area, a part of the lower frontal cortex involved in producing speech. Could this explain why we gesture when speaking, as evidenced by mobile (cell, handy) phone users in the street? And *en passant*, why are some languages more naturally gestural than others? Italian just has to be spoken with dramatic arm gestures. Do we explicitly incorporate this into our second language teaching?

More recent studies have suggested that mirror neurons exist in many other areas of the human brain. In addition to language learning, mirror neurons support a suite of social behaviours including imitation, empathy and 'mind reading'. All of these abilities involve the (mostly) unconscious imagining of other minds – creating mental images of the thoughts and feelings of others (intuition?) To successfully navigate our social environment, prediction, anticipation, pretence and sometimes delusion are all important aspects of our imaginative repertoire. Not surprisingly then, there have been many neuroimaging studies concerned with the neural correlates of other-mindedness or theory of minds. The results, however, have not been entirely consistent, the areas of activation depending on the specifics of the research question of each study. For example, conflicting results have been seen for mental attributions vs. physical attributions; perceptions of self vs. perceptions of others; own self-consciousness vs. self-consciousness of others; first person world-view vs.

third person world-view. Whereas frontal activations were common in all conditions, the main differences were that perceptions of others activated areas in the temporal cortex, whereas perceptions of self activated areas around the junction of the temporal and parietal cortices. One American research group concluded that: 'the data suggest that in addition to joint neural mechanisms, for example, due to visuospatial processing and decision making, third-person and first-person perspectives rely on differential neural processes'.[1] This not unexpected functional modularity of personal perspective raises the question of what neural correlates might be associated with various social interactions between oneself and others. Is it simply a matter of an interaction between the separate neural systems that represent oneself and those that represent others, or do additional neural systems become involved to enable the interaction? One experimental approach has been to investigate the simpler non-linguistic responses to various facial expressions. Using fMRI, Oxford neuroscientist Morten Kringelbach found that the neural correlates of changing behaviour in response to changes in another's facial expression were not located in the fusiform gyrus facial recognition area, but in the frontal areas involved in decision making. Consistently, a PET study by another group who compared subjects' responses to sad stories told by actors with either congruent or incongruent emotional expressions found similar patterns of frontal activations, suggesting that feelings of sympathy rely on separate networks for shared experience and affect. The implication for special education is that effective social learning is especially challenging for children with psychopathologic conditions such as autism which arise from underdeveloped mirror neuron systems.

> [T]he basic response to emotional expressions remains intact but that there is impaired ability to represent the referent of the individual displaying the emotion. In psychopathy, the response to fearful and sad expressions is attenuated and this interferes with socialization resulting in an individual who fails to learn to avoid actions that result in harm to others. In acquired sociopathy, the response to angry expressions in particular is attenuated resulting in reduced regulation of social behaviour.[2]

As a result, children with autism are poor at appropriate reciprocation as an important feedback indicator that one has correctly inferred another's mental states. Appropriate social reciprocation is obviously important for mutually beneficial cooperation. But it is also crucial when playing competitive games, as is counterfactual thinking – imagining what might have been or 'what if'. Evidence for this comes from several fMRI studies which all showed that frontal cortical regions, but no other brain regions, were more active when subjects played games with other human subjects than when they interacted with a computer. The conclusion is that intentionality is critical for the activation of those brain regions involved in imagining the thinking of others. This could explain our predilection for stories, a theme to be discussed in Chapter 7. It certainly is relevant to the daily experience of teachers maintaining good classroom order by anticipating the behaviour of pupils through imagining their intentions. For newly minted teachers, this does not usually come naturally, and therefore needs to be explicitly enacted. For experienced teachers, the professional engagement of their mirror neuron systems is largely unconscious, which is how these brain systems are normally used for non-institutional social learning.

The discovery of mirror neurons in human brains explains a long-standing enigma in the behaviour of newborns. Back in the 1970s, American psychologist Andy Meltzoff made a name for himself in maternity wards by pulling funny faces at babies – poked tongue, pursed lips, mouth yawning, and so on. The babies pulled the same sorts of funny faces right back. Babies from a young age can imitate facial expressions, as parents of newborns know well. The puzzle was to explain this behaviour; the babies have never looked in a mirror. Something in babies' brains knows how to mirror facial expressions that they see. Since to-and-fro facial imitation is a feature of strong emotional bonding between parent and baby, it seems that mirror neuron systems are very important for human development.

It could even be said that a baby's mirror neuron system intuitively solves the problem of other minds – a problem which vexes many philosophers – that our subjective experience of reality cannot necessarily be attributed to others. Consequently, Meltzoff and others suggest that damage to the mirror neuron system could result in an inability to effectively intuit other minds, as observed in syndromes such as autism. Some educational psychologists in the UK have observed that many children who are diagnosed with autism do not seem to show abnormal imitative behaviour as newborns, suggesting that there might be a critical period in which the basis of intuitive socializing is developed, and that an underdeveloped mirror neuron system might compromise the necessary neuronal reinforcement. That said, it could also be noted that many so-called deficits are not a separate syndrome so much as one end of a normal-ish distribution. Certainly there is anecdotal evidence for individual differences in abilities to put one's self in someone else's shoes. Outstanding stage and screen actors and actresses are examples of those with high ability in this area. But how often are we frustrated, when filling in a form, by the ambiguity of a question or the inadequate space to write in our response? And how often when driving in a new town are we baffled by the ambiguous or absent destination signing, of which we only get a fleeting glimpse while negotiating the traffic? Road signage should be positioned by complete strangers to the town, just as a draft form should be trialled by people who have had nothing to do with its preparation. In school, don't we get a colleague to read through our draft examination paper to look out for possible misinterpretations of the questions or instructions before we print it off for our students?

Mirror neurons help us to see the world from the point of view of others. These neural systems enable social learning through imitation, that is, social learning without having to go through trial and error. We could note that the favourite scenarios of young children's pretend play are families, and school (always with a bossy teacher), not to mention dressing up in parents' clothes – literally putting themselves in their parents' shoes. And then there are pre-teens taking careful note of the habits of their older siblings. Recent anti-smoking education campaigns in the UK have used images of young children imitating adults smoking in an attempt to persuade parents not to smoke around the home. We know as teachers that we are role models for our students, and it is thanks to their mirror neuron systems that we are never completely out of school.

However, it is not just social learning through imitation that mirror neurons enable us to accomplish. Learning through imitation is arguably the most basic pedagogy. Eons before there were schools or institutional education, children learned from the adults in their family, tribe or community, through imitation. The master and apprentice arrangement in vocational education reflects this form, as does the newly trained teacher with their senior mentor, and the postdoctoral researcher with their professor. We presumably activate the mirror neuron systems of our students with demonstrations in the language lab, the science lab, the technics workshop, the home science room, the art, dance and music studios, in the gym and on the sports field. The implication from this research is that we should not be shy of showing students how something is to be done.

Nevertheless, 'the' most important outcome of schooling, according to teachers, is that their students socialize well. In an international study of over 300 teachers that I conducted with Miraca Gross we showed that teachers were very concerned about the possible self-restricted socializing of gifted students. We used an evolutionary psychology approach to interpret our results as being indicative of teachers holding a deep-seated social ambivalence towards perceived outsiders. We did not think that this attitude was particularly one of teachers *per se*, but rather that teachers were closer to the action through their daily professional interactions with gifted children. Some previous Australian research found that:

> [T]he major obstacle to [gifted students] receiving appropriate provision was the attitude among educators and the general public that the ability to relate well to others was of prime importance,

with the concomitant fear that any school procedures that single students out as more able might jeopardise this overriding social concern.[3]

Consistently, a more recent study of pre-service teachers in Cyprus found that the student misbehaviour which these teachers anticipated as being of greatest concern was inappropriate socializing, while a lack of interest of students in studying was rated as being of little concern to these new teachers. This result might seem at first glance to be puzzling, but it is not difficult to imagine the evolutionary advantages for our hominid or primate ancestors of group cohesion in environments where survival was a constant struggle. Moreover, pursuing such a generic teaching objective moves the benefits of effective socializing from the interpersonal to the societal level of concern. Thus a central programme for teacher professional development in educational neuroscience might be how a bio–psycho–social model of education could address a broad political question such as:

What are the educational practices most conducive to the promotion of optimum social, cognitive, affective and moral development of children and young people in ways that prepare them for active participation in post-industrial societies?

There seems to be a growing consensus about the qualities required for such participation. The range of abilities required of individuals as a result of this vision of contemporary educational imperatives is vast. Not only are school graduates required to have the age-old skills of literacy and numeracy, but they also are required to demonstrate higher-level reasoning skills as well as self-reliance and emotional resilience in the face of a socially fragmented, unstable and unpredictable world. It is no surprise, then, that social scientists report unprecedented levels of psychological and behavioural disorders among young people. Meanwhile, one political response in the UK to enhancing the role of emotional resilience in education that we could note has been to introduce into the school curriculum lessons in well-being and happiness under the rubric of 'emotional intelligence'. This emotional curriculum involves the reflective regulation of emotions, the analysis and application of emotional knowledge, the emotional facilitation of thinking, as well as the perception, appraisal and expression of emotion. But, it is not clear that emotional intelligence as a construct is reflected in how emotions arise in the brain.

Emotion

We know that our pupils' emotions play a critical role in the quality of their learning. What was not appreciated until recently was the strong neural connection between the emotional and cognitive systems. This connection was suspected, however, for over a century due to the strange but true tale of Phineas Gage. The story is told in many of the books about the brain listed in the Introduction, so a summary here will suffice. Phineas Gage was a construction worker on the railway in the USA in the 1840s involved in laying explosive charges to remove rock from the proposed track bed. His job was to tamp down the charge inside a drill hole once the fuse and compacting sand had been added. His tool was a metre-long iron tamping rod. One day in September 1848 Phineas was apparently momentarily distracted. He tamped the charge before the sand was added, striking the granite rock with a resulting spark. As the *Boston Post* newspaper reported the next day:

> the powder exploded, carrying an instrument through his head an inch and a fourth in circumference, and three feet and eight inches in length, which he was using at the time. The iron entered on the side of his face, shattering the upper jaw, and passing back of the left eye, and out at the top of the head.

The rod landed some 25 metres away. What was amazing about this accident was that Gage survived. After a few minutes he spoke, walked to a nearby cart for the ride into the nearest town with a doctor's surgery. Unsurprisingly, Gage became somewhat of a celebrity.

But, many reports at the time said that 'Gage was no longer Gage'. Previously a quiet, reliable type, he now was short-tempered and quarrelsome, drifting from job to job, and country to country. He died at the age of 38 from an (alcohol-related?) epileptic fit. It seemed that Gage had become someone else, a person who was now unable to make sensible decisions about his life. The question of how this substantial brain injury could have had such a selective effect was investigated by Iowa neuroscientists Hanna and Antonio Damasio. From Gage's preserved but damaged skull they deduced that the tamping iron missed the regions in the frontal cortex involved with language production and motor function, but destroyed sections of the lower inside frontal cortex on the left. This is the part of the frontal cortex which has dense interconnections with the subcortical limbic system, the so-called seat of emotions. Apparently it was this sudden cut in the functional connectivity between the emotional and cognitive areas of the brain that was the cause of Gage's change of personality. Similar frontal damage from disease or surgery in present-day patients results in similar changes. And since the subcortical areas receive direct inputs from the brainstem, which receives nerve signals from the rest of the body, Antonio Damasio advanced a somatic marker hypothesis: that the genesis of emotions in the brain is body states, and the brain uses emotions to create feelings in the subcortical limbic system which mediate our decision making, undertaken in the frontal lobes. That our rational decision making is largely influenced by emotions and feelings seems contrary to the advice we often were given as children: when making a difficult decision we should put our feelings to one side. But as salespeople well know, we make important decisions, such as buying a new car or buying a new house, very much based on our feelings rather than on our bank balance. Some years ago car advertisements stopped featuring content about engineering details and emphasized the hedonic experience: 'Oh what a feeling!' To save ourselves from ourselves, we also now have a cooling off period in legal contracts. And dare we muse over the gut feelings involved with falling in love and choosing a life partner? The point for education is that, unless we are on the lookout for them, these brain processes are unconscious. Thus the misbehaved pupil when asked why they did what they did might shrug their shoulders and mumble, 'Dunno', because, in fact, they don't. So, for the same reason, we might need to literally count to ten when confronted by such an emotionally charged situation of student misbehaviour, rather than let fly with our initial emotionally driven response.

The somatic marker hypothesis is not without criticisms: paraplegics and quadriplegics, whose nerve pathways between body and brain have been severed through accident, still have feelings and emotions. But the principle that emotions are critically involved in learning at a neural level supports the behavioural observations of teachers over the centuries. There is a bi-directional dependency: aspects of emotion rely on cognition, and aspects of cognition rely on emotion. The strong emotional dimension to learning has educational implications for pedagogy. The hippocampus, the subcortical organ responsible for long-term memories, as noted in Chapter 3, has strong reciprocating connections to the amygdala and other modules in the limbic area which are involved in the generation of emotions. This neuroanatomical arrangement explains the well-known phenomenon that memories have an emotional dimension: that pupils learn what they care about. Such truisms are evident everyday in schools, from the excitability of a Reception class after an enjoyable activity – 'Can we do that again, pleeeease?' – to the turgidity of a middle secondary school class where, in some of its 15-year-old members, the egocentredness of adolescence finds expression in more hedonistic activities than are usually provided for at school. School by comparison seems dull and irrelevant, with even the most willing teachers cast in a negative light.

The contrasting feelings in the above examples illustrates an important consequence of our evolution: not all emotions are equal. There is an emotional imbalance favouring negative emotions, particularly fear. It is not difficult to imagine how this imbalance evolved. A fear-induced response to a life-threatening situation – fleeing from a predator – if successful, means you live to reproduce. Stop to sniff the roses and you don't.

An extensive programme of research into the science of emotion led by New York neuroscientists (and occasional rock guitarist) Joseph LeDoux has articulated the evolved role of the amygdala in driving behaviour in response to potential real or imagined threats. No matter what sort of stimulus comes into the brain – visual, auditory, olfactory – the amygdala receives the signal directly from the sensory areas, prior to the signal reaching the decision-making areas of the frontal cortex. The amygdala is programmed to immediately generate a fear emotion in response to any perceived threat, and to communicate that response to the cortex. In general, an unconscious fear reaction can more easily gain control over the cortex and influence our conscious thinking than the reverse. There is neuroimaging evidence to support this claim. FMRI studies show that amygdala activation can easily be triggered in response to seeing pictures of fearful faces. But there is no real threat. Participants in these studies are lying perfectly safely in a brain scanner in a lab looking at pictures. The amygdala apparently ignores all that: the image of bared teeth or an angry expression is enough for it to activate. So, how does the amygdala 'know' what is threatening? Some things seem to be 'hard wired' into our primate brains – the sight of a snake is one. Others are culturally specific, and are therefore learned. As LeDoux summarizes: 'We come into the world capable of being afraid and capable of being happy, but we must learn which things make us afraid and which make us happy'.[4]

But what if the amygdala gets it wrong? From an evolutionary perspective, better a false positive (you run away for nothing) than a false negative (you fail to recognize the threat – end of story). However, evolutionary legacies are not necessarily always helpful in today's society, where very few threats are actually life-threatening. Nevertheless, controlling our amygdalas is no easy task. We lie awake at night worrying about the rowdy Year 8 class on Friday afternoon or the less than amiable exchange with the head at the staff meeting, rather than about the sweet gift of a finger painting by the new pupil after class. LeDoux even speculates that the rise in neuroticism in Western societies, at least in America, is the result of amygdala activations in response to imagined and low-level threats. But the important point is that fear responses win out, and occupy our attention and consciousness wherever possible. Hence the deleterious effects on school learning of a fearful home environment through neglect or abuse, or a fearful school environment through bullying. Adverse or threatening environments can elevate levels of cortisol in the body. There is good evidence for the negative impact of raised cortisol levels on frontal cortical functioning and development that in turn affects attention, working memory, and so on. The mental rehearsal of potential threats will occupy working memory when it should be attending to the lesson content and learning experiences. For example, in studies of early literacy development, low SES as a partial predictor of a poor home environment correlates with lower activations in areas of the frontal cortex when engaged in language tasks. And, as teachers, we have probably all observed extremes of school negativity leading to truancy and/or school vandalism.

What can be done to alleviate this emotional priority of fear? As noted above, an increasingly popular approach in school incorporates emotional intelligence: the capacity to effectively perceive, express, understand and manage emotions in a professional and effective manner. Advocates list a number of factors to be used in determining measures of emotional intelligence. These include: the ability to identify one's own feelings and emotional states, and the ability to express those inner feelings to others; the ability to identify and understand the emotions of others, and those that manifest in response to workplace environments, staff meetings, literature, artwork, etc.; the extent to which emotions and emotional knowledge are incorporated in decision making and/or problem solving; the ability to manage positive and negative emotions both within oneself and others; and to effectively control strong emotional states experienced at work such as anger, stress, anxiety and frustration. Presumably these measures are normative, that is, they are desirable outcomes of educational programmes in emotional intelligence. It all sounds very reasonable, except that it implies that such conscious endeavour can be successful, contrary to what we know about the amygdala and its unconscious hegemony. Nevertheless, there is some evidence of a relationship between emotional intelligence and academic achievement. A team of Australian education researchers found that emotional intelligence measures could distinguish between the relatively higher and lower school final year exam scores of academically gifted students; such a distinction was not so evident for non-gifted final year students. I wonder if this might have more to do with positive emotions, what might be termed 'subject passion' or 'motivation'?

Motivation and self-esteem

How can we as teachers raise and maintain the motivation of reluctant learners? We saw in Chapter 3 that learning as a neural process requires reinforcement of synaptic functioning. From the research of LeDoux and others on amygdala functioning, we also know that learning via synaptic plasticity is strongly mediated by emotion-related processing, by both non-specific neural signals (e.g., dopamine) and specific signals (e.g., attentional gain in the frontal cortex). If such a neural change invokes positive (and negative) affect, then this in turn will strengthen (or weaken) motivation in that subject, as seen in, for example, increasing polarization of children's motivation into a positive or negative attitude towards mathematics.

Such an emotionally charged brain change when understanding is suddenly and consciously recognized – the proverbial 'Aha!' – can be seen by a sudden jump in the intensity of the EEG signal. This jump is presumably indicating the dynamics of neuronal systems which rely on the anatomical interconnectivity between the subcortical limbic regions and the cortex. For slower but more permanent emotional associations with learning, dopaminergic pathways also extend from the limbic subcortex to the cortex, especially the frontal cortex and basal ganglia. Importantly, dopamine affects neuronal firing and thus directly mediates the synaptic plasticity necessary for learning. This is how teachers' praise and encouragement, such as gold stars in the early years classes, bring about reward-seeking behaviour and thus motivation in pupils. Interestingly, the release of dopamine can even be triggered by the environment associated with the reward, without the reward itself having to be present. Dopamine would then be responsible for a whole set of behaviours designed to obtain the reward. For example, a positive, enjoyable class on Monday can result in pupils (and teacher) skipping along to class on Tuesday in eager anticipation of a repeat positive experience. This crucial link between motivation and reward seems to have a genetic basis. Blocking the effects of a particular gene (D2) in monkeys cuts the link between motivation and perceived reward. Humans have the same gene.

But happy feelings are only one of many emotional responses elicited during the average school day. There are multiple emotion systems in the brain, as demonstrated by the separate fMRI activations in response to seeing angry vs. happy faces – located in the inside (medial) vs. outside (lateral) frontal cortex respectively. Given that the medial surface of the frontal cortex is closer to the amygdala, located in the medial part of the subcortex, this neuroimaging result seems consistent with the evolved amygdala-driven priority for processing life-threatening fear responses over other emotions. Joy is not mediated by the fear system. The admittedly saccharine scenario above of skipping to class might readily become, instead, one where pupil and teacher drag their feet with dread. One hopes that the eponymous graffiti 'Skool sux' on the toilet wall was not chalked up by a teacher.

Emotionally mediated decision-making processes are affected differently by the brain's separate systems for processing potential rewards and threats. Rewards do not have to be explicit. For example, learning can be enhanced by challenge, particularly novelty, where the reward is a sense of accomplishment. Humour also can enhance learning through endorphin release in the brain. But, learning can be inhibited by threat which, in school, can include potential punishments. As we've seen, the human brain judges the faces and tones of voice of others for threat levels in a rapid and often unconscious way. This obviously includes the brains of our students judging our facial expressions and voices. The result is that 'positive' motivation can be enhanced through anticipated reward, just as 'negative' motivation can be enhanced through threatened punishment.

Oxford neuroscientist Edmund Rolls represents this bipolarity in diagrams such as that in Figure 6.1(a), where the vertical axis represents 'Reward', while the horizontal axis represents 'Punishment'. They are drawn at right angles to indicate their separateness as neural systems. Note that the end points of the axes indicate that there are two possible outcomes – getting or missing out on – both reward and punishment. If we now put a positive value $(+1)$ on getting a reward, and of avoiding punishment, and then a negative value (-1) on missing out on a reward or receiving a punishment, then as shown in Figure 6.1(b), the top left quadrant gets a $+2$ value representing the proverbial carrot, whereas the opposite bottom right quadrant has -2, representing the proverbial stick. Whereas behaviourism is a most impoverished approach with which to account for human cognition, it is still true that we all respond predictably to carrots and sticks. However, Figure 6.1(b) indicates other possibilities of behaviour, with the top right and bottom left 'neutral' corners providing a personality axis between low and high risk taking, presumably based on task-specific assessments of the likely outcomes. Thus, while we see some pupils always willing to have a go, and others usually preferring to hold back, we might look out for some variance in our expectations depending on the subject area.

Incidentally, since fear and joy involve separate neural systems, I wonder if 'Agreeing' and 'Disagreeing', in response to surveys, also use these or similar separate brain systems? If so, then the ubiquitous Likert 'scale' (*Strongly Agree–Strongly Disagree*) of survey research is not unitary, but in fact consists of two scales: an 'Agreeing' scale and a 'Disagreeing' scale. If this speculation has any foundation, then much Likert scale research is unsound. Who hasn't, when filling in a Likert scale survey, found themselves thinking of instances when they agree, and other instances when they disagree with a particular statement? This is not the place for a lengthy digression into research methods, but if you are a teacher undertaking survey research for a Masters' or professional doctorate degree, my advice is to use another sort of scale for your measurements.

The separate neural systems for the emotions underpinning motivation have implications for our understanding of self-esteem. Self-esteem can be regarded as a non-specific or general motivation. It has been an

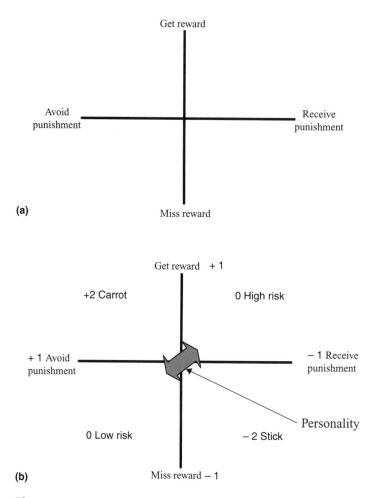

Figure 6.1 Motivation through reward and punishment (after Rolls, 1999)

educational orthodoxy for many years that self-esteem has a causal influence on educational performance.

Consequently, raising self-esteem should concomitantly raise education performance measures such as exam grades. Self-esteem is not a unitary construct, and researchers distinguish between personal, academic, physical and social self-esteem, showing that measures of these various aspects of self-esteem tend to be independent of one another. It is academic self-esteem which is of interest here. American social psychologist Roy Baumeister caused quite a stir in educational circles when, a few years ago, he published the findings of a large-scale study of self-esteem and school performance undertaken in California. The reason that California was chosen as the location was that teaching to raise self-esteem was mandated several years ago, so the opportunity for a positive effect seemed optimal. His results showed that raising self-esteem does not improve grades. Rather, the opposite: improving grades can raise self-esteem. The main reason seems to be that a pupil's self-esteem can be raised as a result of successfully meeting a challenge, be it scaling a cliff or solving a difficult problem. Self-esteem, especially academic self-esteem, is not raised by a pupil being constantly told in class that every remark he or she makes, including answering their name in roll call, is wonderful. Answering the roll call, or doing some time-filling task in class, has no positive emotional association for the pupil, so the teacher's attempt at self-esteem raising in such instances is wasted. Rather, as granny knew well, success breeds success, and failure can lead to more failure.

Positive motivation, then, requires positive feelings, which can be engendered through feedback about success. To this end, there is evidence that vertical curriculum structures based on learning readiness are more motivating than the usual age-lock-step arrangements. As motivation is critically dependent upon affective feedback, so learning will remain compromised while the cycle of low competence generating low confidence, generating low competence and so on, is perpetuated. Consequently, I prefer a more flexible approach to automatic age-based 'progression' in schools, such as a vertical organization of the timetable. Under a vertical organization students, guided by their teachers, can choose a timetable based on interest and level of difficulty rather than what school year they happen to be in by dint of their birthday. Such re-organization within some secondary schools in Australia has achieved a measure of success, particularly with students in the learning extremes. Those students who found the mainstream curriculum too academic, and consequently for whom age-lock-step progression was a recipe for inevitable failure, progressed 'horizontally' with more success and consequently with better motivation. Academically able children who found age-lock-step progression too under-challenging were able to accelerate to an appropriate level, again with higher levels of motivation. The pay-off for teachers was better behaved classes.

Attention deficit hyperactivity disorder

One of the more challenging group of children to accommodate in today's classrooms are children with Attention deficit hyperactivity disorder

(ADHD). The American Psychiatric Association describes ADHD as a pervasive, severe and chronic inattentiveness, impulsiveness and, in some cases, hyperactivity. International prevalence rates vary between 3 and 6 per cent among school-age children. The condition is believed to have a biological component and to be genetically transmissible. Despite claims that ADHD is symptomatic of some contemporary societal malfeasance, the condition was first identified in the UK over a century ago. As psychiatrist Michael Trimble argues:

> It has become fashionable to ascribe much psychopathology to the evils of modern society. Although . . . this is not a new theme, its resurgence reflects the popularity of the simple. Often imbued with political overtones, and rarely aspiring to scientific insights, such a view of the pathogenesis of psychiatric illness ignores the long tradition of both the recognition of patterns of psychopathology and successful treatment by somatic therapies . . . Further, it does not take into account the obvious fact that the biological heritage of mankind extends back many millions of years.[5]

In the classroom, the neuropathology underlying ADHD is made manifest at the social, emotional and motivational levels of expression. Neuropsychological research has focused on impulsiveness as the central feature of ADHD, with the possibility that the neurological aetiology is a dysfunctional response inhibition system. There are a multitude of attentional demands made on a student during a lesson. Attention to a new stimulus requires the inhibition of the previous stimulus. For example, a command for the class's attention such as: 'Now look at the board', has to invoke an inhibition response to the previous command: 'Now, who can remember what we were just doing?' Children with ADHD find this constant shifting of attention particularly difficult. That is, these children experience significantly greater problems than most in inhibiting or delaying a behavioural response.

American clinical psychologist Russell Barkley proposes a model of ADHD wherein ineffective response inhibition leads directly to a cascade of problems in those executive functions of the brain which are essential for self-regulation: working memory, internalized speech, motivational appraisal and behavioural synthesis. As we've seen in Chapters 4 and 5, inhibition is the critical aspect of the informational selectivity (the neural bouncer) which enables working memory to function. Without effective inhibition, children cannot retain and manipulate information for appraisal and planning. Internalized speech is a means of exerting some control over unconscious drives through a process of self-talk, during which possible consequences and implications of impulses can be weighed up. Associated with such explicit decision making about potential behaviour, motivational appraisal refers to the emotional associations generated by an impulse and the extent to which the impulse is likely to produce outcomes we find desirable. Behavioural synthesis concerns planning new and appropriate action on the basis of evaluating the consequences of past behaviours.

There is evidence from neuroimaging studies to support Barkley's model. Structurally, individuals with ADHD have on average smaller brains, and particularly smaller cerebellums, the 'second brain' responsible for mental rehearsal and coordination of action. In fact, one study with ADHD children aged 5 to 18 years found a direct relationship between diminished brain size and the degree of ADHD symptoms. Longitudinal studies show that this difference persists as children grow older, suggesting that ADHD arises from genetic and/or early environmental influences on brain development. Unmedicated children with ADHD also exhibited smaller total white matter volumes – a possible indicator of reduced neuronal maturation or connectivity – compared with non-ADHD children and with medicated children with ADHD. However, these neuroimaging studies found no evidence of brain damage. In other words, these structural correlates are associations, and may as well be a result of the condition and not necessarily a cause. One could also ask whether unmedicated children with ADHD are suitable participants for some forms of functional imaging where voluntary immobility is necessary.

Functionally, ADHD sufferers have reduced activations in the frontal cortex, basal ganglia, the striatum and the anterior cingulate cortex. As we saw in the previous chapters, it is the connectivity between the frontal cortical regions of the brain and the basal ganglia which enable attention and the ability to exercise inhibition. Neurochemical studies have found higher levels of dopamine transporter in the basal ganglia of ADHD children which, after treatment with Ritalin, became normal. That is, the chemical effect of the drug prevents dopamine being mopped up too quickly before the basal ganglia can use it in the neuronal firings involved in making decisions. One American study compared adults diagnosed with ADHD with non-ADHD adults in a conflict task. The control participants showed more anterior cingulate cortex activation than those participants with ADHD, probably due to higher attentional efficiency. The ADHD participants showed greater activation in the anterior insula, a brain region typically associated with responses in more routine tasks not involving conflict. After medication with Ritalin, however, the ADHD participants showed increased levels of activation in their anterior cingulate cortex and lower insula activations, in line with those of the non-ADHD adults. Similar activation trends were observed in children with ADHD following administration of medications – evidence of how Ritalin and other ADHD prescriptions affect the neural systems concerned with inhibition. It might seem contradictory to prescribe psychostimulant drugs such as Ritalin (methylphenidate) to control the behaviour of children who seem way too stimulated in the first place. The effect of the drugs, however, is to 'speed' up inhibitory processes in the brain by blocking dopamine transporters and thereby increasing the available dopamine in the striatum and basal ganglia. That said, Ritalin is no silver bullet. Finding the optimal dosage for each child at each stage of life is no easy matter, but it is crucial for the pharmacology to be effective, since both too little *or* too much dopamine can negatively influence working memory. This could explain why longer-term side effects such as a constraint on general cognition have been observed with older children who have been regular Ritalin consumers.

There is also evidence for the claim of a genetic basis to the abnormal neurological development that leads to ADHD. The condition is more common in biological relatives, especially parents, of children with ADHD than it is in the biological relatives of children who do not have ADHD. In particular, twin and adoption studies have repeatedly shown a much greater incidence of ADHD among MZ (identical) twins than among DZ (non-identical) twins. Consistently, certain genes have been identified as being implicated in the aetiology of ADHD and ADHD type symptoms, and these are genes for the expression of dopamine. This could explain why children suffering from this condition appear to be immune to the effects of commonly used behaviour management strategies such as punishment and counselling. Nevertheless, the possibility of genetic markers suggests that early identification is possible. This, coupled with detailed understandings of the possible cognitive processes involved in the aetiology of the condition, could provide a basis for the development of early psycho-social interventions, a well as providing important indicators for later remedial programmes, such as mnemonic training and rehearsal skills. To this end, a more individualistic curriculum, both in terms of pedagogy and content, may be necessary to cater for the full range of learning needs of children in today's classrooms if schools are to be genuinely inclusive of those children who, through no fault of their own, have genetic predispositions for language delay, attention deficit disorder or some other condition which threatens normal progress in learning – or for that matter who have a genetic predisposition for intellectual precocity. All deserve an education which is best for them, which is much easier said than done, especially when resources for specialist staffing are finite.

Educational neuroscience questions in a box

We know about the interconnections between the frontal lobes and the modules of the limbic system responsible for the generation of emotions. Damasio has described how the functioning of the frontal regions – our so-called rational thinking – is driven by our feelings and emotions. In other words, performance necessitates emotion. What are the neural correlates of passion for an academic subject such as mathematics? How do insights into mathematical understanding generate, and how are they generated by, mathematical passion? Are the neural systems which underpin mathematical passion the same, or similar to, those that underpin passion in other subject areas?

7 Language and Literacy

The area of human cognition most investigated by neuroscience is language usage in its many guises, probably because language use is often regarded as the defining characteristic of humans as a species. This is not to downplay the impressive oral and gestural communication employed by most animals. Rather, it is to highlight the orders of magnitude of the greater facility for communication regularly demonstrated by even very young humans, and their nascent language abilities. That remarkable dexterity of linguistic application, however, poses a challenge for neuroscientists who need to control variables in their neuroimaging laboratory settings. It suggests a caveat to what follows in this chapter: studies of the neural correlates of language usage, given the current limitations of neuroscience technologies, will necessarily fail to capture the richness of linguistic expression of writers, poets, orators, and not to mention teachers of English and second languages. Nevertheless, as the science has often focused on understanding the differences in neural systems of children who fail to achieve normal levels of literacy, the research to date has direct relevance for education.

A second caveat concerns the generalization that language systems in the human brain are exclusively left lateralized. While this is true as a generalization, it is not true for many individuals, and it is not true for all of the neural systems which contribute to speech and literacy in everyone. The generalization that language is exclusively a left-brain activity can be traced back to two famous neuropsychological case studies in the nineteenth century of patients who suffered strokes which dramatically affected their language abilities. One of these patients could no longer speak effectively, while the other spoke fluently but no longer made sense. Postmortem examinations showed that the damage in the first case was in the lower frontal cortex on the left, while the damage in the other case was in the upper temporal cortex, again on the left side. These areas have since been named after the physicians who conducted these cases: Broca's Area and Wernike's Area respectively. Today the roles of these brain regions have been confirmed through many neuroimaging studies of both stroke patients and people with undamaged brains. However, as noted in Chapter 1, all of the latter group are right-handed, for the important experimental reason that 95 per cent of right-handers have their Broca's Area in their left hemisphere. With left-handers, only 60 per cent have their

Broca's Area exclusively in their left frontal cortex, so they are usually excluded from neuroimaging studies. For example, a PET study at the University of Cambridge into how the semantic system is left lateralized not only tested the handedness of participants, but also that of their parents and grandparents to exclude those who might have been born left-handed but were forced to switch handedness at school. The results of this study were consistent with others: the language contributions were a product of activity in the left hemisphere, whereas auditory, graphic and emotional contributions were a product of activity in the right hemisphere. But as the lead researcher Guillaume Thierry emphasized when presenting the group's research at an Oxford research seminar, these data represent: 'A significant quantitative bias found in the brains of extremely right-handed subjects' and therefore, 'It is dangerous to suppose that language processing only occurs in the left hemisphere of all people.' This message, not to apply generalizations to individuals, has been the rationale for pre-surgical assessments for many years. Paediatric surgery to alleviate chronic epilepsy always aims to preserve the child's language areas. Neurosurgeons never assume that these are always nicely located in the left hemisphere. Before neuroimaging, pre-surgical assessment could involve administering a local anaesthetic into each of the carotid arteries leading to the brain in turn to see if that prevented the child from speaking. Now the pre-surgical assessment can be undertaken using fMRI. But with many current neurosurgical procedures, the patient remains conscious so that they can provide real-time feedback about the effects of the surgery on their language functions. The scientific generalizations in the following sections should be noted with these caveats in mind.

Language

All normally developing children learn to talk in their native language or mother tongue(s). As we saw in Chapter 3, babies become more selective in their repertoire of babbling, and presumably listening, during their first 9 to 12 months. There are implications for education arising from this exemplar of Hebbian learning through reinforcement. Coupled with the explosion in lexical development of young children, there seems to be a good case for a sensitive if not critical period for language development. The optimal period for learning languages might be pre-school rather than highschool. In terms of neural systems, learning to talk in a language requires the coordination of many neural systems, not least auditory systems for matching heard sounds from other speakers with motor systems for producing speech, with grammar systems for incorporating specific linguistic conventions, with sensory systems for external referents, with semantic systems of what and where for meaning. How wonderful, then, that so many of us manage this so well and with apparently such little effort. However, given that language requires the coordinated involvement of multiple neural systems, it is perhaps not surprising that some children experience delays in language development, presumably due to genetic predispositions that compromise the efficacy and/or interconnectedness of these multiple systems.

As noted in Chapter 4, genetic contributions to human behaviour can be determined by comparing behavioural similarities of identical and non-identical twins. In one of the largest studies of this type, an Anglo-American team of researchers explored the relative effects of environment and genetic inheritance on language delay among a sample of over 2000 sets of 2-year-old MZ twins born in England and Wales in 1994. A sample of nearly 4000 DZ twins born in the same year was also studied – in total, 44 per cent of the entire population of twins born in that year. The cohort was found to be representative in terms of maternal ethnicity and educational achievement. The age of 2 years is significant because this is the age at which verbal language begins to occur in the general population. The central research question was this: To what extent was the likely variance in levels of language acquisition, as gauged by scores on a standardized vocabulary test, related to genetic differences between individuals? The findings were that for the general population the heritability factor was 25 per cent, compared to 69 per cent for the influence of shared environment. That is, differences in home environment were much more important than differences in genetic variants. For the bottom 5 per cent of the sample, which would place these children in the category of specific language impairment (SLI), however, the heritability factor was 73 per cent, with environmental influence falling to 18 per cent. That is, for the SLI children, the significance of the heritability factors was the reverse of that for normally developing children.

There are important educational implications for the finding that SLI at age 2 years is highly heritable. In principal, it should be possible to predict the likely occurrence of the problem in particular families. This could enable such families to be targeted for preventive action. In particular, early identification could be used to empower parents of at-risk children, through targeted training, to take proactive steps to aid positive language development. Such training might involve instruction on the measures required to develop an enriched language environment. This might in turn lead to the involvement of parent and child in community-based programmes. Given the well-documented association between language delay and emotional and behavioural difficulties in the early years of formal schooling, early identification of language delay could have a positive effect on the development of school-based programmes for behavioural difficulties, with concomitant implications for the mediation of adolescent deviance and delinquency as well as for adult criminality, the latter being significantly correlated with school (mis) behaviour.

The findings of this twin study have been replicated in other international research. One Finish study using ERP showed that differences in the brain waves associated with responses to hearing words within the first week of life could predict later language and literacy difficulties. Again, neural interconnectivity is crucial. Research in language development by English neuropsychologists Andy Ellis and Andy Young has shown the important contribution to language development of non-phonological auditory inputs processed in the right fusiform area, the same area used for the processing of faces and other features of the infant's environment. Hence the value of stories and songs in which 'the cow goes moo, moo, the duck goes quack, quack', and so on. Moreover, consistent with the above account of language development emerging from the interactions of a suite of neural systems, facility with multiple word combinations has a higher heritability than that for speaking isolated single words, suggesting that putting words together into sentences engages a qualitatively different neural system. And consistent with an account of brain development which entails increasingly more specialized functional modules, the variance in the genetic heritability for language at 18 months is shared with that for non-verbal abilities, whereas by 24 months, when language development is blooming, the genetic heritability for language abilities becomes more independent.

For 95 per cent of infants, it must be emphasized, their linguistic environment seems the more important contributor to differences in verbal abilities during their first few years of life. That suggests that infants have genetically expressed neural systems for taking advantage of their linguistic environment, and learning from it. The American linguist Noam Chomsky famously argued that infants have a cognitive predisposition for assimilating the rules of grammar of their native tongue, on the grounds that imitation of adult speech could not account for the countless original sentences that children spoke every day. This has in turn been interpreted by others as implying the existence of a specialized neural system for the processing of grammar, and thus, possibly, a specific gene. One putative candidate was a gene found in mammals and birds labelled FOXP2. Deficits in the FOXP2 gene affect the ability of songbirds to sing, the ability of mice to squeak and the ability of humans to speak. A family in London (known as the KE family) have had this defect transmitted through three generations. Could FOXP2 be a gene for Chomsky's grammar? Genetic research shows that this is not the case. The FOXP2 gene turns out to be a transcription factor – it regulates the expression of a cascade of other genes related to motor routines of various sorts, including some of those that are involved in speaking. The members of the KE family cannot even wipe their upper and lower lips with the tip of their tongues and then put their tongues back in their mouths. And licking your lips hasn't anything to do with grammar.

For almost all children with normal FOXP2 genes there is behavioural evidence that they accurately acquire simple grammatical forms even from an impoverished input. It is not so clear whether children are able to acquire more complex grammar without a relevant, complex grammatical input. Many children are brought up in an environment where there is not a great deal of complex language interaction; many children, and adults, have difficulty in understanding forms such as the conditional. There is some evidence that intentional exposure of children to more complex forms in the classroom can improve their acquisition of grammar. Work on congenitally deaf children has shown that the ability to acquire grammar is best achieved before the age of about 6 years, and that the nature of the language input (oral or signed, Indo-European or other) is irrelevant. The point is that early exposure to language organizes the brain for further language acquisition. That is, exposure to rich language is the optimal stimulator for the expression of the genetic programme for the development of neural systems which enable increasing sophistication of language usage. The implication is that children who have not yet acquired grammatical forms such as the conditional and reversible passives by early primary school years should be exposed to them at school in an interactive way to facilitate their learning. Needless to say, those who do not have full ability to use and comprehend complex grammar are likely to be at a disadvantage when it comes to reading secondary school textbooks, and listening to teachers and lecturers.

Storytelling

'Have you heard the one about … ?' Whether at a party, or in the staffroom, we're 'all ears' to this generic form of humorous short story. The structure of the joke features a sudden violation of the expectation built up during the story preceding the punch line. The neural response is similar to that which generates the 'Aha' when suddenly 'seeing' the solution to a mathematics or science problem, noted in Chapter 5. Canadian neuroscientist Vinrod Goel has shown lateralized differences in the neural correlates of jokes based on linguistic puns, for example, 'Why did the golfer change his socks? Because he had a hole in one' (left frontal cortex), and jokes based on semantics (right frontal cortex). Clearly jokes involve working memory and attentional neural systems as well as those systems necessary for language.

Likewise, the attention of children is easily gained with, 'I'm going to tell you a story. Once upon a time ...' This universal response suggests that humans from a young age are endowed with neural systems for utilizing language in the form of stories. It could be speculated that part of this might involve the mirror neuron system we met in the Chapter 6 where it was suggested that the mirror neuron system could save costly trial and error learning in social situations through enabling mental social simulation. Perhaps the usually predictable structure of stories assists this process, possibly by providing accounts of other people's minds without the listener having to determine this in a real situation where there is always the possibility of misinterpretation or deceit. International cross-cultural research has shown common narrative structures of and assumptions in stories about romantic love and heroic deeds across a great diversity of cultures, including those where marriage customs are very different from one another. This suggests that stories have universal themes which speak to our common neurobiology. This could explain why the sagas and tales from long ago such as the Greek legends from *The Iliad* (e.g., Jason and the Golden Fleece), are still enjoyed by contemporary audiences. A child with an impoverished facility with language is likely to be disadvantaged in benefiting in this way from exposure to stories.

So powerful is the potential benefit from storytelling that Canadian educationist Kevin Egan recommends that stories should form the basis of classroom pedagogy, especially when introducing fresh topics such as a new unit of work in science, or mathematics or history. Egan argues that while the three main aims of school education – personal growth, socializing and acquisition of knowledge – are mutually incompatible, some resolution towards better learning is possible through teacher stories that enable students to recapitulate the psychological, social and philosophical historical development of the new subject matter.

> The first part of story-shaping the content of our topic involves locating some dramatic incident, character, or idea that provides immediate access to the topic by making vividly clear at the beginning some aspect of its basic affective meaning. This story-shaping does not require us to find some fictional story to convey the point of the lesson. I mean by 'story' what the newspaper editor means when she or he asks 'What's the story on this?' We want to know its affective meaning within a narrative context that orients our understanding to the content – whether it is a 'story' involving incidents and people, or a scientific discovery, or a natural phenomenon.[1]

There may well be sound evolutionary reasons to support Egan's recommendations for education. After all, for most of human existence, cultural transmission has been enacted via oral storytelling. Even in today's literate societies, oral storytelling is still the major form of human communication, supplemented by film over print media. And, as UK anthropologist Robin Dunbar has shown, the most popular topic for stories is gossip, especially, it could be noted, among academics, it could be noted. Gossip not only informs us of who is doing what with whom, but lets us entertain mental scenarios about what we've been told, and what we might do under similar circumstances, without necessarily having to be enmeshed in the real thing. Hence stories can stimulate our imagination, and sometimes our motivation for action. We see this in modern advertising which often features emotionally laden narrative instead of fact. It is effective by activating our neural systems which generate our feelings of empathy. In fact, American research has found that individual differences in a capacity to perceive another person's emotions are correlated with how easily listeners are affected by the emotional content of stories and identify with the story's characters. This is consistent with reports from fiction writers who confess that their invented characters seem take on a life of their own in the author's imagination, as noted in Chapter 5.

And as we've seen in Chapter 6, the development of empathy through a theory of other minds, involving mirror neuron systems, is an important milestone in a child's cognitive development. This enables the child to put themselves 'in another's shoes'. This crucial skill for teaching enables us to attribute intentionality and other mental states to the minds of our students, just as it enables them to socialize and to appreciate our stories as practice simulations for real-life experiences. Neuroimaging evidence to support this claim comes from a team at Dartmouth College in America who used fMRI to study brain activations of people watching films of real actors and matched cartoon animations. Interestingly, activations in two areas of the temporal and parietal lobes were significantly higher for the actions of real actors compared with the same actions of cartoon characters. The interpretation of these results is that our neural systems for social engagement can readily distinguish between reality and fiction. This in turn raises the potentially relevant research question of how different kinds of stories might stimulate different kinds of neural responses. One potential application might lie in addressing the perpetual whinge of high school students about the seeming irrelevance of school curricula. By invoking social empathy through activations of the mirror neuron systems of students, the sorts of stories recommended by Kevin Egan might enable students to 'see' the relevance within the wider social context.

That said, a sceptic might ask: Why do we need stories to make sense of the world when we have our highly refined brain sensory systems to do that job? The answer is that consciousness of our response to the world actually lags behind our brain's decision-making processes, by as much as a third of a second. We do things before we know we're doing them. Mostly this is beneficial for social interactions – we could not hold spontaneous conversations if we were self-censoring every utterance before we made it. Haven't we sometimes produced a spontaneous explanation to a student and then thought: 'Gosh, that was clever – where did that come from?' Other times, of course, we wish we could swallow the words that we just spoke – that scathing remark which reduced the misbehaving pupil to tears – especially since the pupil's spontaneous remarks in class are also spoken before they can exert any conscious control. As UK educationist Guy Claxton puts it: Hare brain, tortoise mind. Stories provide a *post hoc* rationale for our uncontrolled actions – a conscious justification for our behaviour. In this way stories help us make sense of our mental and neural world.

Literacy

Learning to read and write – becoming literate – involves the engagement of additional neural systems to the many required for language. Literacy requires decoding and encoding symbol systems which simultaneously correspond with the brain's auditory, visual and semantic networks. This immediately suggests that exclusively employing just one pedagogy for teaching literacy, whether whole language (emphasizing the semantic–visual interconnection) or phonics (emphasizing the auditory–visual interconnection) is unlikely to be effective for all children, given their in-dividual neurological developmental differences. As a personal example, I was confined to a hospital bed for several months of my third year, and I used the time to teach myself to read by a process of rote memory, and phonological and lexical decoding. My favourite story was *Gumpa and the Paintbox* by Ivy Wallace, which I insisted that my mother read to me every day during her visit. Soon I had the whole story memorized. Now it was just a matter of matching the remembered story to the written version, word by word. What afforded generalizability was that *Gumpa*, a teddy bear of the muddle-headed but endearing kind, aka Pooh and Paddington, had suffered a toy room accident and had had his head put on facing back-wards. As a result he spoke in spoonerisms 'frack to bont'. Such verbal jokes can be a great delight for children, and for this child, provided a phono-logical key for decoding the printed version. I have met others who taught themselves to read in a similar fashion. Interestingly, many young choris-ters in cathedral and Oxbridge college choirs learn to read music by first remembering their parts and then decoding the written music as they sing.

However literacy is achieved, it is clear that literacy has the power to change cognition. This was famously demonstrated in Soviet Siberia in the

1930s when Vygotsky's new student and later colleague Alexander Luria reported on his field research with a telegram which was kept hidden from Stalin and the authorities until the 1960s: 'The peasants have no categories.' Luria was sent to Siberia to see how the indigenous peoples responded to standard IQ test items such as the odd one out (e.g., 'saw, log, file, axe'). But when asked which was the odd one out, the typical response was 'None of them.' The explanation would go along the lines that to get a log you first need the axe to fell the tree, but to cut the log with the saw it has to be sharpened by the file, so they are all connected. Only one group of people responded in the 'correct' way that 'log' was different from the other items because it was not a tool. That group was young women who had been to the regional college to learn to use the latest technology: the electric sewing machine. To do this they first had to learn to read the instruction manual. More recent research into the cognitive effects of literacy on primary school children has supported this early Soviet study. Literacy promotes logical inference as a form of deduction, as well as the wider use of analogical thinking, presumably because it requires the interaction of the various relevant neural systems. It might also be noted that the Flynn effect (Chapter 4) has been interpreted as showing a similar literacy-based cultural evolution of logical processing.

However, it is important to note that reading and writing are not synonymous abilities, and while good writers are good readers, research shows that the converse is not necessarily true. This in turn suggests that a focus on etymology as a meta-construct for enhancing a student's personal lexicon could be a productive method of simultaneously enhancing the two sides of literacy in the classroom. This suggestion assumes that connections with the semantic systems are robust, but such an assumption is not true for about 10 per cent of primary school children. Ongoing research led by Dorothy Bishop in Oxford is trying to understand the cognitive processes of poor comprehenders: pupils whose reading skills seem normal but who don't understand the meaning of what they have read. One hypothesis being tested is that the cause of this break between decoding the symbols and relating the words to their meanings lies in difficulties in oral language development back in early infancy, as predicted in the twin studies reviewed above. Another hypothesis looks at the interconnectivity of visual–semantic systems by studying how children with poor reading comprehension look at their visual environment. Perhaps poor comprehenders have trouble using language to categorize multiple sources of information because they do not see the world and its components as normally developing children do?

There is neuroimaging evidence that successful reading requires the integration of multiple neural systems. An American team compared the reading of high frequency words by children (ages 7–10) and adults (ages

18–32). Similar brain regions were activated in both groups, namely, the occipital cortex for visual processing and the temporal cortex for memory of repeated words. This result suggests that children and adults use similar neural systems when processing high-frequency words. However, in the adults, brain regions associated with phonological processing showed less activation while other areas associated with reading showed higher levels of activation, suggesting that as students age, they decrease their reliance on phonology as a means of decoding when reading. And as Hebbian models of learning would predict, word familiarity affects processing. An earlier ERP study of silent reading showed that repeated exposure to words results in changes in neural systems across the lifespan, with the consequence that common words are processed more rapidly (at least 50 ms faster) and more accurately than rarely used words.

That the brain can enable reading is, from an evolutionary standpoint, challenging, since literacy as a cognitive ability is a relatively recent development within human culture. We have genetic predispositions for language, but presumably not for reading. This is delightfully portrayed in the painting *The School of Love*, by the Italian Renaissance artist Correggio, which hangs in the National Gallery, London. The work is more prosaically entitled 'Cupid learns to read and write'. While the concerned mother (Venus) looks on, the teacher Hermes (Mercury) instructs the (perpetual) youngster in the skills of applying a quill to parchment. Even the gifted son of two gods does not have an innate ability for literacy.

It is interesting, then, that numerous neuroimaging studies of the neural correlates of reading have consistently found involvement of a particular area within the left fusiform gyrus, which became known as the visual word form area. Many of the neuroscientists involved in this research such as Stanislas Dehaene in Paris and Bruce McCandliss in America are interested in the potential applications of their work for education. This French–American team used fMRI and ERP with a group of normal participants and a group of patients who had their corpus callosa surgically severed, to show that the visual word form system was left lateralized, and was located in an inferior temporal region which seems specifically devoted to the processing of letter strings. And whereas the visual processing of a read word occurs some 150 ms after presentation, regardless of whether the word is seen in the right or left field of view, the visual word form system enables recognition of the word only 30 ms later. How this system manages this task, it is suggested, is through a pre-lexical recognition of abstract letter strings rather than the recognition of words in the sense that we know them. In fact, fMRI studies show that this visual word form area in the left fusiform gyrus is active during letter reading tasks that do not involve real word processing, suggesting that the neural systems which enable the visual recognition of words require the participation of many other regions throughout the brain. An interesting educational neuroscience example is provided by a structural MRI study in Texas wherein boys with impaired literacy learning had a constricted portion of their corpus callosum – the segment which connected the Broca's Area in the left hemisphere with its homologue in the right. The fact that restricted interconnectivity between the hemispheres is predictive of language learning difficulties is a good demonstration that the neural systems for language are not entirely dependent on left hemisphere activity alone.

Evidence from other studies suggests that the fusiform areas of the brain, being located adjacent to the visual cortices, are sensitive to learning about abstract visual patterns that are important in our environment. Human faces, beginning with the mother's face, is one; familiar objects around the home is another. Learning to recognize written words creates a word recognition system from this evolved function for learning visual patterns. That is, there is a self-reinforcing interplay between the structural repetitions of systems of writing and the developmental trajectories of the human visual and auditory systems. When a parent or teacher points and names objects, a child learns to decode the sounds of speech to discern the syllables and word units in order to create mental associations between the spoken word and its referent. MEG studies in Oxford have shown that activity in the Broca's Area begins before or at the same time as the visual word form area – about a sixth of a second – after reading a word. This suggests that reading relies on top–down processing very early on when deciding whether a word can be pronounced or not. As noted in Chapter 3, functional specificity in the brain is increasingly determined from infancy by the particular experiences of interconnectivity – the inputs and outputs. Hence, for the optimal development of this critical region for reading, being read to as a baby is important, especially with the reader's finger pointing to the words as they are read.

This is not just to reinforce the mechanics of reading, but importantly to instil a sense of enjoyment. Pleasure as a brain function involves anticipation and resolution. This applies across all modes of experience – music, food, sex and literature, to mention a few. Language is but one system which accesses memory systems where correct predictions are rewarded in order to reinforce similar decision making in the future. An ERP study showed that expectation of sentence completion, a typical classroom cloze task, was influenced by semantic relations between expected and unexpected words. Consistent with the 'top–down' interpretation of the MEG study above, this ERP finding suggests that reading involves semantic anticipation. In the classroom this points to the value of cloze exercises for enhancing word meaning and breadth of vocabulary, as well as potential benefits from reader participation stories with decision points for alternate plot trajectories and endings.

Dyslexia

Sadly, not all children are up to the challenge of integrating so many neural systems in acquiring literacy. In school these pupils are often diagnosed as dyslexic. Although enjoying normal intelligence in other respects, dyslexic children have significant difficulties in learning to read and write. Consequently, dyslexia has been a major focus in neuroscientific research about literacy. It should be noted that most children have some initial difficulty in deciphering and writing English script. This is because the human visual system is biased towards recognizing generic forms. Consequently, many children go through a phase in which they write letters such as 'w' and 'm' upside down, and have difficulty in distinguishing between the lowercase letters 'p' and 'q', 'b' and 'd', because these letters are mirrored and rotated variations of each other. Obviously this is not helpful for reading. Consequently, learning to read and write involves teaching the visual system to make such fine distinctions, and to recognize different letters by virtue of their slightly different shapes. Children with dyslexia experience great difficulty in achieving this, as articulated by a thirteenth-century scribe in Figure 7.1.

The main reason is that most dyslexics have low visual sensitivity, which degrades eye control resulting in an impaired acquisition of visual/orthographic skills. That is, the neural system for recognizing letter shape differences, and reproducing them accurately, is either degraded in its efficacy or is not interconnecting sufficiently well with the other neural systems involved in reading. To make matters worse, not only do many dyslexics have impaired motor coordination which compromises eye control affecting orthography, they also have problems with speech articulation which affects phonology. The reason here is that most dyslexics also have a lower sensitivity to auditory frequency and amplitude changes

Reading is a painful task.
It extinguishes the light from the eyes
It bends the back.
It crushes the viscera and the ribs.
It brings forth pain to the kidneys and
weariness to the whole body.

Figure 7.1 Learning to read is difficult according to a thirteenth-century Florentine monk (courtesy of John Stein)

which impairs phoneme discrimination leading to impairments in phonological discrimination.

Readers familiar with UK universities will be unsurprised to learn that researchers at Oxford and Cambridge take contrasting approaches in their research into the neural basis of dyslexia. At Oxford the research has been led by neurophysiologist John Stein. His starting point is that reading is primarily a visual process: words are seen both as a set of separate letters and as a whole, which in turn has to be related to some mental image or construct for meaning. As a visual process, reading relies on one of the brain's most endearing illusions, that our imagery of the world is stationary. In actual fact, our eyes are constantly saccading (jumping about), but our visual system compensates, and we see the world as essentially being still. It's a compelling illusion. With a page of text, we think we see it all clearly, when actually the amount of text in focus at any one moment is much smaller than this paragraph. One of the phenomena that dyslexic children consistently report is that the text does not stand still. Consequently, one of the targets for Stein's neuroscience research has been that part of the visual system which controls eye saccades. It is the subcortical magnocellular system – one of several brain nuclei that convey visual information from the eyes to the visual cortex – which is responsible for stabilizing eye movement (retinal slip) during close work such as reading. One line of research has been to study the brain responses to moving objects. UK neuroscientists Piers Cornelissen and Peter Hansen investigated the relationship between magnocellular function and word reading accuracy using computer-based activities with two whole primary school classes. Those children who were poor at detecting coherent motion, a measure of magnocellular function, were also poorer at detecting anagrams where letters had been swapped around, e.g., OCAEN for OCEAN. That is, one of the features of dyslexia is an inability to accurately encode for the positions of the letters in a word.

This research-based analysis suggests several diverse interventions to help dyslexic children learn to read. One is eye fixation exercises to improve visual stability while reading. Another is to occlude one eye while reading to reduce the conflict within the visual cortex from receiving two incompatible inputs. A third intervention is based on the fact that magnocellular neurons are sensitive to the optic nerve signals which differ depending on the frequency of the light falling on the retina. Hence, yellow or blue filters can compensate for magnocellular deficits depending on the specific nature of the impairment. Perhaps the most controversial intervention is taking omega 3 long chain polyunsaturated fatty acids (LC-PUFAs), that is, fish oils, as a nutritional supplement. It has been shown that PUFAs speed up the output signalling of magnocellular neurons. And while nutritionists have argued that there is a deficiency of PUFAs in modern Western diets, Stein has shown that dyslexics are particularly deficient in PUFAs. To test his hypothesis that a course of fish oils could improve the reading abilities of adolescents with long-term poor reading skills, Stein conducted a 'blind' trial of adding fish oil supplements to the meals of half of the boys in a UK reform home (borstal). After only six months of this study, significant improvements in reading skills were recorded in the group that had received the fish oil intervention.

Meanwhile, at Cambridge, Usha Goswami's research into the relationships between phonological awareness and reading is also potentially informative. Her research uses ERPs to study the patterns of brain function of auditory inputs involved in reading. The rationale for this research focus is that the development of phonological skills in infants seems to follow a set sequence regardless of the language. Awareness of syllables and onset/ rimes (e.g., 'd' – 'og') develops prior to literacy, whereas awareness of phonemes develops with learning to read. Consequently, phonemic development depends on linking sounds to letters or syllables (orthographic transparency). And of all of the acoustic properties of a spoken word, the syllable onset is critical for understanding. Syllable onset in the brain can be measured as the rise time of the ERP signal stimulated by listening to that syllable in a spoken word. Goswami has shown that the rise times of the auditory signals in the brains of dyslexic children are longer than those for normal readers of the same chronological age and, importantly, for the same reading age. This demonstrates that the brains of dyslexic children operate in qualitatively different ways to those of children who learn to read without such difficulties.

Goswami's research could be interpreted as suggesting that children with dyslexia experience continual novelty with what should be familiar sounds. Could this affect access to orthographic memory in a manner similar to that in which children who are poor at arithmetic fail to see that number facts generalize, e.g., $19 + 3$ calls on the same number facts as $9 + 3$? If so, then it could be expected that neuroimaging of the brains of dyslexic children would show differences for culturally specific symbol learning in those regions of the fusiform gyrus previously identified as involved in word recognition. And this turns out to be the case. FMRI studies show that the visual word form areas in dyslexic people are less activated than those of non-dyslexics when reading text. Interestingly, a 2008 American fMRI study has found that when confronted with incongruous sentences, dyslexic readers had higher levels of activation in their left hemisphere language areas, but when reading meaningful sentences, their left hemisphere activation fell while activations in the right hemisphere temporal areas rose. It's as though the neural systems for reading in dyslexics are not able to take advantage of, or establish, the functional specificities that are enjoyed by normal readers in supporting reading comprehension. Cornelissen and Hansen describe the multiple interactions of neural systems required for reading in terms of multichannel information processing:

> [V]isual processing, phonological processing, and short-term memory are all necessary components. The amount of information that can flow through each channel can vary continuously between a minimum and maximum value. Since reading requires several channels ... if an individual's information processing capacity falls below some critical value, then they may experience difficulty with reading ... This model avoids that problem of forcing a division between phonological and visual impairments when trying to explain children's reading problems.[2]

That said, it is important not to lapse into 'biology is destiny' thinking. Other American research has shown that as long as a diagnosis of dyslexia is made early, the plasticity inherent in children's brain development can be exploited with specific interventions of phonics *together with* whole-language to improve the reading skills of these children. As post-intervention fMRI analyses have shown, these improvements have not altered the previous weak activations in the left fusiform areas. Rather, adaptive plasticity seems to have been utilized for the enhanced functioning of other regions to produce some degree of educational compensation.

Second language learning

As noted in Chapter 3, the ease with which infants acquire their mother tongue seems largely due to synaptic pruning. This applies also to a considerable extent with learning a second language. Thus the learning of native and second languages exhibits sensitive periods, unlike other school subjects, with performance falling from 7 years of age. At 6 months all infants discriminate the phonetic contrasts of all languages, but by 12 months, only native language phonemes are noticed, or babbled. In between, there is great individual variability, with some infants already showing language learning, while others do not.

Some parents in bilingual families express concern that speaking two languages to their baby will cause neural confusion. They needn't worry. Evidence from fMRI studies shows that areas of cortex involved with a second language are spatially separated from those brain areas involved with native language speech. The reason is that like all learning, language growth depends on learning from experience. One critical experience for language advancement, in addition to social cognition, is the statistical learning which enables implicit learning of grammar, and the discrimination of the different grammars of different languages. This means that the orthographic relationships between sounds and symbols are language-specific, ranging from unique mappings in Italian, to the many phonetic ambiguities of English (e.g., 'though', 'through', 'bough', 'thorough', and so on), not to mention the various pictographic languages such as Mandarin or non-Romantic languages such as Thai. For example, an fMRI study comparing the neural responses to reading nouns vs. verbs found several contrasts with English, including activations in the cerebellum in response to reading verbs, but no differences when reading Mandarin Chinese characters. In fact, ongoing cross-language research at Oxford questions the assumption that onsets and rimes are special decoding units, or that children's phonological development is dependent on an onset/rime structure. But, however organized in terms of neural systems, the sensitive periods for language acquisition arise from the developing brain's ability to integrate these various experiences.

Consequently, the ability to acquire a second language by immersion, that is, beyond the limited exposure possible in a classroom, fades with age, particularly with respect to the acquisition of grammar. The implications are that second language teaching at school should be ideally situated in the early years classroom, and involve bilingual teaching on a daily basis. But if left to the later years, then second language teaching needs to involve, instead, a top–down curriculum of grammar rules and vocabulary which are less likely to be acquired implicitly since the brains of older language learners lack the large degree of neuronal plasticity available in the brains of young children.

Behavioural evidence in support of this claim comes from a large-scale UK study by Oxford educationist Lynn Erler on the difficulties many secondary school students have in reading written French. The major finding was that many children were employing English phonological referents to read written French. Interviews with students produced statements often similar to those of dyslexics learning to read: 'I'd just pronounce them like English words, just to help me', 'the letters are all muddled', and 'when they are on the board they look like a different word than what you've been repeating'. These results were interpreted as suggesting that the difficulties that the children experienced in reading written French could be explained by a dissociation between French orthography and phonology, resulting in a failure to establish automaticity in learning the orthographic form. It was suggested that these outcomes arose from the current emphasis in second language curricula on conversation over grammar. At a meeting of the Oxford Forum where Erler presented her findings, hypotheses were proposed of a dissociated activity between the superior temporal gyrus for assembled phonology, and the middle temporal gyrus for addressed phonology in students failing to learn to read written French. It was suggested that these hypotheses could be tested through MEG neuroimaging of such students and comparing the data with MEG scans of English dyslexic students. Regrettably, none of the many funding bodies approached were interested in supporting such educational neuroscientific research that might have significant implications for the teaching of second languages. Nevertheless, second language learning at school could be better recognized for the hard work that it is, since the 'magic' learning period of early infancy may be largely past. And learning a second language is well worth the effort because there is evidence for general and specific cognitive benefits from bilingualism, with positive effects not only for language abilities, but also for mathematical processing and general learning in school.

Educational neuroscience questions in a box

Some children do not develop very sophisticated writing skills while at school or university. Yet, many of these students embark on professional careers such as engineering which require writing detailed and unambiguous reports or policy documents. It could be interesting to investigate the neural systems involved in the development of advanced writing skills. Could an fMRI study compare the brain activations of an experienced professional author to see if there are interpretable differences from the activations of a non-writer? Presumably there are neural correlates to match these differences in writing abilities. Perhaps these findings could be insightful for teaching functional and creative writing?

---

8   Numeracy and Mathematics

As with literacy, the brain needs to coordinate multiple neural systems in order to be numerate. Effective neural interconnections are critical for success at mathematics in general. This chapter will discuss which systems in the brain have been identified for mathematical processing, how computation and creativity as different contributions to mathematical thinking are supported by separate but overlapping networks in the brain, and implications from the relevant research for structuring introductory and remedial mathematical curricula.

Before reviewing some of that research, we should ask, just what is entailed in mathematical thinking? As mathematics teachers we often find ourselves asking our charges if they 'get it'. Get the correct answer? Well, yes, but more than that: get the idea of how and why the solution works. In primary school arithmetic, this mostly involves decimal number sense – how numbers go in base 10. Here, some children 'get it' much more easily than others. I met William (then aged 4) a decade ago while observing trainee primary teachers on their practicum school placements in Australia. In a Central School (Years Kindergarten (K) to 10), I was observing a Kindergarten (Reception) class on digit recognition where the children were colouring in large copies of 1 to 9. William was clearly bored. Sitting down beside him on the floor, I whispered in his ear: 'What's the biggest number you know?' 'Oh' he said, 'one mil...wait...a hundred thousand'. 'Well,' I replied (thinking that his understanding of 'biggest' might be 'longest number name' rather than 'largest sized number'), 'do you know a million?' 'Of course,' he shot back. 'OK then,' I continued (wondering if he was just parroting some recent conversation with his parents), 'write a million down on the back of your paper'. Without hesitation William wrote down 1,000,000. So we went on to talk about billions, trillions, zillions, and so on – that all-important lesson where you confirm your suspicion that powers of 10 can increase indefinitely. It's just that most people aren't ready for that lesson until they are much older than 4 years.

And then having decimal number sense on board, there is its application to computation. Another day, another school, and I was observing another trainee teacher presenting a lesson on factors to a composite Year 4/5 (9–10 years of age). She was giving examples on the board, '30 = 5 × ?; 28 = 4 × ?', with pupils sitting on the floor. Jake sat at the back and couldn't stop wriggling. It struck me that Jake was more than 'bored out of his brain', he was bored out of his whole body. The trainee teacher (probably because her university supervisor was present) wrote his name on the bad behaviour list, and sent the class back to their seats to complete worksheets of similar problems. Jake sat with the new girl Sally; they each completed their sheet in less than 20 seconds, the time it took them to write down the answers, hers neatly, his in a mess. I sat down with them. 'How would you like to do something harder?' Salvation! 'Oh, yes please!' 'OK then,' I said, hastily improvising, '$225 = 15 \times ?$' And after they had the answer we went on to do as many double-digit factors as I could generate in my head: '$238 = 14 \times ?$', '$247 = 19 \times ?$' and so on. How did Jake and Sally's brains do these problems? Clearly it was not just a matter of 'mindlessly' employing a multiplication algorithm. Why is '$247 = 19 \times ?$' possible for a few 9-year-old children, and difficult if not impossible (without a calculator) for most (and most adults if it comes to that)? Are their brains different and, if so, how and why?

Neuroimaging studies reveal at least ten separate areas of the cortex, from the rear to the front, and across both sides, that contribute to the simple task of subtracting one number from another. In an early fMRI study, French cognitive neuroscientist Stanislas Dehaene put himself in the scanner to investigate which parts of his brain were involved in repeated subtraction: 100 take away 7, take away 7, take away 7, and so on (actually a psychiatric test for normal brain function following a head injury). Areas of increased activation included the left and right fusiform gyri (imagining the numbers), left and right parietal cortices (number sense), lateral and medial parts of the temporal lobe (arithmetic memories), and inferior (lower) parts of the frontal lobes (working memory and decision making).

Whereas it is interesting to delineate the functions of these various parts of the brain which contribute to the task of subtraction, what is more important to note is the fact that there are at least ten of them, distributed around the brain, side to side, and front to back. That it takes so much distributed brain effort for such a typical primary school computation underscores the point that our brains did not evolve to do schoolwork such as subtraction. But nevertheless, if you do the sum in your head, 100 minus 7 takes only a fraction of a second. The neuroscience question is: How do these (at least) ten separate regions with different neural functions communicate with one another so quickly and efficiently to come up with the correct answer? The neuroscience short answer is: We don't (yet) know. The neuroscience longer answer is: There is good evidence for several ways in which functional modules transfer information – anatomically, bio-chemically, bio-electrically, rhythmically. But, as noted in Chapter 1, how the intermodular information 'content' is coordinated and updated remains an enigma.

Nevertheless, the principle of neural interconnectivity underpins the emergence of the various neural systems required for all facets of school learning. Where connections are not robust, this could lead to limits for understanding. Arithmetic is perhaps the easiest to investigate in a neuroimaging laboratory due to its emphasis on unambiguous correctness. A better understanding of the connectivity between the functional modules involved in doing arithmetic could be instrumental in the design of new approaches to teaching this crucial area of basic mathematics. Such an approach might aim to develop arithmetical competence through work on number patterns and relations (e.g., factors), which feature conceptual connectivity, which in turn presumably is achieved through strengthening the supporting neural links.

Moreover, a better understanding of the neural interconnectivities required for arithmetic could point the way towards more focused remedial interventions which target weaknesses in a particular interconnectivity in the brains of those children who don't 'get it'. The hope would be that such interventions could exploit the brain's remarkable plasticity to build new connections, just as we saw in Chapter 3 with the music students repractising to overcome errors. Such interventions might be quite different from many of the present strategies of giving such children more and more of the same problems that they cannot seem to master in the first place, with predictable negative effects on motivation. At this stage, it has to be said, this is an ambitious claim, but as we noted in the Introduction, some neuroscientists are optimistic that one day enough might be known about how the brain learns for such a programme to be put into effect. But as we've seen in Chapter 1, any such brain-based remedial programme will be neither simple nor simplistic.

Arithmetic

There is evidence for differences between the neural networks associated with each of the four basic arithmetic operations: addition, subtraction, multiplication and division. This is not to say that these networks are completely independent from one another. They all overlap, notably in the frontal and parietal areas, but they also include areas of brain which seem to be unique to each arithmetical operation. There is also evidence for separate neural networks for estimation (involving the lower parietal cortices bilaterally), and computation (involving the parietal and frontal cortices on the left). In other words, there is no specific brain area or module for doing arithmetic. Rather, arithmetical brain functioning relies on the cooperation of neural systems supported by various functional modules located in many different parts of the brain across both hemispheres.

The evidence for these separate systems for arithmetic operations is mostly neuropsychological in the form of double dissociations. Double dissociations are seen in patients with localized brain injuries or disease which impair specific cognitive behaviours. For example, consider patients A and B who before brain injury could both perform behaviours α and β, say, addition and multiplication. After their strokes, patient A with injury to brain area X can still perform behaviour α but not behaviour β (say, addition but not multiplication), whereas patient B with injury to brain area Y can still perform behaviour β (multiplication), but not behaviour α (addition). This suggests that brain area X is critical for the performance of behaviour α (addition), while brain area Y is critical for the performance of behaviour β (multiplication). Importantly, because there was no injury to other brain areas J, K, L, etc., all of which might or might not be involved in doing addition and multiplication, this kind of comparison can only tell us about which parts of the brain are necessary for particular arithmetic operations, but not which parts are sufficient, and not which parts are shared.

As Oxford psychologist Ann Dowker summarizes, there are not only double dissociations for the four major arithmetic operations, there are also double dissociations for strategies employed in arithmetic processing, in particular, reliance on factual vs. procedural vs. conceptual number knowledge. Different brain systems are involved in solving problems presented orally or in a written format, whether the problems require number comprehension or number production, and whether the task demands reading or writing numbers vs. calculation. Could preferred arithmetic computational strategies reflect individual differences in the strengths of neural connectivities, for example, doing multicolumn addition from the left or doing mental subtraction by rounding off before taking away? A challenge for arithmetic education is that not all of these strategies generalize.

This was demonstrated in schools in Japan, as 'discovered' in 1995 by American researchers from the Trends in International Mathematics and Science Study (TIMSS). TIMSS sought international age-normed comparisons of the mathematics and science achievements of US school students. Over the 20 years since its beginning, children from schools in Japan, Taiwan, Singapore and China have consistently outperformed children from Western countries. The SIMSS researchers wanted to know why, so they went to Japan to observe mathematics classes in action. What they saw was that Japanese mathematics classes featured whole-class diagnoses of student strategies in order to demonstrate those which generalized, and thus could be adopted, and those which did not, and therefore should be abandoned. The point of this at a neural level, as noted in Chapter 3, is that Hebbian reinforcement through repetition is no judge of correctness if there is no feedback about errors. Repeatedly using an incorrect number fact is like the music student practising the wrong note. Moreover, Hebbian reinforcement certainly cannot prejudge the usefulness of a particular strategy for situations yet to be encountered. For example, a trap that some new teachers fall into is to use small numbers in explanatory examples which can be readily misunderstood by their students, for example, introducing squared numbers with 2^2 equals 4, implying to some students that this is just another way of writing familiar multiplication, and therefore 3^2 should equal 6.

Small numbers do not necessarily make the best exemplars. One of the fascinating double dissociations is between small numbers 1 to 6, literally a handful, and larger numbers 7, 8 and 9, and zero. This dissociation in our brains seems best explained by evolution. Look at the number of objects on the table or desk in front of you. If there are five or fewer, you can tell this at a glance – you don't need to count. But if there are more, say, a dozen, then you will need to count, or at least to break them into a couple of smaller groups. Young infants, even a few months old, seem to be able to distinguish between 1, 2, 3, 4 and 5 objects. The evidence comes from habituation studies, where newborns, sitting comfortably on mother's lap, will stare at toys disappearing behind a screen and then re-appearing. So long as the number of toys remains the same, they quickly get bored of this and look around at their surroundings, as infants will. But if the number of toys appearing from behind the screen suddenly changes to no longer match the number of toys disappearing behind the screen, then the infants resume staring, and stare longer, suggesting that they register the difference. Interestingly, the crafty experimenters can change the toys, say, two teddy bears disappear, two trucks 're'-appear, but this does not have any noticeable effect; staring is longer only when the number is changed, such as when two teddy bears disappear, three teddy bears 're'-appear. Moreover, once the number of objects exceeds five or six, then the staring time is no different, suggesting that there is no perception that the number has changed. This is not to say that infants have a sense of absolute number magnitude. Presumably they do not. But it is to suggest that they do have some 'inbuilt' sense of small number in at least a relative manner. Perhaps pre-school and Reception/Kindergarten classes could assume this basic knowledge in their pre-numeracy curriculum?

And not only do humans have an 'inbuilt' number sense up to around five, so do most mammals it seems, from the variety of those tested, which include apes, monkeys, dogs, cats, rats and horses. One could conjecture that this sense of a handful might have evolved under the adaptive pressure of keeping track of one's children or immediate relatives. Another suggestion is that such a small number sense enables an animal, when faced with a group of prey, to immediately compute the odds of success at standing and fighting, or fleeing. Surrounded by hungry lions there is no time to add up the units and carry the one. Of course, these speculative accounts are not incompatible. And, interestingly, chimpanzees in the laboratory have been taught to recognize numbers of objects up to nine, and to order them by relative magnitude, although there is no clear evidence for them doing this in the wild.

Moreover, many birds (pigeons, magpies, parrots, crows) have also demonstrated a similar small number sense, both in the lab and in the wider world. A nice example in the French countryside is of crows nesting in the tops of grain storage silos. They frustrate the farmer's efforts to shoot them *in situ* by flying off and not returning to their nest until they apparently spot the farmer leaving his hiding place in the silo. Combining forces with neighbouring farmers so that a couple go into the silo, and one comes out, does not fool the crows. It takes about six farmers to enter, and then five to leave before the crows will return – to their demise. Given the evolutionary independence of birds and mammals, perhaps this number sense is an example of the convergent evolution of a cognitive trait, in this case from the adaptive pressure of keeping track of the number of eggs in the nest as well as of chicks to feed. The speculation is not important. What is important is that a strong 'inbuilt' number sense can be both a cognitive strength on which to build an early number curriculum and a cognitive weakness, in that it could bias number processing away from less intuitive constructs.

Statistics

A notable educational example of where our unconscious predilection for small numbers can lead us astray is in the area of statistics. This can happen in several ways. First, our cognitive bias towards perception of small numbers seems offset by a poor ability to comprehend large numbers. We know that a billion is a thousand times larger than a million, but it doesn't feel that way. But numbers seem uncountably large. Such indifference affects our responses to scientific data involving large numbers, e.g., the number of stars in our galaxy, the number of galaxies in our universe or the number of years that life has evolved on Earth. And this in turn affects how poorly we appreciate probabilities, say, of finding life supporting planets. It affects how we respond to the high likelihood of low probability events occurring over a very large tract of time. For example, a period of millions of years is plenty of time for animal vision to have evolved, albeit through a series of low probability events. In fact, animal vision has evolved independently many times over in different forms of animal life: insects, spiders, crustaceans and fish, as well as in the ancestors of mammals. Our inability to process large numbers can present a particular challenge for science teaching.

Second, our intuitive bias towards small numbers might well fuel our predilection to generalize from the particular – someone has to win the lottery, why not me! – and consequently to subjectivize the improbable – my chances of winning the lotto will increase if I choose special numbers for me, for example my children's birthdays. Australian research on lottery winning payouts has shown that winning combinations which include the numbers from 32 to 48 receive larger prizes on average because they are less likely to have to share them with other winners. And one could construct an evolutionary story about generalizing from the particular. Imagine an early prehominid family group. It's evening, and the group is preparing the evening meal. Going down to the local water hole, the mother sees a sabretooth tiger also heading for the same water hole. Mother has never seen a sabretooth at this water hole before. But what is the message that she conveys, with some emotional emphasis one imagines, to her children? Despite seasons of happy play around that water hole, never go there again without an adult. Of course, the sabretooth might have just been passing by, but the risk is obviously much too great to assume that. Once (nearly) bitten, twice shy! Another example of one shot aversive non-Hebbian learning (Chapter 3).

Third, generalizing from the particular, combined with our parietal driven ability to see patterns, could well explain our attraction to winning streaks: what has become known in American sport betting on basketball matches as the 'Hot Hand' effect, after supposed streaks of successful shots at basket. In fact, statisticians have found no correlation between the successful outcome of a given shot and the results of the prior attempt. But true randomness is not equivalent to the complete absence of any bias over short intervals. Computer software programs – so-called random number generators – will produce occasional series of repeated numbers, or repeated patterns (e.g., 123123123). It's just that these are not predictable *a priori*. Even random processes with inanimate objects, such as coin flipping, can yield occasional long streaks. But try telling that to our brains. FMRI studies of people experiencing a streak of the same outcome show increased activation in the anterior cingulate, an area of brain involved in decision making. As cognitive psychologist Bruce Burns has noted, people's future choices are often influenced by a streak of events (e.g., betting in a casino).

The implication for teaching statistics is that the computational results can run counter to the intuitive. I suggest that there might be value in making such feelings explicit. An example I've used in teaching probability is to imagine a friend gives you a Lotto ticket with the numbers 1, 2, 3 4, 5, 6. How do you feel about your chances of winning? Everyone says that they feel that they have no chance. OK, what about the numbers 7, 14, 21, 28, 35, 42? A few in a class will say that these seem 'better' numbers, until they see the catch. Then, what about 8, 15, 22, 29, 36, 43? Many will admit that they do feel OK about the chances of these numbers – they feel more spread out, less ordered – despite the simple generative algorithm. Finally, what about 8, 17, 21, 27, 37, 44? Most agree that such a set feels like it should have a good chance of winning, while at the same time acknowledging that the chance of winning is as good as any other combination, including the original 1, 2, 3, 4, 5, 6. The rational and irrational analyses simply do not agree in our minds, because our brains process them rather separately.

Fractions

Another notable watershed in mathematics education is computation with vulgar fractions. The contrast with real-world fractionating is fascinating. Imagine a young child's birthday party where half the cake has been eaten, and there are five children who at the end of the party want to take a slice of cake home. Even a very young child (with a little help wielding the knife) can divide half a birthday cake into five pieces for the remaining guests at the party. Yet, how many adults, (perhaps fewer than 50 per cent?) can compute one-fifth of one-half? I wonder if this could be due to the separateness of neural systems which enable the recognition of objects and symbols. As noted in Chapter 7, convergent neuroimaging evidence suggests that a function of a specific subregion of the left fusiform gyrus is the processing of symbols. In mathematics, this area enables the neural representation of numerals representing numbers, and pairs of numerals representing fractions. In contrast, its homologue on the other side of the brain, the right fusiform gyrus, contains subregions which enable the recognition of important and familiar objects, including faces, especially mother's face for a newborn, animals, tools, and so on. It would seem that if the interconnections across the hemispheres between the left and the right fusiform gyrus are not strong, or reinforced, then the conceptual links between a teacher's concrete example (e.g., diving the cake at the party) and the same problem posed in abstract symbolic form (e.g., 1/5 of 1/2) might not necessarily be made in the brains of the pupils.

The implications for education are challenging. Perhaps Piagetian approaches to the teaching of fractions need to be reconsidered? Perhaps abstract mathematical thinking does not develop from concrete mathematical thinking and, hence, moving from the concrete to the abstract might not be of much help to many children. There is some evidence in support of this conjecture from teachers in Denmark who have used a direct symbolic approach, introducing fractions as a symbol system without real-world examples. This non-concrete approach might actually help reduce children's working memory load when dealing with fractions. We saw in Chapter 4 that working memory capacity was a critical individual difference variable in academic achievement and, therefore, the pedagogic strategy of limiting potential working memory load when introducing new work could assist children's success in getting to grips with the new topic. The challenge of fractions is that the numerator and denominator, although both expressed as numerals, represent quite different types of number system. They have different meanings – quantity and category respectively – and so are manipulated differently. Keeping track of these two number systems when adding or subtracting fractions and finding common denominators, or multiplying and cancelling common factors, much less dividing by inversion, is highly demanding of working memory load.

This working memory challenge was well demonstrated in a study by Oxford educational psychologist Terezinha Nunes with 6-year-old children who were asked to solve the following three-part problem. Part 1: On Monday you have 3 blue marbles and 3 white marbles – what fraction is the blue marbles of the total? Most got the answer of 1/2 correct. Then, part 2: On Tuesday you have 2 blue marbles and 2 white marbles – what fraction is the blue marbles of the total? Again, most got the answer of 1/2 correct. Now for the third part, the real question of interest: Does the fraction of blue marbles change from Monday to Tuesday? Intriguingly, 45% of children asked said 'Yes'. It seemed for nearly half of the children, when reviewing the two parts of the problem, the salience of the 3 and 2 dominated their working memory load to the exclusion of their answers.

Fractions also run counter to our inbuilt number sense: 4 is larger than 3, but $1/4$ is small than $1/3$. The latter example, where a larger denominator represents a smaller fraction, seems to be in contradiction to our well-evolved representations of magnitude. The magnitude–distance effect is a robust research finding: people take longer to decide which is the larger of two numbers the closer the pair are together, e.g., deciding which is the larger between 46 and 43 takes longer than between 67 and 98. Curiously, it does not matter whether the problem is posed in numerals or number names, e.g., 'forty-six vs. forty-three' takes longer than 'sixty-seven vs. ninety-eight'. But with fractions, it is quite difficult for most people to judge which is the larger of, say, $2/7$ vs. $1/5$.

In sum, there might be understandable neural reasons for why vulgar fractions present such a learning challenge for so many children – and adults. The teaching of fractions might require rethinking in terms of mastering a different, and possibly counterintuitive, symbol system. I suggest that the way to introduce fractions is via percentages. Some time spent on percentages could provide neural reinforcement of a numerical representation of one familiar category (1%) which can be relatively easily manipulated, and then rewritten in terms of fractions of 1/100. And percentages would therefore be sequenced after decimals, which do not involve categorical representations or different rules of arithmetic – just one new rule of keeping track of the decimal place.

Algebra and geometry

It seems reasonable to predict that the neural systems which we as teachers help develop in the brains of our students should resemble those of adults who are competent, even expert, in the subject area in question. An fMRI study led by American neuroscientist Yulin Qin tested this conjecture by investigating the changes in brain activation patterns as children learned algebra equation solving. The participants were ten pre-algebra adolescents who were tutored for five days in linear algebraic equations. These were presented in three levels of difficulty in terms of the number of steps required to reach a solution (e.g., 0-step: $1x + 0 = 4$; 1-step: $1x + 8 = 12$; 2-step: $7x + 1 = 29$). Pleasingly, there was a significant reduction in the solving time required over the five days. During this period, the students' patterns of brain activations while solving similar algebraic equations were compared with the activation patterns of adult algebra 'experts' solving the same equations. The areas of significant activation were very similar – and included the lower parietal cortex, the frontal cortex and the anterior cingulate. But what was interesting was that there was a significant reduction in the activation in the parietal and frontal cortices of the adolescents over the five days, consistent with the Hebbian model of synaptic reinforcement for learning by children of new subject matter.

Of course, these algebraic equations are quite trivial as equations go, and being successful at school mathematics, much less beyond, requires a far greater facility at complex reasoning. To better understand how this process differs between experts, proficient problem solvers and novices, another American fMRI study investigated complex reasoning in Euclidean geometric proof. Here 15 young adults attempted to provide proofs for the equality of length for pairs of sides in triangular figures (as reviewed in Chapter 4). The knowledge required was the Euclidean properties of triangles. The experimental design not only varied the degree of difficulty (and impossibility), but had the relevant sides highlighted in colour in half the figures. The results showed a beneficial interaction effect for the highlighting, suggesting that proficient problem solvers integrate problem givens and diagram information to support their logical inferences. The areas of the brain which were the most responsive were the left parietal and right prefrontal cortices, the same areas involved in arithmetic and algebraic problem solving.

As noted in Chapter 4, the implication for teaching geometric proof is that highlighting the objects of the proof in the diagram might help maintain focused attention, especially for students with less expansive working memory capacities. Moreover, this recommendation can be generalized for introducing all new work: provide target answers for the first examples to be worked by the students. In Chapter 3 it was noted that Hebbian learning is blind to errors unless there is immediate feedback. So, having all the class do all of Set 1 before seeing any answers might well reinforce erroneous methods in those students who didn't 'get it' from the erudite explanations by the teacher on the white (black) board. Such reinforced erroneous methods can then be very hard to undo. It might be better for all of the answers of Set 1 to be available, item by item. For example, the first item of Set 1 of a new unit on simultaneous equations might begin: $3x + y = 7$, $x + y = 3$, with answers $x = 2$, $y = 1$ displayed beside the question to provide some immediate feedback. Of course, this will not guarantee that the recommended generic method of solving the equations was employed, but it could prevent completely erroneous methods getting established in the students' brains.

The fact that similar areas of the brain, notably the frontal and parietal cortices, are involved in different types of mathematical thinking is interesting for the educational neuroscientist researcher. So much so, that mathematical problems are used as stimuli in other neuroimaging studies aimed to further understand the functioning of these brain areas. It is a good example of education usefully contributing to neuroscience. At the time of writing, one such study by Jacqueline Wood and Jordan Grafman of the US National Institute of Health is using calculus problems to test a model of how the frontal cortex engaged in knowledge-binding and neural plasticity is required to process multiple representational perspectives while learning. The results of this ongoing research could well hold implications for making calculus more accessible to more students.

Mathematical thinking

These two brain areas, the (right) parietal and frontal cortices, have been the focus of neuroscientific studies into the highest levels of mathematical thinking. An early study of the brain functioning of high mathematical abilities used PET to study the brain metabolism of two groups of college students, one group of 20-year-old maths majors with high mathematical abilities, the other group with normal mathematical abilities, while solving Scholastic Aptitude Test – Math (SAT-M) problems. The PET profiles of the brain activations of the mathematically group were significantly different from their age-matched peers, notably in their frontal cortices, prompting the researchers to conclude that the frontal cortex is critically involved in mediating high mathematical intelligence.

For many years, the University of Iowa has held a summer school for young mathematically gifted adolescents. These 13-year-olds who are just beginning their secondary education score as high on the Scholastic Aptitude Test – Math (SAT–M) as college students (average age 20 years) who are majoring in mathematics: both groups average 1100 out of 1400. Neuropsychologist Michael O'Boyle used EEG to record the brain's electrical activity of the mathematically gifted 13-year-olds and age-matched subjects while engaged in a series of psychophysical tasks. Mathematically gifted adolescents did not differ from the 20-year-olds in terms of overall brain activation, but had superior levels of brain activation in their right parietal areas, as well as the frontal lobes when compared to age-matched, average ability peers. In sum, these Iowa studies indicate that mathematically precocious individuals rely more on their right hemisphere for basic information processing, and that the frontal lobes play a prominent role in mediating their high levels of mathematical ability. As noted in Chapter 5, a follow-up study led by O'Boyle, then at the University of Melbourne, used fMRI to study the brain functioning of mathematically able boys performing number sentence completion and spatial rotation tasks (i.e., imagining how a group of blocks might appear once they've been turned around). This is the sort of thinking involved in doing 3D geometry, whereas number sentence completion involves pre-algebraic thinking. Consistent with the previous EEG studies, O'Boyle's group found that, among other areas, the right parietal and frontal areas of the brain were involved in both pre-algebraic *and* geometrical thinking of able young mathematicians. But, whereas previous neuroimaging studies had shown that mental block rotation tasks induce only parietal activity on the right, these gifted subjects demonstrated bilateral activation of the parietal lobes and frontal cortex, along with heightened activation of the anterior cingulate, during mental rotation. The researchers conjectured that:

> [I]t may be that enhanced (and bilateral) activation of the parietal lobes, frontal cortex, and the anterior cingulate are critical parts of an all-purpose information processing network, one that is relied upon by individuals who are intellectually gifted, irrespective of the nature of their exceptional abilities.[1]

Further evidence for enhanced bilaterality as a neural characteristic of mathematical giftedness includes the results from psychophysical studies aimed to elicit laterality biases in gifted subjects. In sum:

> [E]nhanced development and subsequent processing reliance on the specialized capacities of the right hemisphere, coupled with a fine-tuned ability for rapid and coordinated exchange of information between the hemispheres, are hypothesized to be unique processing characteristics of the mathematically gifted brain.[2]

In other words, mathematical thinking requires the coordinated participation of several neural systems, which in the brains of gifted mathematicians, seem more extensive throughout both right and left hemispheres. These neural systems involve at least the temporal cortices for the storage and retrieval of number facts and computational rules and algorithms, the parietal cortices for number sense and conceptual interrelationships, especially of a quasi-spatial representations, the anterior cingulate, a region involved in emotionally weighted decision making, and the frontal cortices for working memory, creative analogizing and cognitive coordination of the other non-frontal systems.

An important educational question follows: If frontal cortical functions are critical for mathematical thinking, how might we enhance these, or at least optimize these in our students? Since a critical frontal function is to enable working memory, one suggestion is to try and optimize working memory capacity, or at least that part involving short-term memory. The suggestion will sound very old-fashioned: Mentals! For readers not sufficiently ancient, these are mental arithmetic problems, usually delivered at a fast pace, no writing allowed (e.g., what's the cost of $1\frac{1}{2}$ kilos of sugar at £1.50 per kilo?) A well designed 'mental' will not only require calculation of at least one intermediary step, and holding that result in a memory buffer, but also allow for several different computational strategies (e.g., in this case, squaring 15 (intermediary step) and then adjusting the decimal place, or, 1×1.5 (intermediary step 1), then $\frac{1}{2} \times 0.5$ (intermediary step 2), and then addition of the intermediate results). For younger children, chanting multiplication tables from memory, and doing mentals of operational number facts, serves the same purpose.

In offering the above suggestion, it must be kept in mind that to enable working memory, frontal cortical systems work in synchrony with parietal systems. All of the neuroimaging studies reviewed in this chapter have found activations in the parietal region when subjects solved mathematical problems, whether arithmetic, algebraic or geometric. An American fMRI study of spatial imagery in deductive reasoning found that reasoning activated an occipito–parietal–frontal network, including the pre-frontal cortex, the cingulate gyrus, the superior and inferior parietal cortex, and the visual association cortex. This network of brain systems enables reasoners to envisage and inspect spatially organized mental models to solve deductive inference problems. So, one specific contribution of the parietal cortex seems to be as a mental 'draughtsman' for spatial, and quasi-spatial, perceptions. But, as we've seen above, the parietal cortex also acts as a substrate for a number sense. This has been well demonstrated in several neuroimaging investigations. For example, in one event-related fMRI study, the researchers presented numbers, letters and colours in the visual and auditory modality, asking subjects to respond to target items within each category. In the absence of explicit magnitude processing, numbers compared with letters and colours across modalities activated a bilateral region in the horizontal intraparietal sulcus. The researchers concluded that this intraparietal response encodes magnitude information which is independent of the presentation modality, or how the idea of number is represented.

This dual role for the parietal region raises an evolutionary question: Why does the parietal cortex compute magnitude *and* create mental visualization? The answer is that the parietal cortex enables us, as it did for our evolutionary ancestors, to find our way home. Both sorts of information processing are necessary to find our way in the world. A mental map of where we are going seems obvious, but without a sense of magnitude of the distances we have travelled, and the orientations of our turns, our mental map reading is likely to go astray. In the real world we are helped, of course, by remembering landmarks. This integrative process of navigation has been the subject of French research, which found that, during locomotion, mammals update their position with respect to a fixed point of reference, such as their point of departure, by processing inertial cues, proprioceptive feedback and stored motor commands generated during locomotion. This so-called path-integration system (dead reckoning) helps the animal to return to its home, or to a familiar feeding place, even when external cues are absent or novel. However, without the use of external cues, the path-integration process leads to rapid accumulation of errors involving both the direction and distance of the goal. Therefore, path-integration and familiar visual cues are combined to optimize navigational performance. The dual roles of the parietal cortex seem to have evolved to help us find our way by engaging whole-body propriocentrism to perform geometry and trigonometry in the real world.

Thus the educationally relevant role of the parietal cortex is to transform sequential information where meaning is embedded in the order, such as a series of landmarks used to find one's way home, into a quasi-spatial whole where the meaning is no longer reliant on the order of the original information. In music, the order of notes creates the melody which is then perceived as a whole. In spoken language, when listening to a person tell a story, the order of the speaker's words can convey meaning – my father's brother is a different person from my brother's father – but once the words are 'in', the overall meaning can then be put into one's own words when retelling the story.

This leads directly to a highly recommendable classroom application: LOGO Turtle! When Seymour Papert introduced LOGO he was at pains to point out that this was not simply an exercise in computer programming, but a cognitive task requiring children to step out the geometric shape required in order to devise the LOGO commands for the turtle (a moveable computer-graphic icon) on the basis of the child's propriocentric experience. For example, a square is so many steps in a straight line, then a right- or left-hand turn through 90 degrees, then the same number of steps, then another 90 degree turn in the same orientation, and repeat until back at the starting point. The LOGO program, with some careful thought, can reduce to an algorithm such as '[FWD, RT90] × 4'. The point is that LOGO might well be particularly useful in helping students 'see' geometric problems, and their solutions, as, first, a propriocentric exercise, leading to mental representations.

Consistently, a research group in Germany used fMRI to investigate the role of spatial imagery in deductive reasoning. These researchers concluded that when reasoning, humans envisage and inspect spatially organized mental models to solve deductive inference problems through a parietal-frontal network, in which a part of the frontal cortex mediates task attention, possibly by inhibiting irrelevant information.

Similarly, neuroscientists in Canada found that relational reasoning tasks, both concrete and abstract, activated bilateral parietal-frontal networks. They described this process as bypassing the language system and using Venn diagrams and spatial mental models to gain insight – to literally see the problem.

A good classroom resource which encourages children to think spatially, and to be rewarded with 'Aha' insight experiences from seeing the problem, are the puzzles of the Russian cognitive psychologist Mikhail Bongard. Bongard was interested in spatial insights arising from visual cognition. In his puzzles, two sets of six shapes are drawn side by side. All of the shapes have something in common, but those in the set on the left have a variation in the theme which makes them a distinct set from the shapes on the right which have a different variation. The challenge is to figure out what the theme and variations are. A trivial example is shown in Figure 8.1 – all of the shapes on the left side are triangles, whereas all of the shapes on the right side are quadrilaterals, other variables such as shading or size, or orientation being irrelevant. Most of the other 99 Bongard patterns are far more engaging, for example, number 20 shown in Figure 8.2 (solution in Endnotes). Analytic approaches do not seem to work as well as looking at the shapes until an 'Aha' insight occurs.

I've shown some of the easier Bongard patterns to children as young as 5 years of age, so there does not seem to be any age restriction on their use in school. There are several websites, the one in the References and Further

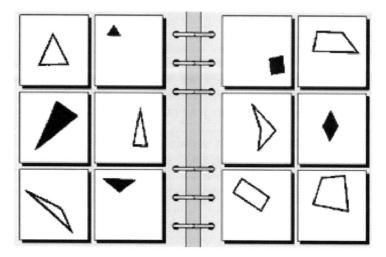

Figure 8.1 Bongard pattern #6

Reading was created by American cognitive scientist Harry Foundalis. In addition to Bongard's original 100 patterns, it shows newer puzzles created by other Bongard pattern solvers. The website encourages creative responses, and I've seen children in primary school setting original Bongard patterns for their classmates to solve.

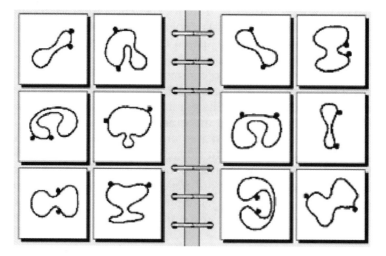

Figure 8.2 Bongard pattern #20

Mathematical creativity

Without invoking the Platonic debate over the ontological independence of mathematical entities, it might be conjectured that, to the extent to which mathematics is a human construct, the source of the deep underlying interconnectedness between areas of mathematics is the common brain functioning which supports mathematical thinking: the temporal cortices which have been shown to be involved in the different arithmetical operations; the parietal cortices enabling spatial insights, of which a number sense is one example; and the frontal cortices and their capacity to support creative thinking in general.

That mathematical problems can have multiple solutions is itself quite wondrous, and suggests that there are deep conceptual connections between different branches of mathematics. I can still recall my epiphany as a young adolescent reading that marvellous book *Mathematics and the Imagination* and first encountering Euler's substitution in De Moivre's theorem to realize $e^{i\pi} + 1 = 0$. The apparent convergence of imaginary, transcendental, irrational, counting numbers and zero into a simple relation is strongly suggestive, it seemed to me at the time, of a deep underlying connection between the different branches of mathematics. Moreover, Andrew Wiles's proof of Fermat's Last Theorem involved establishing *inter alia* that elliptical equations were modular, thus connecting two hitherto separate areas of number theory. The lesson from Wiles's work is that progress in one area of mathematics might be achieved through analogy with another. In terms of brain functioning, this seems another example of how mathematical thinking requires the interplay of a number of generic neural systems.

The suggestion that creative analogizing is critical for mathematical thinking has a basis in research into brain functioning. In particular, there is evidence that the frontal cortices support analogical and related types of reasoning. For example, in a recent PET study, researchers at the American National Institute for Health found that analogical mapping was mediated by areas in the left lower frontal cortex. The results suggest that these frontal areas control the creation and mapping of both semantic and visuospatial relational representations, thus providing the structural consistency (correspondence) and isomorphism (uniqueness) required for successful mathematical reasoning. Other neuroscientists in California using fMRI to study complex reasoning reported distinct frontal activations for integrating complex relations. Similarly, an fMRI team at Stanford University investigating neural correlates of geometric analogy tasks found major right frontal activations associated with figural and analytic reasoning. It was conjectured that distinct pre-frontal areas are involved in goal management or representing intermediate solutions with fluid reasoning, in conjunction with other frontal areas associated with rehearsing and storing information, as well as areas associated with executive or self-initiated control of working memory systems. And as a last example, fMRI researchers at the Institute of Neurology, London, in a study of rule learning, concluded that the fronto-polar cortex mediates implicit rule learning within generic reasoning and problem-solving tasks, (i.e., tasks characteristic of mathematical thinking). In other words, to solve higher-level problems, the cognitive processes involved include meta-cognition, a highly valued educational strategy, and one that is invaluable for monitoring one's efforts in solving mathematical problems.

In sum, the results of all of these studies converge on the suggestion that creative mathematical thinking, just like computational processing, is reliant on a network involving the parietal and frontal areas of the brain. This network is distinct from another involving the temporal and frontal areas which seems to use memory of number facts and rules to support computation, probably the main aspect of school mathematics. This is consistent with the earlier PET study of US college students with high vs. average scores on the SAT–M. For the high SAT–M scoring group, there were significant differences in frontal metabolism while doing a set of SAT–M questions in the PET scanner. However, there were no temporal lobe hemispheric differences between the two groups of students. This suggests that there are two separate kinds of mathematical thinking, supported by different brain systems: high-level creative and basic-level computational. If there are, then quite different classroom strategies might be necessary to promote either one.

Israeli mathematics education researchers Nava Livne and Roberta Milgram categorize individual differences in mathematical abilities into four levels. An ordinary level of mathematical talent is one in which an extrinsically motivated student with low task commitment engages in unchallenging activities utilizing popular and low quality convergent thinking. The fourth level is characterized by a profoundly gifted level of mathematical talent in which an intrinsically motivated student with high task commitment engages in challenging activities utilizing unusual divergent thinking towards high quality outcomes. Livne and Milgram's studies of children's mathematical abilities show that they fall into two independent factors: academic and creative. Academic mathematical ability is related to general intelligence, and is manifest in computational accuracy, symbolic manipulation, memory for number facts, and so on. Creative mathematical ability is related to measures of creative thinking, involving fluidity in mathematical ideas such as finding multiple solutions to a problem or engaging in real-world problem solving.

The suggestion that mathematical thinking requires contributions from both academic and creative abilities might explain some popularized extremes in mathematical performance. First, there are the autobiographical reports of some great mathematicians, such as Benoit Mandelbrot of fractals fame, who performed relatively poorly at primary school arithmetic, where presumably opportunities for creative input were largely absent. In contrast, it is certainly the case that calculation savants (as portrayed in the film *Rain Man*) cannot do mathematics in the constructive and creative manner that professional mathematicians do. It could be hypothesized that in some cases of mathematical genius, ordinary performance at primary school arithmetic, and even poor adult performance at adding up the shopping bill, might be indicative of a relatively underdeveloped academic ability, at least in the specific task of number computation, whereas the case of the autistic–savant who can calculate calendar week days or square roots of large numbers, the creative side of mathematics might be impaired, along with a normal ability to engage in social interaction. But this is not to say that extremes in these two aspects of mathematical ability are always incompatible. Far from it. There are many professional mathematicians who are 'calculating geniuses'. Perhaps the best known is Richard Feynman, Nobel Laureate in theoretical physics. Their biographical accounts show how they employ their intellectual skills to re-organize calculation strategies based on their deep numerical knowledge.

So, although we might be on the lookout for evidence of separate sets of neural processes that roughly correspond to academic and creative mathematical abilities, this may not be fruitful because of the high degree of overlap of the systems involved. Creative mathematical thinking requires extensive and thorough mathematical knowledge. Gifted mathematical thinking involves a high degree of creativity: the application of unusual divergent thinking towards high quality outcomes. But outstanding mathematical talent can only be manifested, even in an intrinsically motivated student with high task commitment, through engagement in challenging mathematical activities, requiring an in-depth knowledge of mathematics. And what is good for the gifted might well indicate what is good for all. There seems no reason why all mathematics students cannot enjoy the emotional satisfaction of the 'Aha!' experience on solving a mathematical problem. As noted in Chapter 5, the neural activity behind such a subjective feeling has been investigated with fMRI, to locate the regions within the brain especially involved, and with EEG to record the temporal dynamics. The stimuli were problems which could be solved with insight vs. those whose solutions were obvious or non-insightful. FMRI revealed increased activity in the right temporal area during initial solving efforts, and this activity remained when the solution was insightful compared with a non-insightful solution. EEG recordings revealed a sudden burst of high-frequency neural activity in the same area beginning

0.3 seconds prior to an insightful solution. Given that this right temporal area is associated with making connections across distantly related information during comprehension, it seems that the sudden flash of insight occurs when these distinct neural systems are suddenly coupled, enabling cognitive processes that allow perception of conceptual connections that had previously not been apparent.

To this end, I cannot recommend too highly the online mathematics club NRICH (see References and Further Reading) run by a team of mathematics educators in the Faculty of Education, University of Cambridge. Established in 1998, NRICH has an international membership of tens of thousands of school students of all ages. Each month new sets of problems are posted on the website. The problems are graded in four levels in terms of the UK school mathematical knowledge used to set them. Usually, but not always, this is indicative of the level of mathematical knowledge required to solve them. The problems for the beginning level are deliberately open-ended, and all of the problems are designed to have multiple solutions or strategies for solution. Importantly, there is no age restriction on who can attempt any problem, so mathematically gifted students can be challenged to their limit. The website incorporates Java plug-ins so that the site is interactive online. In addition to the new problems, the monthly web posting also includes student solutions of the previous month's problems, along with an archive of past problems and their solutions, with flags on which problems have yet to be solved. And there is also a challenging 'Weekly Problem' for those members who cannot wait out the month. But at any time children can email the NRICH tutors, all Cambridge mathematics undergraduates and graduates, to discuss their mathematical thoughts. It is therefore very much to the credit of the NRICH project that it provides such a high level of interactivity. As an exemplar of best educational practice it was recognized with a Queen's Anniversary Prize in 2006. Membership is free – it's as simple as logging on.

Educational neuroscience questions in a box

Most of the neuroimaging studies of mathematical thinking have understandably focused on simple forms of mathematics such as arithmetic. What about recording the neural activations involved in undertaking higher levels of mathematics such as calculus, analysis, matrix algebra, topology, Boolean logic and so on?

9   Arts Curriculum

The current politically driven emphasis on education for 'the basics' has perhaps cast a curriculum shadow over the arts, despite the widely held belief by educators and the wider community that engagement with the arts should be a central part of every child's basic education. From a neuroscientific perspective, our enjoyment of the arts presents an enigma. The evolutionary advantages of significant cognitive investment in the arts are not obvious beyond the enjoyment that comes from personal expression of feelings and mental states, and of the consequent social bonding that such expression might induce in others. One intriguing suggestion is that activating the neural systems involved in artistic endeavour might confer some benefit on general cognitive abilities through the reinforcement of interconnectivity between otherwise cognitively distant functional modules. This chapter presents some of the neuroscientific evidence that supports this claim.

Music

Despite its importance in popular culture, music plays a Cinderella role in most schools' curriculum and timetable allocations. Nevertheless, there is compelling evidence that music might be one of the most important subjects for general cognitive development. In particular, music could be the means of enhancing the development of cerebral interconnectivity in infants' brains. This proposal is based on the observation that mothers naturally sing to their babies. This is true in all cultures, and whether or not a mother regards herself as musical, or a good singer. Interestingly, tape recordings of mothers singing after intervals of 6 to 12 months reveal a remarkable stability in the pitch and tempo of the mothers' songs, even with the so-called non-musical women. Presumably, significant interpersonal bonding is developing here. This seems to be one important benefit we derive from music. In social gatherings, music permits the suspension of taboos against spontaneous singing in public, making physical contact with others (even complete strangers) through dancing, which can be quite sexually suggestive depending on the setting. In a social context then, music creates social connectivity through a temporary dissolving of social barriers. Cambridge music cognition researcher Ian Cross argues that, in a parallel manner, music facilitates intermodular bonding in the brains of babies. That is, Cross suggests, music in a cognitive context enables cognitive connectivity, for which an infant's brain is particularly plastic. Indirect evidence for this provocative speculation comes from the work of a London-based team of researchers in music cognition led by Laura Stewart. They found that babies' musical discrimination becomes more culturally specific with development. We could note that this is similar to how babies' babbling becomes more culturally specific over time (Chapter 3) which, like babbling, can be accounted for by Hebbian reinforcement of babies' aural environment.

The question that has engaged researchers for much of the past century is how the development of musical abilities affects more general cognitive functioning. Before the advent of neuroimaging this question was pursued through various forms of musical and psychometric testing. It was noted from several studies that the correlation between measures of musical aptitudes and general intelligence was positive and statistically significant, but rather low. However, in the 1970s, music cognition researchers Desmond Sergeant and Gregory Thatcher drew attention to the relationship in statistics between correlation indices, r, and the reliability of the measures being correlated, namely, that r is constrained to be less than the reliability. Since the reliability of music aptitude tests is often 'disconcertingly low', typically around 0.4, r cannot rise above about 0.4. Taking this into account, Sergeant and Thatcher showed that corrected correlations between musical aptitude and intelligence are actually rather high, with r exceeding 0.8. Anecdotally, music teachers say that musically talented students seem to have high levels of general intelligence. My research of precocious young 'Mozarts' in Australia found them to be high academic achievers at school. Musical ability presumably develops from the interaction of intelligence with other factors, especially a musical environment in the home. Sergeant and Thatcher's point is that this is a one-way association: a highly developed musical ability implies an underpinning high level of general intelligence, but not the converse. 'A favourable musical environment cannot redeem the absence of the level of intelligence necessary for musical cognition, nor can intelligence alone suffice for the development of musicality.'[1]

In terms of the multitude of neural systems involved in all aspects of cognition, this seems quite a reasonable overview. However, the effect of music on measures of general intelligence has been highlighted in recent years in response to American research which has come to be known as the Mozart effect. The Mozart effect refers to the temporary enhancement of spatial reasoning abilities immediately after listening to a piece of music by Mozart. It was first measured with American university students in a laboratory in the 1990s. The researchers Frances Rauscher and Gordon Shaw attributed the phenomenon to the organizing effect of Mozart's music on brain function, perhaps some kind of auditory cross-modal cohesion. They emphasized that the effect is temporary, and that it was limited to measures of temporo-spatial reasoning and not full-scale IQ. Perhaps unsurprisingly, these caveats were lost in the resulting media hype about boosting babies' IQ by playing them music by Mozart, or any classical music for that matter.

Many other researchers were eager to investigate this finding, but only 50 per cent of follow-up studies were able to replicate the original results. That is, about half of these studies, including some which carefully replicated the original experimental conditions, failed to find any Mozart effect. A postgraduate student of mine decided to undertake a Mozart effect study with primary school children in their classrooms: younger children rather than university students and in a more naturalistic setting than that of a university laboratory. She found a temporary improvement in scores on a spatial processing test while listening to music by Mozart, and also found the same result when children listened to music of Bach. Likewise, others have found effects from listening to classical music by composers other than Mozart, but not from listening to popular music. The consensus, if any, is that the music might help focus attention, although the neural mechanism is not so obvious. One experiment which challenges musical rather than auditory interpretations of Mozart's compositions as a stimulus found a Mozart effect in the ability of rats to run mazes faster.

The onus, then, is on researchers to provide some evidence of associated neural change with listening to and performing music, particularly as one of John Bruer's specific claims (Chapter 1) is that neuroscience cannot tell us whether Mozart or popular music is better for general brain vigour. There are, however, a range of studies which are informative about the neural processes associated with music. My studies of musical prodigies, ranging from middle primary to junior secondary school students, looked at how they perceived musical coherence. The point of focusing on musical coherence is that in order to make sense of music, what is being heard in the time window we call 'the present' – about a third of a second – is compared with what was heard just prior, and what was heard before that and so on over longer time periods back to the beginning of the piece. This constant comparing is aided by compositional structures such as the temporal organization of the music. One of the tests which my young 'Mozarts' performed significantly better than age-matched peers who were also playing music was a Stroop-type test for attention (Chapter 4). I concluded that: 'For gifted young musicians, it is their superior use of executive or metacognitive strategies such as inward-directed attention, that contributes most towards their remarkable abilities.'[2]

Directed attention, we know, is a process mediated by activity in the frontal cortex. But, in classical and jazz music at least, the various heard segments are not identical. Hence, I suggest, high-level musical information processing involves fluid analogizing, as outlined in Chapter 5, to sustain the coherence of complex music. Confirming evidence for this comes from a study by a team of neuroscientists and music cognition researchers who used EEG to compare the frontal brain waves of musically experienced university students with musically inexperienced students listening to both complex chaotic music and simple rhythmic music. Their results were two-fold. First, the most complex (pseudo-classical) music elicited the most complex brain waves in all participants. So, contra Bruer, neuroscience can distinguish which types of music have more effect on brain function, and complex classical music (including that of Mozart) is better. Second, differences in the brain waves between the two groups of students supported the seemingly provocative hypothesis that:

> Complex music produces complex brain activity in complex people, simple music excites simple brain activity in simple people, [where the brain activity referred to involves a] delay of immediate reinforced behaviour and active working memory. Both cognitive functions are more or less exclusively frontally located.[3]

The point that these researchers are making is not that the world is divided into 'complex' and 'simple' people, but rather that individual differences in abilities build on minute differences in potential (here, auditory acuity) through feedback over time. As school education is a major provider of the feedback that drives the increasing divergence of individual abilities, music is but one subject area where we observe a progressive spread of ability levels in our students as they develop through the school years. One of the characteristics of musical prodigies is an extraordinarily steep learning curve which is supported by their high levels of motivation as part of a positive feedback cycle where success builds on success: these students enjoy their practice. Focused inhibition of occasional errors means that they are not repeated, as are done by more typical music students, and so not inadvertently reinforced as per Hebbian plasticity (Chapter 3).

There is evidence for the involvement of various brain systems in the development of musical abilities from several neuroimaging studies into the neural correlates of music. Am American fMRI study used VBM to map structural differences between a group of professional musicians and age- and gender-matched non-musicians. The musicians had more neurons in their sensorimotor regions, their cerebellum, and in their left parietal and basal ganglia regions. The researchers concluded that since professional musicians begin their practice at an early age, these structural brain differences demonstrate that musical training during childhood influences brain growth. This is not to say that there weren't differences present from birth that supported the development of their musical talent through the feedback processes outlined above. But, consistently, previous neuroimaging studies have also found similar structural differences between pianists and violinists and non-musicians in sensorimotor areas of the brain. In the American VBM study, enhanced neural density in the basal ganglia could explain the highly developed capacity for 'instant' decision making for motor responses required for musical performance. Together, these results explain a UK study into the effect of feedback on the musical memory of experienced musicians. For these professionals, their memory for pieces of music was not affected by the withdrawal of auditory or visual feedback, but was negatively affected by the disruption of the timing of tactile feedback from their instrument.

The other neural system of interest, as evidenced by parietal and cerebellum activations, involves spatial or quasi-spatial processing. Spatial metaphors are essential for conveying musical meaning. Pitch is conceptualized in intervals and scales, pitch contours rise and fall in sound as well as in musical notation, intonation can be sharp or flat, voices need to project, and so on. Further evidence for this claim comes from one of the studies of Stewart in which a group of non-musicians were taught to read music and play the keyboard for a period of 15 weeks. A comparison of fMRI scans before and after the training showed enhanced activations in bilateral parts of the parietal cortex. These results suggest that music reading involves the translation of music notation as a spatial code into motor responses as a sequence of piano key presses. In Chapter 8 we noted a similar role for the parietal cortex in supporting mathematical reasoning involved the conversion of sequential into quasi-spatial information. Could the frequently observed correlation between mathematical and musical abilities be explained as an outcome of parietal functioning? I don't buy the often-raised argument that music is mathematical – despite the use of numbers and counting, music is musical. But I do find persuasive the suggestion that in our brains, maths and music might both have a parietal-based neural system of quasi-spatial processing in common.

The cerebellum also plays an important coordinating role for the many neural systems which underpin the various simultaneous musical skills of sight reading notation, listening to aural feedback from other players and one's own playing, and preparing the fingers, arms, lungs, etc., for

Figure 9.1 PET arrangement for musicians to 'play' Bach while undergoing a brain scan (courtesy Larry Parsons)

appropriate and temporally coordinated action. In a series of PET studies of piano performance of Bach preludes from memory (Figure 9.1), neuroscientist Larry Parsons found bilateral activations of the temporal cortex for long-term memory, and significant activations in the cerebellum. Parsons suggests that the neural systems required for processing the musical components of harmony, melody and rhythm are distributed throughout the brain. The difference between musicians and non-musicians lies in the extent of the activations in these areas. The cerebellum, of which many studies have shown is necessary to coordinate fine motor control and movement, is involved in music through determining timing, the structural feature of music essential for coherence. Interestingly, professional musicians have a larger cerebellum (by 5 per cent) than non-musicians.

A New Zealand study of students learning to sing simple songs from memory provides a good illustration that some of the neural systems for music are available to both musicians and non-musicians. To memorize the songs, the students had unconsciously grouped them according to their similarity of pitch contour – how the notes rise and fall. Both musicians and non-musicians grouped the songs in this same way. Furthermore, since this involved exploiting a quasi-spatial characteristic of the music, the researchers suggest that singing in school might be beneficial for other spatial reasoning-based subjects such as mathematics, as speculated above. In fact, a number of studies have demonstrated improvements in academic outcomes from learning to play a musical instrument, especially the piano. This has been shown across the school-age span, with pre-school children, primary school pupils and university students. One study by the Mozart effect researchers showed that the most benefit from piano lessons for primary pupils came if combined with computer games involving mathematics puzzles of proportion and ratios. Four months of piano lessons and computer interactions was sufficient for relative gains of 27 per cent on mathematics tests of proportion over other children who had not had the instrumental training. The researchers point out that since music involves ratios, fractions, proportions and thinking in space and time, it is likely to involve the same brain systems as required to be successful at this critical aspect of primary school mathematics on which much of secondary school mathematics depends. Consistently, a longitudinal study of over 25,000 high school students led by American education researcher James Catterall found that students who played musical instrumentals from an early age had significantly higher mathematics test scores in their final year of high school. Interestingly, the effect was more noticeable for students from lower SES backgrounds than higher. The study also found benefits for reading and more positive attitudes towards social inclusivity from participation in any arts programme. Perhaps this is another illustration of the power of music for social bonding, as discussed above?

Some of the neural systems engaged in the expression of musical abilities are those involved in working memory, as outlined in Chapter 4. A widely used age-normed test of musical abilities based on working memory capacity is the Gordon's Musical Aptitude Profile (MAP). Each item requires listening to short phrase played on a violin, and then choosing which is the better response phrase from a pair. In another of my studies of young 'Mozarts' I used the MAP to compare their musical abilities with those of children of similar age. The 'Mozarts' had significantly higher scores on musical tests of pitch and rhythm which require better working memories for musical information – hardly surprising. But on the MAP subtest for aesthetic preference there were no differences between the gifted musicians and their peers: evidence for yet another neural system which operates similarly in the brains of musicians and non-musicians?

Both cognitive and theoretical analyses of musical compositions converge on the notion of balance between predication and surprise. Musical expectations need to be met, but not all the time. Rock music is typically high on prediction and low on surprise, making it compelling to dance to. Contemporary art music is typically the reverse, perhaps accounting for the muted response of audiences, at least in terms of sales and requests for repeat performances. More generally we could note that how various commentators have suggested over the years that in many aspects of life we seek a balance between the stimulation of novelty and the security of the well known. And as a non-musical application of this principle, UK neuropsychologist Paul Howard-Jones has devised a non-musical computer game for school students as an application of educational neuroscience to the fostering of creativity in the classroom. (A high school music program which explicitly used the tension between novelty and prediction in composing musical variations is described in an article by Andreasen and Geake (1988), Chapter 9 References.)

But in the here-and-now demands of live musical performance, it is not easy for a music student to achieve an optimal balance between unengaging safety, on the one hand, and risky but interesting interpretation on the other, particularly in a competition or for an examination. The experience is understandably anxiety-forming. Some interesting research led by London cognitive psychologist John Gruzelier has used EEG neurofeedback to reduce performance anxiety and stage fright in student musicians. The idea is that the student concentrates on a visual display of one of their EEG waveforms on a computer monitor and, through deliberately enacting a sense of calm, tries to reduce the amplitude of the signal. The results have been quite promising. All of the students who received neurofeedback training were found to have improved their performances. But those who had received the neurofeedback using the waveforms with the longest and shortest wavelengths improved their performance the most, up to 17 per cent. The researchers suggest that the benefits of neurofeedback go beyond simply alleviating stage fright to more general enhancement of artistic expression.

Visual arts

Visual literacy, the comprehension and production of visual art in its many forms, requires a similar degree of cerebral interconnectivity as does music, but with the obvious difference being the centrality of visual over auditory information. The brain's visual processing systems of how and what we see, and how we separately understand features and form, have been one of the most studied of all of the brain's neural systems. Visual information from the retinas of each eye is transmitted along the optic nerves through the optic chiasma, where information from the same half visual

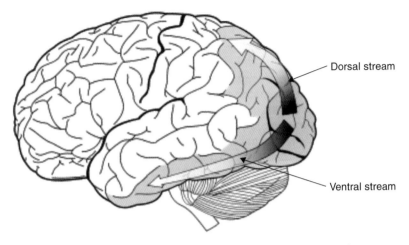

Figure 9.2 Dorsal and ventral streams of processed visual information

field from each eye is combined. Then in the lateral geniculate nucleus, parvo-magnocellular systems separate various aspects of the information, including contrast sensitivity, temporal resolution and acuity. These separate information streams are then fed to relevant parts of the visual cortex. In the visual cortex, columns of neurons process these inputs to select image features through the inhibition of surrounding cells. For example, to select an edge which is perfectly upright, the 'upright' cells inhibit the surrounding cells for 'leaning a little bit to the right' and 'leaning a little bit to the left'.

Neuroscientists recognize five different functional areas of the visual cortex: V1, the primary visual cortex, which processes basic spatial patterns through contrasts; V2, the secondary visual cortex which processes complex spatial patterns through associations; V3, which processes the relevant visual field from the spatial context; V4, which employs selective attention from the frontal cortex to assess the salience of the visual information; and V5, which undertakes motion detection and guidance of eye movements. As noted in previous chapters, we are visually biased primates. Our visual systems are our predominant means of getting information about our changing world. They provide this information by interconnecting functional areas along two pathways labelled 'where' and 'what' to produce a spatial map and a categorization of what's in it respectively (Figure 9.2). The 'where' pathway connects V1 to V2 to V5 to the lower part of the parietal lobe resulting in a dorsal stream of information. A good example of its use is in the representation of object locations when visual information is used to guide reaching. The 'what' pathway connects V1 to V2 to V4 to the inferior temporal lobe to form a ventral stream of information. This enables the recognition of form and objects, and their storage in and retrieval from long-term memory.

The neural systems in our brains have one agenda: to make sense of our world. This is readily demonstrated with human (and presumably most animal) ability to continually recompute head position so that the visual world remains the same way up. The combining of outputs from all of the functional areas in the visual cortex to achieve this feat requires many neuronal systems to function in concert.

With so many neural systems involved, how do our brains integrate all of this information, especially when most of the time the information is incomplete and sometimes contradictory? Our brains make up stories! Our brains fill in what's missing with a best guess from what is being seen. Evidence for this is part of our everyday experience, and not just with clever visual illusions in psychology books such as the famous Necker cube which appears to oscillate inside out. The very compelling moving reality of cinema and television imagery is a visual illusion comprised of static images shown too fast for our visual system, evolved in slower times, to notice. And the other visual arts are no exception in playing to our highly adapted but necessarily limited visual systems. A nice illustration is given by any of the sidewalk chalk drawings by American artist Julian Beever, popular on the Internet. You have to be at the correct viewing angle on the sidewalk to get the 3D effect, as shown here.

Art education, then, involves a blending of the cognitive with the practical aspects of art. Like an accomplished musician, an aspiring visual arts student must acquire manual dexterity and confidence with techniques. Like the musician with their instrument, this involves the cerebellum to coordinate the fine motor control and muscle coordination to employ a paintbrush or chisel in a deliberative fashion. To employ these tools with artistic purpose, high visuo-spatial awareness must incorporate the difference between 'looking' and 'seeing'. Research into the neural systems involved in the detection of symmetry led by American vision scientist Christopher Tyler is illustrative. Humans need less than a twentieth of a second to detect symmetry in an image, regardless of how it is presented for viewing. This is too fast for mental comparison, so it implies that symmetry processing is 'hard-wired', in other words, undertaken by a highly adaptive neural system. An fMRI study of symmetrical dot images vs. unsymmetrical dot images produced significant activations in a dorsal region of the visual cortex, but not in the other regions of the visual cortex. It seems that evolution has produced a specialized brain region for processing visual symmetry. Why? For a newborn the most important visual image is that of its mother's face, and human faces are highly symmetrical. In fact, there are specialized areas of the brain overlapping the visual cortex, the fusiform and occipital face areas, dedicated to processing images of faces. A Taiwanese fMRI study, among several, has shown that symmetry is the key variable in processing images of faces, and that viewing faces from any angle makes no difference. And if viewing mother's face is the evolutionary driver for our hard-wired sense of symmetry, then this could explain an earlier finding of the Tyler group in which general spatial processing became more focused when processing symmetry out of the corner of one's eye, just as a baby has to do when viewing their mother's face while breast feeding. Our evolved neural system for symmetry detection presumably explains our predilection for symmetry as a basis for our sense of aesthetics, at least when it concerns the human form. This is turn suggests a feature for critique and guidance in portraiture and life drawing classes.

Art teachers also want their students to develop an understanding of the terms of visual language: line, tone, colour, shape, space, texture, form, dimensionality, balance, composition and pattern. One novel fMRI study has used individual 'translations' from image to visual language as patterns of brain activation to predict which picture out of a large set that a particular individual is looking at while in the scanner. From the visual features of a particular image such as the relative placement of objects, their orientation, their luminescence, and so on, the software predicts which visual neuronal systems will be activated. For example, a picture of a relatively complex cityscape would generate a significantly different pattern of activation from a picture of a misty rainforest. Before it can begin, however, the software has to be 'tuned' to the visual predilections of each individual, highlighting the point in Chapter 1 that no two brains are ever exactly the same. Nevertheless, this achievement was regarded so highly that the report of this research was published in *Nature*, the world's top-ranking science research journal. It provides neuroscientific support for the common maxim in art education that drawing is thinking, both in terms of visual problem solving, and in terms of technical and interpretive creativity.

One focus of research into visual thinking has been fractal form – the geometry of natural shapes such as coastlines, clouds, branching rivers, branching trees, mountain profiles, and so on. The term 'fractal' was coined by French mathematician Benoit Mandelbrot in the 1970s to refer to shapes which exhibited self-similarity with changes of scaling, at least within a range. For example, zooming in on a coastline reveals yet more wriggles of inlets and promontories, from national maps down to one particular headland and the waves lapping the shore. The contrast

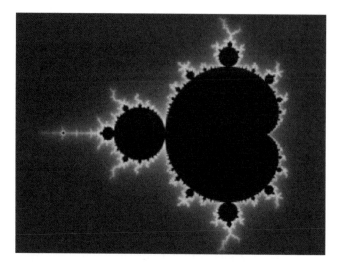

Figure 9.3 Mandelbrot set at zero zoom level

with urban environments is that the latter tend not to be fractal. Mathe-matically, fractals have a fractional dimensionality (i.e., not 2D or 3D, but 1.4D or 2.7D for example). Interestingly, fractals can be gener-ated as computer graphics of incredible complexity. The Mandelbrot set (Figure 9.3) is iconic. Zooming in on any part of the boundary reveals figures and shapes arrestingly suggestive of natural forms. Remarkably, this infinite complexity is generated by iteration of a simple equation: the solutions of one iteration are put back into the equation for the next round.

The insight this affords is that many natural phenomena are formed through iterative processes: erosion of coastlines and mountains, cellular division, are typical. The point for visual literacy is that we evolved in a fractal environment, so perhaps our visual systems have also evolved to notice fractal form in a similar way to our noticing symmetry whenever it is present. Certainly some of the early researchers into fractal geome-try such as Michael Barnsley claimed that after learning about fractal ge-ometry, you will see everything in the natural world differently. Clouds, trees, rivers, especially seen from the air, take on a new meaning. One of my first pieces of research tested this claim by investigating how expo-sure to a programme of fractal computer graphics affected primary school children's paintings. The children zoomed around the fractal computer graphics on their new colour monitors whenever they had a few minutes inbetween lessons over a month. Their teacher had the inspired idea of recording her pupils' impressions with watercolour paintings at the beginning and end of the four-week period. I showed the two sets of paintings to my colleague and art educator Jim Porter, who knew nothing about the research at that stage. I asked him to analyse the children's art work in terms of what imagery they might have been exposed to. Porter suggested that the source imagery was either some natural forms such as seen down a microscope, or in space such as the red spot of Jupiter, or the early works of pioneering abstract artist Vassily Kandinsky in which he was attempting to capture the forms of nature. Porter's analysis suggests how well the fractal computer graphics evoke natural forms. In fact, Mandelbrot in his first book on fractals speculated that the aesthetic appeal of Beaux Art and Baroque artists lies in their unconscious use of fractal form in their art. What, then, of contemporary art one could ask? Australian physicist Richard Taylor has undertaken fractal analyses of the works of Jackson Pollock, and found them to have a fractal dimensionality, unlike the works of many of Pollock's contemporaries. Taylor suggests that this can explain the unconscious aesthetic appeal of Pollock's abstracts. Interestingly, the fractal dimensionality of his paintings increased from 1.0 to 1.7 over Pollock's working life, presumably from an increasing confidence in his drip-paint technique to produce works of engaging aesthetics.

The preceding research highlights the main objective of art education: to develop artistic creativity through fostering an interpretive ability which connects process with outcome. An American team led by neuroscientist Mark Samco used DTI to map neural interconnectivity in 36 participants who then took the Torrence Tests of Creative Thinking, tests which ask participants to produce novel visual and lexical solutions to semantically challenging problems. The correlational analysis revealed that the participants who scored higher on the creativity tests showed more highly directed white matter connections in their right hemispheric brain areas, especially their right frontal areas. Mapping the connectivity fibres showed that creative individuals use an extended network of right hemisphere functional areas to produce novel solutions to complex problems. In contrast, the solutions of the less creative participants seemed to rely more on long-term memory of past ideas, consistent with more of their related white matter tracts being located in the left temporal cortex. The researchers note that creating art is among the most complex expressions of visual and other brain functions.

Also with relevance for art education, American neuroscientist Robert Solso used fMRI to observe the brain of an artist while he drew a portrait while lying inside the scanner. The aim was to try an understand how an experienced painter uses his visual neural systems. The point of the study is that we all possess visual neural systems which we use for perception and cognition of art. This aesthetic evaluation is done rapidly, and mostly unconsciously. Consequently, the artist's brain activations were compared with those of a non-artist also drawing faces while lying inside the scanner as the control condition, necessary in all fMRI studies (Chapter 1). Unsurprisingly, activations in the fusiform face areas were seen in both participants. But, in the artist's brain, these activations were less intense, suggesting a degree of automaticity in processing facial information, just as we've seen with other examples of Hebbian reinforced learning (Chapter 3). Furthermore, consistently with Samco's creativity DTI study above, the artist showed more activation in the right frontal area, indicative of using creative cognitive functions such conceptual associations when drawing faces.

This account of the neural basis of artistic expression is both supported and challenged by the artistic proclivities of people whose brains have been affected by disease or abnormal development. One case involved a professional artist with a non-senile type of dementia which affected her frontal and temporal cortices. While she progressively lost her abilities for language and social skills, her paintings became more colourful and less inhibited. The implication is that the functioning of the frontal and temporal cortices concerned with language and social skills might concomitantly be suppressing artistic expression, possibly through imposing social norms aka Freud. Other similar cases have been reported whereby non-artist dementia patients spontaneously develop artistic interests and talents while simultaneously losing social skills as their dementia progresses. Since in most of these cases the disease symptoms were located in the left hemisphere, one interpretation of this phenomenon is that these enhanced artistic abilities might arise from the right hemisphere compensating for the loss of cognitive functions concerning language and social skills.

Further support for this interpretation comes from the remarkable artistic endeavours of child savants, as illustrated in Figure 9.4. Before trying to generalize from such particulars, it has to be said that artistic talent in savants is extremely rare. Moreover, like all children who take to drawing, artistic savants demonstrate persistence, practice and self-motivation, while needing encouragement, praise and tuition. 'Blind' assessments of the works of artistic savants compared with normal high ability artists demonstrate little difference in artistic execution, the main difference being cognitive in the understanding of meaning, symbols and context of the work. Interestingly from a developmental perspective, sometimes these prodigious talents disappear, as was the case with 'Nadia' who lost her drawing ability once she started to talk later on

Figure 9.4 Horse by 'Nadia', aged 3 years

in childhood. Australian psychophysicist Alan Snyder argues that, taken together, the dementia and savant cases provide compelling evidence that artistic abilities can be unlocked in all of us by closing down our brain connections with our social world. To test this hypothesis, Snyder has used TMS to temporarily suppress activity in the left temporal cortex of participants to see if this causes an improvement in their drawing abilities. He claims that it does. In contrast, I am not convinced; my viewing of the results leaves me sceptical. Surely the point of art, and thus of art education, is to make connections between the life experiences of the artist as expressed in each particular work, and similar life experiences of the viewer? Closing down the brain's social networks and neural systems would seem to compromise possible connections between artist and viewer. Moreover, examples of occasional so-called 'mad' artists like Vincent Van Gough notwithstanding, most artists do not lack language and social skills: look at the life of Picasso. It seems that other factors must contribute to an artistically creative brain. There is no future in TMS machines in school art classroom zapping our students' brains to get them to stop socializing.

Educational neuroscience questions in a box

Conducting a school band requires considerable imagination on the music teacher's part about what the music ought to sound like. Conducting a school band, then, is no easy task since the skill levels of the student players can be quite variable, and their individual preparation less than optimal. In a performance, the band conductor has to communicate his or her imagined music through the gestures of conducting.

What distinguishable neural processes underpin the performance of band and orchestral conductors, where the desired sound is being continually anticipated, and a corresponding arm motion made, a fraction of a second (about 300 ms) ahead of the response by the musicians?

10 A Future for Educational Neuroscience

Of course, writing scenarios about the future is a guarantee for retrospective embarrassment. Nevertheless, we can hope that future generations will use our increasing knowledge of the brain to enhance mental qualities which add meaning to our lives, and to reduce those that are destructive. As London neuroscientist Paul Fletcher conjectured on possible developments arising from the imaging of neural activation: 'One day there might be enough known about brain activity to show the process of learning, and whether it was taking place efficiently'.[1] To this end, John Bruer has outlined an interdisciplinary research approach:

> A reasonable position would be to admit that traditional cognitive science should be supplemented by cognitive neuroscience from below and by cognitive anthropology or cultural psychology from above. Biological theories, functional theories, and sociocultural theories proceed at different levels of analysis that for now cannot be seamlessly linked. Research at these levels should proceed in parallel, with each level looking to the other for possible constraints on its own theorising. If this is to be scientific research, all that is required is that the disciplines at each level share a belief in an external reality that can be discerned through careful use of qualitative and quantitative research methods. All participants should share a conviction that their collaborative discourse is indeed about something.[2]

In this case, the 'something' is learning within formal education. There are some implications for learning from current educational neuroscience that could help shape schools of the future. Of course, the best predictor of the future is the present, and many of the predictions that follow are already in place in some educational institutions right now. Moreover, a school whose practice embraces educational neuroscience could provide valuable opportunities for the school's teachers to make important contributions to the neuroscientific research agenda, crucial if we are to have educationally relevant educational neuroscience in the future. But, it should be noted, none of this is to ignore the many caveats in the

Introduction, especially that neuroscience is a laboratory-based endeavour. Even with the best of intentions, extrapolations from the laboratory for the classroom need to be made with considerable caution.

With that in mind, here are four predictions for the future.

- understanding of brain functioning will increase dramatically;
- brain imaging technology will become more user-friendly;
- cognitive neuroscience will become more influenced by educational concerns as a subdiscipline of educational neuroscience;
- educational practice will become more influenced by educational neuroscience.

For a first prediction of the future, it would seem reasonable to expect that our understanding of brain functioning will continue to increase dramatically. Hopefully, this will entail a more holistic understanding of brain function, featuring explanatory relationships between function and structure. With many thousands of studies producing data every year, this in turn might depend on developments in data mining search engines. Of course, there is always the possibility that some of this enterprise will be blocked by some critical conceptual or interrogative ceiling. As pointed out in Chapter 1, there are already conceptual limits to neuroscientific experimental design, especially the nature of the stimuli, and interpretation of neuroscientific data, from the black box models of cognition that we are necessarily constrained to employ. But as neuroscientist Colin Blakemore has conjectured, it might be that to cross the mind–brain interface, to solve the so-called 'hard problem' of how so much biological wetware gives rise to the thoughts and mental experiences of consciousness, we will need a brand new science, an interrogative framework as different from our present scientific repertoire as the quantum mechanics of the early twentieth century was different from the classical mechanics of Galileo and Newton.

But if we are to deeply understand how individual brains enable individual individuality, then we have to hope that brain imaging technology will become more user-friendly. At present, having a brain scan is not necessarily a pleasant experience. An fMRI scan involves lying inside a very strong magnetic field subjected to an experience which is noisy, physically restrictive and uncomfortable, not to mention claustrophobic. A PET scan involves having an injection of a radioactive isotope. The question of any possible long-term side effects from either of these procedures was raised in Chapter 1. For all of the preceding reasons, user-friendly neuroimaging technology would certainly be desirable. Will it happen? One of Arthur C. Clarke's predictions, made when computers occupied large air-conditioned basements, was that one day computers would be sufficiently miniaturized to fit onto a desk. Of course at the time, in the 1970s, everyone laughed. Seymour Paper took that a step further to predict that one day every child at school would have such a miniaturized computer on his or her desk in the classroom. As he stated at the World Conference on Computers in Education, Sydney, 1990: 'Conferences about computers in education will become as redundant as a conference about pencils in education.' And it's certainly not clear how the essential technology of an fMRI scanner, the large superconducting magnet, or the circular radiation counter of a PET scanner, could be readily miniaturized in a vaguely parallel manner to the way in which a computer chip miniaturizes the electronic and logic functions of large arrays of the thermionic valves of those original computers.

One relatively new approach in brain scanning technology which holds some promise for direct use in educational settings – classrooms, playgrounds, and so on – is near optical infra red (NOIR) scanning. The technique involves shining low-powered laser beams in the infra-red waveband through the skull on to the cortical surface, and then reading differences related to function in the reflected wave. This, it has to be said, restricts study to the cortical grey matter, with the possibility that interactions of the laser beam with the intermediate scalp and skull tissue might distort the findings. Nevertheless, NOIR technology is already in use in hospitals to scan newborns for possible brain damage if they have suffered some trauma during birth. The potential benefits for educational neuroscience are several. The kit consists of a relatively inexpensive headset, so a class set of 30 would be affordable. With its protruding mini-lasers, some types of NOIR headsets look like space helmets out of a science fiction movie, so could have appeal to children. From a health and safety perspective, subjects can be examined repeatedly or even continuously for long periods. While the spatial resolution is relatively poor, one important advantage of this technology is that the headsets can be worn in classrooms or school playgrounds. The headset is connected to the data collecting monitor via a wireless link, so subjects are not confined to lying still. Head motion is not a problem. Of course, obtaining data of a whole class of children during, say, a mathematics lesson only compounds the problems of interpretation. The development of analytic software which could handle such diverse group data, therefore, would be a valuable step forward for a genuine educational neuroscience.

Another neuroimaging technological development with potential applications for educational neuroscience is a miniaturized MRI device, about the size of a briefcase, the nuclear magnetic resonance mobile universal surface explorer (NMR-MOUSE). For several years now the NMR-MOUSE has been used for scanning non-biological materials for defects. Further development should soon realize a helmet NMR-MOUSE scanner for use in medical emergencies, and a hand-held device for use in the home, much like home blood pressure monitors. How long before a school purchases one?

A third prediction, although it is probably more of an aspiration, is that cognitive neuroscience will become more influenced by educational concerns. That is, educational neuroscience as described here will become a recognizable research interdiscipline in its own right. But that requires money, which in the research community is a seemingly sparse, sought-after commodity. If this prediction is to come true, then it will require changes in the allocation of money on at least two levels: competitive funding within research granting programmes, and political prioritizing for targetted budget allocations to research grant programmes. At the time of writing, the average chance of getting a UK national funding council research grant for your cherished project is about 1 in 20 – not good odds. But if your project is interdisciplinary, then those odds become almost prohibitively longer. The members of any discipline-based funding council want their limited budget to be spread as far as feasible, so an interdisciplinary project will usually be regarded as better left to be supported by the funding council of the other discipline. The only way to break this impasse is at the political level – for a portion of the funding councils' budgets to be earmarked for interdisciplinary areas such as educational neuroscience. This in turn requires politicians to be persuaded that the potential applications of educational neuroscience research are likely to receive public approval, that is, that there are appreciable benefits for voting teachers and parents.

The converse prediction/aspiration, that educational practice will become more influenced by cognitive neuroscience, seems at first blush to be more likely if the enthusiasm with which the teaching profession has embraced brain-based schemes, regardless of their scientific validity, is any indication. One can only hope that applications based on real science will be similarly embraced. The main threat could be that if high expectations of instant applications are not met, science taking as long as it does, many in the teaching profession might turn their backs on neuroscience as a source of innovation, just when it eventually is ready to deliver. As we have seen in the preceding chapters, cognitive neuroscience is still in its relative infancy, and while brain imaging can be employed to assist in the identification of some specific learning disabilities, it is a long way short of being able to predict the learning needs of every individual child, not least when under-achievement or cultural difference affect conventional means of assessment.

The main reason for limitations on the ultimate utility of educational neuroscience is, I predict, that the problem of how the brain works will never be completely resolved. Our brains, as clever as they can be, did not evolve under adaptive pressure to undertake neuroscience research. The

fact that we can do any science *of* our brain *with* our brains is wonderful. And there's even a silver lining to this cloud: cognitive neuroscience
as a career for gifted students. What sort of career advice can a teacher
offer to a bright young child, when we know that most careers that this
child will be confronted with when grown have not yet been invented? If
I'm correct in this prediction about the ongoing challenge of completely
describing our brain's function, then there will always be positions as cognitive, possibly educational neuroscientists. Moreover, the very nature of
this interdiscipline, which requires in-depth interconnected knowledge
of physics, computing, mathematics, statistics, neuroanatomy, neurophysiology, cognitive psychology and philosophy to be combined with
education, is particularly suitable for the interconnected brains of our
academically able students. Hopefully some of them will then go on to
join the teaching profession.

To that end, some years ago Paul Cooper and I presented two possible
future scenarios.[3] The scene is a parent–teacher night at a local primary
school. A parent is discussing the poor maths results of her child, Chris,
with Chris's class teacher. In the first scenario, the teacher acknowledges
that Chris's maths performance has been under surveillance for a while.
The teacher has available Chris's event-related neuroimaging report captured in the school's neuroimaging assessment room. Here, the whole class
regularly undertakes their term assessment tasks while wearing individual
neuroimaging headsets. The school bought a class set of NMR-MOUSE
neuroimaging headset scanners some years ago. They've been set up in
the former class computer room, long abandoned when all students were
issued with hand-held computer note pads with infra-red links to their
teacher's classroom PC. The class set of individual images is statistically
analysed by a dedicated computer, and parent–teacher reports generated.
After scanning Chris' report, the teacher brings her professional knowledge to bear, and recommends a course of real-time bio-feedback utilizing
mental multistep arithmetic problems to strengthen Chris's' short-term
memory circuit for number solutions, which the imaging has shown to
be relatively weak. Ongoing neuroimaging assessment during the next
month will determine the effectiveness of this individually specific intervention. The parent is pleased with the professionality of the teacher,
especially that the teacher knew what was the matter, and could do
something about it. The teacher was pleased to be able to act in such
a professional manner. Her considerable training, including an MPhil in
educational neuroscience had been worth it, especially her research thesis
on the neural correlates of learning difficulties in mathematics.

In the second contrasting scenario, the teacher is at a loss to explain
why Chris might be having maths learning problems. 'Could it be motivation?' the teacher offers. 'Obviously,' says the frustrated parent, 'but

that is circular. If Chris had more maths success, Chris would be better motivated.' 'I suppose so,' replies the teacher. 'I barely scraped through the lowest level of maths at my School Certificate.' 'Well,' says the parent, 'what are you going to do about it?' 'Me?' says the teacher, 'How would I know what to do? After all, I'm only a teacher. I don't know what is causing the problem. Why don't you take Chris for an assessment with Cognitive Services Inc? Here is their card. They'll know best what to do.'

In either case, the remedial intervention is undertaken by bio-feedback with the subject viewing a suitable neuroimage while undertaking the remedial learning task. In the first future scenario, teachers have developed a similar professionality to that of doctors and engineers, and are accorded commensurate social status (and salary?). Obviously, there are corresponding issues regarding selection for teacher pre-service courses. In the second future scenario, the professionality of teachers has been usurped by other professionals, including those with some training in educational neuroscience. The change in the social status of doctors came last century with the profession's adoption of scientific evidence-based practice. The move for teachers to scientific evidence-based practice is still to come. Will it be this century?

Schools of the future

The mission for a school of the future (or the present?) should be to optimally meet children's learning needs. That carries the implicit recognition that every child's brain is unique. And whereas most brains follow a normal developmental trajectory, each is also idiosyncratic in its strengths and weaknesses for learning particular types of information. Hence, to meet individual learning needs, the most important and radical change in the way schools operate will be to de-couple age from stage. A school of the future will be structured around multi-age classes within a vertical curriculum structure that has children moving between academic levels for different subjects as needs be. Since brain development is driven by life experiences, rather than chronological age *per se*, individual children's learning needs are best addressed by having them engage in appropriate curriculum for their stage of learning readiness, largely independent of their birthday. This, it is acknowledged, is a provocative suggestion, since age-stage progression is deeply embedded in our educational culture, especially in school organization. Except, of course, when it isn't, as in school representative sporting teams, school musicals and choirs, national competitions such as the science and mathematics Olympiads, and school art exhibitions. In all of these school activities, ability is the criterion for selection, and age is irrelevant. And everyone gets along just fine. Of course, such an argument is also employed to support a currently fashionable call for personalized education, with its attendant definitional inexactitude, not to mention pragmatic challenges from externally imposed curriculum and assessment protocols. However, replacing birthdays with learning needs is a principle for student grouping which survives the transience of education fashion.

To elaborate a little, the most compelling reason for organizing school classes on a basis of learning readiness, is, as teachers readily acknowledge, that the considerable variance in cognitive abilities and prior knowledge observable at school entry increases with every subsequent school year. It therefore makes sense to group children for teaching in terms of relative homogeneity of learning needs, that is, by ability, experience and interest rather than by chronological age alone. Such a vertical curriculum organization (VCO) has been used with considerable success in schools in Australia, in both elementary and secondary schools. In a VCO, classes in one subject area, varied in level and focus, are offered on the same timetable line. For example, in mathematics, there might be classes ranging from basic arithmetic to introductory algebra, together with classes on maths around the home, maths in DiskWorld, maths for PlayStation, and so on. Advanced classes require challenge testing for entry. Each student chooses an individual timetable, under guidance from teachers, to suit their levels of ability in their various subjects. A young student gifted in maths would take the advanced classes along with many older students. A student whose academic strength lies in English and not in maths might opt for a class in maths around the home, but sign up for an advanced class on Shakespeare's tragedies timetabled for next lesson. Ideally, while each student does the required amount of maths, few fail or get turned off maths: their chosen classes are at the right level of challenge. Teachers in schools which have adopted VCO speak highly of the improved behaviour and motivation of children in learning needs-based classes, the reduction in disciplinary distractions more than off-setting the additional counselling and screening necessary to determine class placements. Interestingly, it is the less able academic students who seem to benefit most from having classes pitched at their level, although academically gifted students can be readily catered for by attending classes advanced for their age. Furthermore, transition between levels can then be made in response to learning achieved, rather than the next inevitable birthday. In a school of the future, VCO could be readily implemented where much of the class delivery is via a virtual ICT classroom.

As noted in Chapter 3, an important implication of a Hebbian account of adaptive plasticity is that repetition is necessary for reliable learning; therefore in curriculum design, depth should preside over breadth. Thus a spiral curriculum could benefit learners by presenting learning experiences which are more in accordance with natural brain processes. A VSO with mixed age classes and independent learning plans would enable the curriculum of a school of the future to be conceptually spiral, with individual student progress closely monitored through a matrix of teacher mentoring and formative feedback. Another feature of Hebbian plasticity that could influence the conduct of a class in a school of the future is that long-term memories take longer, about 30 minutes, to consolidate, suggesting that every 30 minutes or so students should take a break to do something completely different (e.g., run around outside) for 5 minutes or so to give their brains a chance to 'catch up'. At least one UK secondary school is doing just that to good effect, with learning outcomes enhanced, and popularity with the students high.

As society becomes ever more dependent on information communication technology (ICT), so will our schools. This will increasingly impact on management and curriculum. In a school of the future, the actual hours of operation could be quite flexible. For example, flexible timetabling and off-site downloading would be welcomed by adolescents whose circadian rhythms and sleep patterns are at odds with current school timetable hours. Virtual classrooms could allow timetabling to be more in accordance with well-documented adolescent patterns of sleep – at least nine hours per night, but beginning several hours later than in childhood, and continuing well into the morning when, traditionally, school has begun. Although adolescent culture through late night socializing reinforces this pattern, its underlying aetiology is biological, with endocrine-induced alterations to internal biological clocks being associated with the onset of puberty. Adolescent sleep deprivation can have deleterious consequences on learning outcomes. First, there is good evidence that sleep is important for memory consolidation. Second, daytime sleepiness negatively affects powers of concentration to learn. Nevertheless, school operating hours have ignored this fact, resulting in adolescents being among the most sleep-deprived populations in our society. To support such flexibility, curriculum delivery could utilize ICT such as virtual classrooms, chatroom discussion groups, smart chips to track students' attendance, palm pilots for downloads of administrative communication, and so on.

In a school of the future, individual feedback and monitoring could include neuroimaging diagnoses of neural structures and functions which might be contributing to learning difficulties. Assessment procedures could take advantage of increased understanding of factors that affect memory and performance under stress. As we saw in Chapter 9, promising research involves neurofeedback whereby students use visual imagery of their EEG (alpha and gamma band) output to control brainwaves affecting concentration and motivation, and, in curricula involving physical performance such as gymnastics and music, reducing fluctuations associated with performance anxiety.

Another possibility for a school of the future involves changes to the physical classroom environment, particularly with lighting. Our eyes evolved to be particularly sensitive to blue light from the sky. Since daylight heralded the potential presence of both predators and prey, it is perhaps not surprising that research has found that exposure to blue light can improve alertness and performance in sleep-deprived subjects, such as our sleepy adolescents at school, especially in the morning. This suggests that the current widespread use of overhead neon strip lighting in school classrooms might need to be re-assessed.

Lest all of these scenarios for schools of the future sound unrealistically utopian, there are, of course, predictable negatives. As society is also becoming ever increasingly dependent on drugs, both medically prescribed and illegally trafficked, so the use of cognitive-enhancing drugs is likely to become an ever-increasing aspect of education. Cognition-enhancing drugs are already marketed as therapeutic agents for use in clinical settings: memory enhancers for Alzheimer's disease, drugs to increase wakefulness in narcolepsy and stimulants for ADHD. These psycho-active compounds work by targeting receptors and other biochemical mechanisms in the brain to alter the subtle balance of neurotransmitters involved in nerve signalling. The precise mechanism of cognitive enhancers on this complex and sensitive system of neurochemistry is poorly understood, presenting the risk of a range of unforeseen side-effects. Nevertheless there is already a black market trade in Ritalin on some American school campuses, and it is predicted that memory-enhancing medications prescribed to offset the effects of dementia in the elderly will soon be seen in the playground with disturbing regularity. No longer the quick fag down behind the bike shed, but a round of granny's yellow dementia pills on the morning of the maths test. Needless to say, drugs designed for a demented brain are likely to have deleterious side effects on growing brains. So does that mean we can predict a designer drug market for so-called 'smart drugs' for the competitive student? Interestingly, one of the points made by some of the hundreds of teachers who participated in the Teaching and Learning Programme's Seminar Series on Neuroscience and Education in the UK was that if hand-held computers are approved brain extensions, why not chemical ones? The moral issues seem less clear-cut, but they will be unavoidable.

Consequently, teacher professional development in a school of the future would include educational neuroscience to provide up-to-date and scientifically accurate information, in contrast to fads based on misinterpretation as currently abound. Hopefully, in a school of the future, neuro-scientifically informed teachers will reject fads and claims made without a proven scientific basis, such as the currently popular brain gym. Whereas it does not need a neuroscientist to point out that nutrition impacts on learning, and good nutrition is better than bad, or that physical exercise is good for learning due to increased oxygenation of the brain, most of the specific claims of brain gym are scientific nonsense. For example, contra brain gym, water has no energy because water has no calories. Drinking water has no direct effect on cognition. Obviously severe thirst will negatively affect attention. But too much water can also negatively affect brain function by flooding the intercellular space and compromising the actions of the glial cells. And processed food, like most food, is full of water. The torso does not feature 'brain buttons'. Having your students prod their ribs, or pull on their ear lobes, is not going to 'turn on' their language learning neural systems in their brains. That requires a language task.

One piece of educational research that is crying out to be done, therefore, is to determine to what extent school teachers base any of their practice on their understanding of cognitive neuroscience. UK psychologists Sue Pickering and Paul Howard-Jones surveyed teachers and other education professionals at a large brain-based learning convention, and other teachers attending a session of the Teaching and Learning Research Project's seminar series on neuroscience and education, about how important they thought it was to consider the workings of the brain in their educational practice. Around 90 per cent of respondents said it was, and that both mainstream and special educational classes could benefit from neuroscientific understandings from fMRI and other neuroimaging studies of how children learn. However, it was not so evident that the teachers surveyed got their information from scientific reports. Many teachers using so-called brain-based pedagogies in their classrooms such as brain gym and VAK learning styles only considered the information from the promoters of these schemes. And many teachers said they had found them very beneficial, especially for children who did not seem to respond well to traditional teaching methods. Nevertheless, most teachers who were interviewed said that they wanted to find out more about the science of how the brain worked. To that end, some teachers expressed frustration in finding out that the so-called brain-based pedagogies that they had been using were not scientifically valid. The researchers concluded that scientific communication with teachers is likely to be critical for the success of applying neuroscientific understandings about the brain and learning in the classroom.

An agenda for educational neuroscience

Such a school of the future, or in the future, will presumably only come into being from concomitant developments in educational neuroscience – that is, from parallel developments in relevant cognitive neuroscience and education. For this to happen, I argue, teachers must contribute educationally relevant questions to the neuroscience research agenda. Without such input the educational implications of neuroscientific research will be disappointingly limited. However, there is a feedback loop implied here. For any pedagogy to be effective, much less the type of future-oriented pedagogy proposed here, the work of teachers should be informed by as secure and as reliable an understanding of how children learn as science is able to provide. Such a scientific account of children's learning is obviously far from complete. There is much for educational neuroscience to understand about intelligence, learning, memory and emotions, and how these cognitive characteristics are driven by human genetics. A good deal of this future research will focus on the development of literacy and numeracy in particular. Thus an in-principle educational neuroscience agenda which, following the action research plan of Chapter 1, could look like this:

1   Identify some educational problems, controversies or debatable issues about which poor understanding or irresolution could be impeding educational success.
2   Determine which of these educational bottlenecks might be usefully informed by neuroscience research findings.
3   Analyse which of these neuroscientific problems is tractable given previous research and current resources.
4   Take a step back: what are some educational success strategies which are deliberately unconventional?
5   Determine what sort of neuroscientific evidence could support or refute the general applicability of such strategies.
6   Ask what tractable neuroscientific research could provide such evidence.
7   Look at deeply embedded assumptions: What implicit school educational conventions might be challenged by current neuroscientific understanding of brain function and learning? (e.g., age lock-step progression? One teacher to 30 children?)
8   Analyse what new neuroscientific research could provide such evidence.
9   Identify genetic markers for conditions which can result in learning disabilities and assist the early intervention of psycho-socio-environmental learning strategies that can complement rather than antagonize such genetic predispositions.
10 Analyse what are some of the ethical issues in educational genetics.
11 Extend research into how neuroimaging can play a diagnostic role in assisting educational psychologists to determine effective interventions of each individual child in their care.

Work on the last item has already begun. The cortical representations of memory involved in some classroom tasks (e.g., arithmetic) can already be mapped by event-related fMRI or MEG, where the time course of the relevant brain functions can be determined. Cortical visual areas are first involved with scanning the board or problem sheet, followed by the cortical areas involved in the recognition of numbers and number facts, followed by the pre-frontal areas responsible for executive functions which determine the problem-solving strategy, and so on. Might it be informative to compare high-ability performance on mathematics problems with lower-level performance in order to determine the nature of interventions which might be maximally helpful for children with low mathematics achievement? That is, by tracking the types and strengths of neural connections laid down earlier, the possibility of individually tailored curricula might become an actuality. One type of consequent intervention already noted is that of bio-feedback whereby the student can see their brain working on a screen while performing a particular learning task. With head-only scanning devices a technological possibility, perhaps such bio-feedback regimes might one day be available for all children with learning difficulties. In fact, such a scenario has been recently explored in the lab. Subjects were able to learn to voluntarily control neural activations in their somato-motor cortices from feedback provided by real-time fMRI. Importantly, this positive learning effect was shown to be additional to improvement due to practice-based neural plasticity. In other words, neuroimaging can be used, not just to measure learning, but also to influence it.

Last word

Another city, another international education research conference, and the more papers I listened to, the more I found my mood progressing from boredom to annoyance to extreme irritation. Part of what was getting my goat was the absence of critical argument and analysis – the sort of argument and defence that characterizes papers at a science conference. There was nothing like A says X, but B says Y, so we devised this experiment to see which holds, X or Y. Instead, there was this seemingly endless stream of embedded uncontested received 'wisdom', which, on reflection, makes an inconsistent nonsense. For example, how often do we hear educationists advocate individualizing the curriculum with learning styles, and Vygotsky's ZPD, and Bloom's taxonomy, and so on? Yet how can a mentor who is operating at the lowest of Bloom's levels help a student traverse the ZPD to a higher level? Or with a different learning style, if there were such a thing? These different ways to cut the cake are not necessarily compatible. Yet I rarely hear an education/practitioner researcher stand up and say that a particular theoretical position, much less a piece of research, is wrong, or silly, or useless in the classroom. Or say that here is evidence that this particular pedagogic approach is ineffective. Instead, it all gets added into a cornucopia of unpredictable flubber recently expanded, to make matters worse, with the latest neuromythologies.

This fortunately is not true in every education research conference. Special interest groups in educational neuroscience, long-standing in the American Education Research Association and recently formed in their British counterpart, have papers which do focus on scientific findings and their implications, or on educational projects based on neuroscientific understandings. One such project by the Institute for the Future of the Mind at the University of Oxford, UK, involved advanced skills teachers (ASTs) in Gloucestershire. Each week these ASTs heard lectures from Oxford neuroscientists. Then they broke into small groups for discussions of how the previous week's information was used in their classrooms, and to what effect. A nice example was the use of physical embodiment of history and geography content in dance, consistent with the role of the parietal cortex in learning with programmes such as LOGO (Chapter 8). The teachers summarized their professional findings for publication on the Institute's website. The two-way flow between the science and the classroom makes this project one of best-practice in educational neuroscience. Similarly, the seven years of meetings between educators and neuroscientists at the Oxford Forum have set a promising future for educational neuroscience. It is my hope in writing this book that it might contribute in some small way towards such a realization.

Educational neuroscience questions in a box

For the past decade, a number of UK schools have been embracing brain gym programmes. This immediately suggests a preliminary programme of research:

- What is the current level of knowledge of cognitive neuroscience among the education community?
- To what extent do school teachers base any of their practice on their understanding of cognitive neuroscience?
- To what extent do university educationists in teacher preparation programmes incorporate cognitive neuroscience into their courses?
- To what extent do parents expect teachers to employ cognitive neuro-scientific evidence-based practice?
- To what extent do students perceive their teachers as being in or out of touch with modern developments in understanding brain function?

Another topic for research could be a rigorous evaluation of existing interventions in schools which claim to be based on neuroscientific evidence (e.g., brain gymnastics which purport to increase cerebral blood flow). Would a psychometric analysis of a well-designed (e.g., using matched controls) quasi-experiment find the same level of benefit in school performance that anecdotal reports indicate?

Endnotes

Introduction

Quotations

1   Bruer 1994: 273.
2   Carter 1999: 207.

Chapter 1

Quotations

1   James 1899: 7.
2   Eisenhart and DeHaan 2005: 10.

Chapter 2

Quotations

1   Sherrington 1938: 181.

Chapter 3

Quotations

1   Thelan and Smith 1994: 264.
2   Changeux 1985: 249.

Chapter 4

Quotations

1   Dehaene et al. 1998: 14529.
2   Sherrington 1938: 217.
3   Kratzig and Arbuthnott 2006: 245.

4   Duncan 2001: 824.
5   Waterhouse 2006: 213.
6   O'Boyle, Benbow and Alexander 1995: 438.
7   O'Boyle et al. 2005: 586.

Answer to the Wason card selection task

The correct response is to turn over the E and the 7. Most people choose to turn over the E and the 4, which is wrong. Turning over the E is correct, because it's necessary to verify that the E, a vowel, has an even number on the other side. But turning over the 4 is unnecessary, because it's not important to show that a card with an even number on one side has a vowel on the other side – the 'reverse' of the rule. However, turning over the 7 is necessary, because if the 7 has a vowel on the other side, then it refutes the rule.

Chapter 5

Quotations

1   Mitchell 1993: 240.
2   James [1890] 1950: 530.
3   Hofstadter 2001: 499.
4   Csikszentmihalyi 1998: 59.
5   Lotze et al. 2003: 1817.
6   Borg et al. 2003: 1965.

Fluid analogy letter strings

The various responses can be analysed in terms of the number of transformations required to construct it. For example, in the example **abc** → **abd, pqqrrr** → **?**, plausible responses could include:

- **pqqrrr** (new letter sequence);
- **pqqrrd** (new letter sequence, last letter copy);
- **pqqrrs** (new letter sequence, alphabet preservation, letter advance);
- **pqqsss** (new letter sequence, alphabet preservation, grouping, letter advance);
- **pqqssss** (new letter sequence, alphabet preservation, grouping, numerical increase, letter advance).

Note that the last response captures the meta-level analogy of three- to four-ness. Consequently, one would expect presentation of fluid analogies to humans (in contrast to an AI computer programs) to elicit considerable variance in plausible responses. This was demonstrated by psychologist Bruce Burns where, among 74 respondents, **abc => abd, kji => ?** received 12 different responses (**kjh**, **kjj**, **lji**, etc.), and **abc => abd, mrrjjj => ?** received 20 different responses (**mrrkkk**, **mrrjjk**, **mrsjjk**, **jjmrr**, etc.).

Chapter 6

Quotations

1 Vogeley et al. 2004: 817.
2 Blair 2003: 561.
3 Goldberg 1981: 18.
4 LeDoux 2000: web ref.
5 Trimble 1996: 41–2.

Chapter 7

Quotations

1 Egan 1997: 246.
2 Cornelissen and Hansen 1998: 185.

Chapter 8

Quotations

1 O'Boyle et al. 2005: 586.
2 Singh and O'Boyle 2004: 676.

Bongard pattern solution

Dots on the same/other side of the neck.

Chapter 9

Quotations

1 Sergeant and Thatcher 1974: 56.
2 Geake 1996: 41.
3 Birbaumer et al. 1996: 269, 277.

Chapter 10

Quotations

1 *Daily Telegraph*, 8 September 1998.
2 Bruer 1994: 289.
3 Geake and Cooper 2003: 17–18.

References and Further Reading

Introduction

UK websites

Oxford Cognitive Neuroscience Education Forum
http://www.brookes.ac.uk/schools/education/rescon/ocnef/ocnef.html
Centre of Education and Neuroscience, Faculty of Education, University of Cambridge
www.educ.cam.ac.uk/research/centres/neuroscience/
Centre of Learning Science, University of Nottingham
http://www.sciencelearningcentres.org.uk/
Institute for the Future of the Mind, University of Oxford
http://www.futuremind.ox.ac.uk/

US websites

Brain, Neuroscience and Education Special Interest Group (SIG) of the American Education Research Association (AERA)
http://www.tc.umn.edu/~athe0007/BNEsig/
International Mind, Brain and Education Society, Graduate School of Education, Harvard University, Boston
http://www.gse.harvard.edu/ppe/highered/programs/mbe.html
US National Science Foundation (NSF) Science of Learning Centers program
http://www.nsf.gov/slc
Center of Excellence for Learning in Education, Science, and Technology (CELEST)
http://cns.bu.edu/CELEST/
Center for Learning in Informal and Formal Environments (LIFE)
http://life-slc.org/
Pittsburgh Science of Learning Center for Robust Learning (PSLC)
http://www.learnlab.org/index.php
Spatial Intelligence and Learning Center (SILC)
http://spatiallearning.org/
Temporal Dynamics of Learning Center (TDLC)
http://tdlc.ucsd.edu/portal/

Visual Language and Visual Learning Center (VL2)
http://vl2.gallaudet.edu/

Further reading

Blakemore, S-J. and Frith, U. (2005) *The Learning Brain: Lessons for Education*. Oxford: Blackwell Publishing.
Byrnes, J. P. (2001) *Minds, Brains, and Learning: Understanding the Psychological and Educational Relevance of Neuroscientific Research*. New York: The Guilford Press.
Carter, R. (1999) *Mapping the Mind*. London: Weidenfeld and Nicolson.
Della Sala, S. (ed.) (2007) *Tall Tales about the Mind and Brain: Separating Fact from Fiction*. Oxford: Oxford University Press.
OECD (2002) *Understanding the Brain: Towards a New Learning Science*. London: OECD.
OECD (2007) *Understanding the Brain: Birth of a Learning Science*. London: OECD.

Research references

Bruer, J. T. (1994) Classroom problems, school culture, and cognitive research, in K. McGilly (ed.) *Classroom Lessons: Integrating Cognitive Theory and Classroom Practice*. Cambridge, MA: MIT Press.
Byrnes, J. P. and Fox, N. A. (1998) The educational relevance of research in cognitive neuroscience, *Educational Psychology Review*, 10(3): 297–342 (and following commentaries to p. 412).
Geake, J. G. (1998) Implications of cognitive neuroscience for education. School of Education seminar, University of Cambridge, UK, November.
Geake, J. G. (2000) Knock down the fences: Implications of brain science for education. *Principal Matters*, April: 41–43.
Geake, J. G. (2003) Adapting middle level educational practices to current research on brain functioning, *Journal of the New England League of Middle Schools*, 15(2): 6–12.
Geake, J. G. (2004) Cognitive neuroscience and education: two-way traffic or one-way street? *Westminster Studies in Education*, 27(1): 87–98.
Geake, J. G. and Cooper, P. W. (2003) Implications of cognitive neuroscience for education, *Westminster Studies in Education*, 26(10): 7–20.
Goswami, U. (2004) Neuroscience and education, *British Journal of Educational Psychology*, 74: 1–14.
Goswami, U. (2006) Neuroscience and education: from research to practice? *Nature Reviews Neuroscience*, 7: 406–13.

Howard-Jones, P. (2007) *Neuroscience and Education: Issues and Opportunities, Commentary by the Teacher and Learning Research Programme.* London: TLRP. Available at: http://www.tlrp.org/pub/documents/Neuroscience%20Commentary%20FINAL.pdf

Kirshner, P. A., Sweller, J. and Clark, R. E. (2006) Why minimal guidance during instruction does not work: an analysis of the failure of constructivist, discovery, problem-based, experiential, and inquiry-based teaching, *Educational Psychologist*, 41(2): 75–86.

Chapter 1

Further reading

Calvin, W. H. (1988) *How Brains Think*. London: Phoenix.

Freeman, W. J. (1999) *How Brains Make Up Their Minds*. London: Weidenfeld & Nicolson.

Frith, C. (2007) *Making Up the Mind: How the Brain Creates our Mental World.* London: Blackwell.

Fuster, J. (2003) *Cortex and Mind: Unifying Cognition.* Oxford: Oxford University Press.

Greenfield, S. (2000) *The Private Life of the Brain*. Harmondsworth: Penguin Books.

James, W. (1899). *Talks to Teachers on Psychology: And to Students on Some of Life's Ideals.* New York: Henry Holt and Company.

Sherrington, C. (1938) *Man on His Nature*. Cambridge: Cambridge University Press.

Research references

Eisenhart, M. and DeHaan, R. (2005) Doctoral preparation of scientifically based educational researchers, *Educational Researcher*, 34(4): 3–13.

Geake, J. G. (2004) How children's brains think: not left or right but both together, *Education 3–13*, 32(3): 65–72.

Geake, J. G. (2005) Educational neuroscience and neuroscientific education: in search of a mutual middle way, *Research Intelligence*, 92: 10–13.

Gura, T. (2005) Big plans for little brains, *Nature*, 435: 1156–8.

O'Boyle, M. W. and Gill, H. S. (1998) On the relevance of research findings in cognitive neuroscience to educational practice, *Educational Psychology Review*, 10(3): 397–409.

Chapter 2

Further reading

Gazzaniga, M. S. (ed.) (2004) *The Cognitive Neurosciences*, 3rd edn. Cambridge, MA: MIT Press.

Gregory, R. L. (2004) *The Oxford Companion to the Mind*, 2nd edn. Oxford: Oxford University Press.

Jezzard, P., Matthews, P. M. and Smith, S. M. (2001) *Functional MRI: An Introduction to Methods*. Oxford: Oxford University Press.

Kolb, B. and Wishaw, I. Q. (1996) *Fundamentals of Human Neuropsychology*, 4th edn. New York: W. H. Freeman & Co.

Rugg, M. D. (ed.) (1997) *Cognitive Neuroscience*. Sussex: Psychology Press.

Zigmond, M. J., Bloom, F. E., Landis, S. C., Roberts, J. L. and Squire, L. R. (1998) *Fundamental Neuroscience*. San Diego: Academic Press.

Chapter 3

Further reading

Barnet, A. B. and Barnet, R. J. (1998) *The Youngest Minds*. New York: Simon & Schuster.

Changeux, J-P. (1985) *Neuronal Man: The Biology of Mind*. Princeton, NJ: Princeton University Press.

Edelman, G. (1987) *Neural Darwinism: The Theory of Neuronal Group Selection*. New York: Basic Books.

Hebb, D. O. (1949) *The Organization of Behavior*. New York: Wiley.

Thelen, E. and Smith, L. (1994) *A Dynamic Systems Approach to the Development of Cognition and Action*. Cambridge, MA: MIT Press.

Zull, J. E. (2002) *The Art of Changing the Brain: Enriching the Practice of Teaching by Exploring the Biology of Learning*. Sterling, VA: Stylus.

Research references

Baxter, J. (1989) Children's understanding of familiar astronomical events. *International Journal of Science Education*, 11: 502–13.

Berninger, V. W. and Corina, D. (1998) Making cognitive neuroscience educationally relevant: creating bi-directional collaborations between educational psychology and cognitive neuroscience, *Educational Psychology Review*, 10(3): 343–54.

Bruer, J. T. (1997) Education and the brain: a bridge too far, *Educational Researcher*, 26(8): 4–16.

Draganski, B., Gaser, C., Busch, V. et al. (2004) Changes in grey matter induced by training, *Nature*, 427(6972): 311–12.

Driver, R., Guesne, E. and Tiberghien, A. (eds) (1985) *Children's Ideas in Science*. Milton Keynes: Open University Press.

Jacobs, B., Schall, M. and Scheibel, A. B. (1993) A quantitative dendritic analysis of Wernike's area in humans: gender, hemispheric, and environmental factors, *Journal of Comparative Neurology*, 327: 97–111.

Johnson, M. and Hallgarten, J. (2002) *From Victims of Change to Agents of Change: The Future of the Teaching Profession*. London: Institute of Public Policy Research.

Kay, J. and Phillips, W. A. (1997) Activation functions, computational goals and learning rules for local processors with contextual guidance, *Neural Computation*, 9: 763–8.

Maguire, E. A., Woollett, K. and Spiers, H. J. (2006) London taxi drivers and bus drivers: a structural MRI and neuropsychological analysis, *Hippocampus*, 16: 1091–101.

McClosky, M. (1983) Intuitive physics, *Scientific American*, 248: 114–22.

Phillips, W. A. and Singer, W. (1997) In search of common foundations for cortical computation, *Behavioral and Brain Sciences*, 20(4): 657–722.

Shapiro, M. L. (2001) Plasticity, hippocampal place cells, and cognitive maps, *Archives of Neurology*, 58: 874–81.

Chapter 4

Further reading

Clark, B. (1997) *Growing up Gifted*, 5th edn. Upper Saddle River, NJ: Prentice Hall.

Flynn, J. R. (2007) *What Is Intelligence?* Cambridge: Cambridge University Press.

Gross, M. U. M. (2004) *Exceptionally Gifted Children*, 2nd edn. London: Routledge Falmer.

Luria, A. R. (1973) *The Working Brain*. New York: Basic Books.

Mackintosh, N. J. (1998) *IQ and Human Intelligence*. Oxford: Oxford University Press.

Plomin, R. (1994) *Genetics and Experience: The Interplay Between Nature and Nurture*. London: Sage Publications.

Sternberg, R. J. and Grigorenko, E. (eds) (1997) *Intelligence, Heredity, and Environment*. Cambridge: Cambridge University Press.

Wright, G. (2007) *The Anatomy of Metaphor*. Cambridge: Clare College.

Research references

Baddeley, A. and Sala, S. D. (1998) Working memory and executive control, in A. C. Roberts, T. W. Robbins and L. Weiskrantz (eds), *The Prefrontal Cortex: Executive and Cognitive Functions*. Oxford: Oxford University Press, 9–21.

Calvert, G. A., Campbell, R. and Brammer, M. J. (2000) Evidence from functional magnetic resonance imaging of crossmodal binding in human heteromodal cortex, *Current Biology*, 10(11): 649–57.

Christoff, K., Prabhakaran, V., Dorfman, J. et al. (2001) Rostrolateral prefrontal cortex involvement in relational integration during reasoning, *NeuroImage*, 14: 1136–49.

Coffield, F., Moseley, D., Hall, E. and Ecclestone, K. (2004) *Learning Styles and Pedagogy in Post-16 Learning: A Systematic and Critical Review* (Report No. 041543). London: Learning and Skills Research Centre.

Dehaene, S., Kerszberg, M. and Changeux, J-P. (1998) A neuronal model of a global workspace in effortful cognitive tasks, *Proceedings of the National Academy of Sciences USA*, 95: 14529–34.

Duncan, J. (2001) An adaptive coding model of neural function in prefrontal cortex, *Nature Reviews Neuroscience*, 2(11): 820–9.

Duncan, J., Seitz, R. J., Kolodny, J. et al. (2000) A neural basis for general intelligence, *Science*, 289: 457–60.

Dunn, R., Dunn, K. and Price, G. E. (1984) *Learning Style Inventory*. Lawrence, KS: Price Systems.

Frangou, S., Chitins, X. and Williams, S. C. (2004) Mapping IQ and gray matter density in healthy young people, *NeuroImage*, 23(3): 800–5.

Gathercole, S. E. (2008) Working memory in the classroom, *The Psychologist*, 21(5): 382–5.

Geake, J. G. (2004) How children's brains think: not left or right but both together, *Education 3–13*, 32(3): 65–72.

Geake, J. G. (2006) The neurological basis of intelligence: a contrast with 'brain-based' education, *Education-Line*. Available at: www.leeds.ac.uk/educol/documents/156074.htm

Geake, J. G. (2008) Neural interconnectivity and intellectual creativity: giftedness, savants, and learning styles, in T. Balchin and B. Hymer (eds), *Companion to Gifted Education*. London: Routledge, pp. 10–17.

Geake, J. G. and Dodson, C. S. (2005) A neuro-psychological model of the creative intelligence of gifted children, *Gifted & Talented International*, 20(1): 4–16.

Gilmore, C. K., McCarthy, S. E. and Spike, E. (2007) Symbolic arithmetic knowledge without instruction, *Nature*, 447: 589–91.

Goswami, U. (2001) Analogical reasoning in children, in D. Gentner, K. J. Holyoak, and B. N. Kokinov (eds), *The Analogical Mind: Perspectives from Cognitive Science.* Cambridge, MA: MIT Press, pp. 437–70.

Gray, J. R. and Thompson, P. M. (2004) Neurobiology of intelligence: science and ethics, *Nature Reviews Neuroscience,* June, 5: 471–82.

Gray, J. R., Chabris, C. F. and Braver, T. S. (2003) Neural mechanisms of general fluid intelligence, *Nature Neuroscience,* 6(3): 316–22.

Haier, R. J., Jung, R. E., Yeo, R. A., Head, K. and Alkire, M. T. (2004) Structural brain variation and general intelligence, *NeuroImage,* 23(1): 425–33.

Kanevsky, L. S. and Geake, J. G. (2005) Validating a multifactor model of learning potential with gifted students and their peers, *Journal for the Education of the Gifted,* 28(2): 192–217.

Kayser, C. (2007) Listening with your eyes, *Scientific American Mind,* 18(2): 24–9.

Kratzig, G. P. and Arbuthnott, K. P. (2006) Perceptual learning style and learning proficiency: a test of the hypothesis, *Journal of Educational Psychology,* 98(1): 238–46.

Lee, K. H., Choi, Y. Y., Gray, J. R. et al. (2006) Neural correlates of superior intelligence: stronger recruitment of posterior parietal cortex, *NeuroImage,* 29(2): 578–86.

O'Boyle, M. W. (2000) Neuroscientific research findings and their potential application to gifted educational practice, *Australasian Journal of Gifted Education,* 9(1): 6–10.

O'Boyle, M. W., Benbow, C. P. and Alexander, J. E. (1995) Sex differences, hemispheric laterality, and associated brain activity in the intellectually gifted, *Developmental Neuropsychology,* 11(4): 415–43.

O'Boyle, M. W., Cunnington, R., Silk, T. et al. (2005) Mathematically gifted male adolescents activate a unique brain network during mental rotation, *Cognitive Brain Research,* 25: 583–7.

Rypma, B., Prabhakaran, V., Desmond, J. E., Glover, G. H. and Gabrieli, J. D. (1999) Load-dependent roles of frontal brain regions in the maintenance of working memory, *NeuroImage,* 9: 216–26.

Singh, H. and O'Boyle, M. W. (2004) Interhemispheric interaction during global–local processing in mathematically gifted adolescents, average-ability youth, and college students, *Neuropsychology,* 18(2): 671–7.

Strange, B. A., Henson, R. N., Friston, K. J. and Dolan, R. J. (2001) Anterior prefrontal cortex mediates rule learning in humans, *Cerebral Cortex,* 11: 1040–6.

Vandervert, L. R. and Liu, H. (2008) How working memory and the cognitive cerebellum collaboratively produce the child prodigy, in

L. Shavinina (ed.) *International Handbook of Giftedness*. New York: Springer Science (in press).

Waterhouse, L. (2006) Multiple intelligences, the Mozart effect, and emotional intelligence: a critical review, *Educational Psychologist*, 41(4): 207–25.

Zhang, Q., Shi, J., Luo, Y., Zhao, D. and Yang, J. (2006) Intelligence and information processing during a visual search task in children: an event-related potential study, *Neuroreport*, 17(7): 747–52.

Chapter 5

Further reading

Borg, J., Andrée, B., Soderstrom, H. and Farde, Lars (2003) The serotonin system and spiritual experiences, *American Journal of Psychiatry*, 160: 1965–9.

Hofstadter, D. R. (1995) *Fluid Concepts and Creative Analogies*. New York: Basic Books.

James, W. ([1890] 1950) *The Principles of Psychology*. New York: Henry Holt.

Mitchell, M. (1993) *Analogy-Making as Perception: A Computer Model*. Cambridge, MA: MIT Press.

Roth, I. (ed.) (2007) *Imaginative Minds*. London: British Academy.

Steptoe, A. (ed.) (1988) *Genius and the Mind: Studies of Creativity and Temperament*. Oxford: Oxford University Press.

Stewart, I. and Cohen, J. (1997) *Figments of Reality: The Evolution of the Curious Mind*. Cambridge: Cambridge University Press.

Research references

Burns, B. D. (1996) Meta-analogical transfer: transfer between episodes of analogical reasoning, *Journal of Experimental Psychology: Learning, Memory and Cognition*, 22: 1032–48.

Carlsson, I., Wendt, P. E. and Risberg, J. (2000) On the neurobiology of creativity: differences in frontal activity between high and low creative subjects, *Neuropsychologia*, 38: 873–85.

Carson, S. H., Peterson, J. B. and Higgins, D. M. (2003) Decreased latent inhibition is associated with high-functioning individuals, *Journal of Personality and Social Psychology*, 85(3): 499–506.

Csikszentmihalyi, M. (1998) Creativity and genius: a systems perspective, in A. Steptoe (ed.), *Genius and the Mind: Studies of Creativity and Temperament*. Oxford: Oxford University Press, pp. 39–64.

Geake, J. G. (2008a) Neuropsychological characteristics of academic and creative giftedness, in L. V. Shavinina (ed.), *International Handbook of Giftedness*. New York: Springer Science (in press).

Geake, J. G. (2008b) High abilities at fluid analogising: a cognitive neuroscience construct of giftedness, *Roeper Review*, 30(3): 187–95.

Geake, J. G. and Dodson, C. S. (2005) A neuro-psychological model of the creative intelligence of gifted children, *Gifted & Talented International*, 20(1): 4–16.

Geake, J. G. and Hansen, P. (2005) Neural correlates of intelligence as revealed by fMRI of fluid analogies, *NeuroImage*, 26(2): 555–64.

Geake, J. G. and Hansen, P. C. (2006) Structural and functional neural correlates of high creative intelligence as determined by abilities at fluid analogising, paper presented at Society for Neuroscience Annual Meeting, Atlanta, Georgia, 17 October.

Geake, J. G. and Hansen, P. (in progress) Neural correlates of fluid and crystallised contributions to creative intelligence as determined by abilities at fluid analogising.

Geake, J. G. and Kringelbach, M. L. (2007) Imaging imagination: brain scanning of the imagined future, in I. Roth (ed.), *Imaginative Minds*. London: *Proceedings of the British Academy*, 147: 307–26.

Hofstadter, D. (2001) Analogy as the core of cognition, in D. Gentner, K. J. Holyoak, and B. N. Kokinov (eds), *The Analogical Mind: Perspectives from Cognitive Science*. Cambridge, MA: MIT Press, pp. 499–538.

Holden, K. J. and French, C. C. (2002) Alien abduction experiences: some clues from neuropsychology and neuropsychiatry, *Cognitive Neuropsychiatry*, 7: 163–78.

Jung-Beeman, M., Bowden, E. M., Haberman, J. et al. (2004) Neural activity when people solve verbal problems with insight, *PLoS Biology*, 2(E97): 500–10.

Knauff, M., Mulack, T., Kassubek, J., Salih, H. R. and Greenlee, M. W. (2002) Spatial imagery in deductive reasoning: a functional MRI study, *Brain Research: Cognitive Brain Research*, 13: 203–12.

Kuhtz-Buschbeck, J. P., Mahnkopf, C., Holzknecht, C. et al. (2003) Effector-independent representations of simple and complex imagined finger movements: a combined fMRI and TMS study, *European Journal of Neuroscience*, 18: 3375–87.

Lotze, M., Scheler, G., Tan, H. R., Braun, C. and Birbaumer, N. (2003) The musician's brain: functional imaging of amateurs and professionals during performance and imagery, *Neuroimage*, 20: 1817–29.

Luo, Q., Perry, C., Peng, D. et al. (2003) The neural substrate of analogical reasoning: an fMRI study, *Brain Research: Cognitive Brain Research*, 17: 527–34.

Puri, B. K., Lekh, S. K., Nijran, K. S., Bagary, M. S. and Richardson, A. J. (2001) SPECT neuroimaging in schizophrenia with religious delusions, *International Journal of Psychophysiology*, 40: 143–8.

Samco, M. R., Caplovitz, G. P., Hsieh, P.-J. and Tse, P. U. (2005) Neural correlates of human creativity revealed using diffusion tensor imaging (Abstract), *Journal of Vision*, 5(8): 906.

Silberstein, R. B. (2006) Dynamic sculpting of brain functional connectivity and mental rotation aptitude, *Progress in Brain Research*, 159: 63–76.

Wharton, C. M., Grafman, J., Flitman, S. S. et al. (2000) Toward neuroanatomical models of analogy: a positron emission tomography study of analogical mapping, *Cognitive Psychology*, 40: 173–97.

Chapter 6

Website

http://www.scholarpedia.org/article/Emotional_memory

Further reading

Barkley, R. A. (1997) *ADHD and the Nature of Self-control*. New York: Guilford Press.

Cohen, D. and Maxwell, T. (eds) (1985) *Blocked at the Entrance: Context, Cases and Commentary on Curriculum Change*. Armidale, NSW: Entrance Publications.

Cooper, P. and Ideus, K. (1997) *Attention Deficit/Hyperactivity Disorder: Medical, Educational and Cultural Issues*. East Sutton: The Association of Workers for Children with Emotional and Behavioural Difficulties.

Damasio, A. (1994) *Descartes' Error: Emotion, Reason, and the Human Brain*. New York: Gosset/Putnam.

Gerhardt, S. (2004) *Why Love Matters: How Affection Shapes a Baby's Brain*. London: Routledge.

Goleman, D. (1996) *Emotional Intelligence*. London: Bloomsbury.

LeDoux, J. E. (1996) *The Emotional Brain*. New York: Simon & Schuster.

LeDoux, J. E. (2001) *Synaptic Self*. New York: Viking.

Rolls, E. T. (1999) *The Brain and Emotion*. Oxford: Oxford University Press.

Trimble, M. R. (1996) *Biological Psychiatry*, 2nd edn. Chichester: Wiley.

Research references

Adolphs, R. (2002) Trust in the brain, *Nature Neuroscience*, 5: 192–3.

Baumeister, R. F., Campbell, J. D., Krueger, J. I. and Vohs, K. D. (2003) Does high self-esteem cause better performance, interpersonal success, happiness, or healthier lifestyles? *Psychological Science in the Public Interest*, 4(1): 1–44.

Bechtereva, N. P., Korotkov, A. D., Pakhomov, S. V. et al. (2004) PET study of brain maintenance of verbal creative activity, *International Journal of Psychophysiology*, 53: 11–20.

Berns, G. S., McClure, S. M., Pagnoni, G. and Montague, P. R. (2001) Predictability modulates human brain response to reward, *Journal of Neuroscience*, 21: 2793–8.

Blair, R. J. (2003) Facial expressions, their communicatory functions and neuro-cognitive substrates, *Philosophical Transactions of the Royal Society of London B Biological Science*, 358: 561–72.

Bush, G., Frazier, J. A., Rauch, S. L. et al. (1999) Anterior cingulate cortex dysfunction in attention-deficit/hyperactivity disorder revealed by fMRI and the Counting Stroop Task, *Society of Biological Psychiatry*, 45(12): 1542–52.

Decety, J. and Chaminade, T. (2003) Neural correlates of feeling sympathy, *Neuropsychologia*, 41: 127–38.

Fletcher, P. C., Happe, F., Frith, U. et al. (1995) Other minds in the brain: a functional imaging study of 'theory of mind' in story comprehension, *Cognition*, 57: 109–28.

Gallagher, H. L., Happe, F., Brunswick, N. et al. (2000) Reading the mind in cartoons and stories: an fMRI study of 'theory of mind' in verbal and nonverbal tasks, *Neuropsychologia*, 38: 11–21.

Goldberg, M. L. (1981) *Issues in the Education of Gifted and Talented Children in Australia and the United States*. Canberra: Commonwealth Schools Commission.

Greenberg, M. T. and Snell, J. L. (1997) Brain development and emotional development: the role of teaching in organising the frontal lobe, in P. Salovey and D. Sluyter (eds), *Emotional Development and Emotional Intelligence*. New York: Basic Books.

Kokkinos, C. M., Panayiotou, G. and Davazoglou, A. M. (2004) The effects of trainee teachers' personality characteristics on their appraisals of pupils' undesirable behaviours, paper presented at British Psychological Society Annual Conference, Imperial College London, April.

Kringelbach, M. L. (2004) Learning to change, *Proceedings of the Library of Science Biology*, 2: 577–9.

LeDoux, J. E. (2000) *The Future of the Study of Emotion*. Available at: http://www.loc.gov/loc/brain/emotion/Ledoux.html

Maxwell, T. W., Marshall, A. R. A., Walton, J. and Baker, I. (1989). Secondary school alternative structures: semester courses and vertical grouping in non-state schools in New South Wales, *Curriculum Perspectives*, 9(1): 1–15.

Mayer, D. and Salovey, P. (1997) What is emotional intelligence? in P. Salovey and D. Sluyter (eds), *Emotional Development and Emotional Intelligence: Educational Implications*: New York: Basic Books.

Morris, J. S., DeGelder, B., Weiskrantz, L. and Dolan, R. J. (2001) Differential extrageniculostriate and amygdala responses to presentation of emotional faces in a cortically blind field, *Brain*, 124: 1241–52.

O'Connor, T. G., Neiderhiser, J. M., Reiss, D. et al. (1998) Genetic contributions to continuity, change and co-occurrence of antisocial and depressive symptoms in adolescence, *Journal of Child Psychology and Psychiatry*, 39: 323–36.

Palmer, B., Donaldson, C. and Stough, C. (2002) Emotional intelligence and life satisfaction, *Personality and Individual Differences*, 33(7): 1091–100.

Raz, A. (2004) Brain imaging data of ADHD, *Psychiatric Times*, 21(9): 1–3.

Rilling, J. K., Sanfey, A. G., Aronson, J. A., Nystrom, L. E. and Cohen, J. D. (2004) The neural correlates of theory of mind within interpersonal interactions, *Neuroimage*, 22: 1694–703.

Rizzolatti, G., Fadiga, L., Gallese, V. and Fogassi, L. (1996) Premotor cortex and the recognition of motor actions, *Brain Research: Cognitive Brain Research*, 3: 131–41.

Ruby, P. and Decety, J. (2003) What you believe versus what you think they believe: a neuroimaging study of conceptual perspective-taking, *European Journal of Neuroscience*, 17: 2475–80.

Saxe, R. and Kanwisher, N. (2003) People thinking about thinking people: the role of the temporo-parietal junction in 'theory of mind', *Neuroimage*, 19: 1835–42.

Vogeley, K., Bussfeld, P., Newen, A. et al. (2001) Mind reading: neural mechanisms of theory of mind and self-perspective, *Neuroimage*, 14: 170–81.

Vogeley, K., May, M., Ritzl, A. et al. (2004) Neural correlates of first-person perspective as one constituent of human self-consciousness, *Journal of Cognitive Neuroscience*, 16: 817–27.

Chapter 7

Further reading

Claxton, G. (1997) *Hare Brain, Tortoise Mind: Why Intelligence Increases When You Think Less*. London: Fourth Estate.

Egan, K. (1997) *The Educated Mind: How Cognitive Tools Shape Our Understanding*. Chicago: University of Chicago Press.

Goswami, U. (2002) *Blackwell Handbook of Cognitive Developmental Psychology*. Oxford: Blackwell.

Research references

Bishop, D. V. M. (2006) What causes specific language impairment in children? *Current Directions in Psychological Science*, 15: 217–21.

Church, J. A., Coalson, R. S., Lugar, H. M., Petersen, S. E. and Schlaggar, B. L. (2008) A developmental fMRI study of reading and repetition reveals changes in phonological and visual mechanisms over age, *Cerebral Cortex*, 18(9): 2054–65.

Cohen, L., Dehaene, S., Naccache, L. et al. (2000) The visual word form area: spatial and temporal characterization of an initial stage of reading in normal subjects and posterior split-brain patients, *Brain*, 123: 291–307.

Cohen, L. and Dehaene, S. (2004) Specialization within the ventral stream: the case for the visual word form area, *Neuroimage*, 22(1): 466–76.

Cornelissen, P. L. and Hansen, P. C. (1998) Motion detection, letter position encoding, and single word reading, *Annals of Dyslexia*, 48: 155–88.

Dale, P., Simonoff, E., Bishop, D. et al. (1998) Genetic influence on language delay in two-year-old children, *Nature Neuroscience*, 1: 324–8.

Ellis, A. W. (2004) Length, formats, neighbours, hemispheres, and the processing of words presented laterally or at fixation, *Brain and Language*, 88: 355–66.

Fine, J. (2005) Reading deficits predicted by differences in structure of the corpus callosum, paper presented at the AERA, Montreal.

Green. M. (2004) Transportation into narrative worlds: the role of prior knowledge and perceived realism, *Discourse Processes*, 38(2): 247–66.

Hsu, J. (2008) The secrets of storytelling: why we love a good yarn, *Scientific American Mind*, 19(4): 46–51.

King, J. W. and Kutas, M. (1998) Neural plasticity in the dynamics of human visual word recognition, *Neuroscience Letters*, 244(2): 61.

Kutas, M. and Hillyard, S. A. (1984) Brain potentials during reading reflect word expectancy and semantic association, *Nature*, 307: 161–3.

Mar, R. A., Kelley, W. M., Heatherton, T. F. and Macrae, C. N. (2007) Detecting agency from the biological motion of veridical versus animated agents, *Social Cognitive and Affective Neuroscience*, 2: 199–205.

McCandliss, B. D., Cohen, L. and Dehaene, S. (2003) The visual word form area: expertise for reading in the fusiform gyrus, *Trends in Cognitive Sciences*, 7(7): 293–9.

Pammer, K., Hansen, P. C., Kringelbach, M. L. et al. (2004) Visual word recognition: the first half second, *Neuroimage*, 22: 1819–25.

Price, C. J. and Devlin, J. T. (2003) The myth of the visual word form area, *Neuroimage*, 19(3): 473–81.

Pulvermüller, F., Assadollahi, R. and Elbert, T. (2001) Neuromagnetic evidence for early semantic access in word recognition, *European Journal of Neuroscience*, 13, 201–5.

Richardson, U., Thomson, J., Scott, S. K. and Goswami, U. (2004) Auditory processing skills and phonological representation in dyslexic children, *Dyslexia*, 10: 215–33.

Rimrodt, S. L., Clements-Stephens, A. M., Pugh, K. R. et al. (2008) Functional MRI of sentence comprehension in children with dyslexia: beyond word recognition, *Cerebral Cortex* (Advance Access published online) 30 May.

Shaywitz, S. E. (1996) Dyslexia, *Scientific American*, 275(5): 98–104.

Shaywitz, S. E., Shaywitz, B. A., Pugh, K. R. et al. (1998) Functional disruption in the organization of the brain for reading in dyslexia, *Proceedings of the National Academy of Science of the United States of America*, 95: 2636–41.

Stein, J. (2001) The magnocellular theory of developmental dyslexia, *Dyslexia*, 7: 12–36.

Stein, J. (2003) Visual motion sensitivity and reading, *Neuropsychologia*, 41: 1785–93.

Thierry, G., Giraud, A. L. and Price, C. (2003) Hemispheric dissociation in access to the human semantic system, *Neuron*, 38: 499–506.

Chapter 8

Websites

http://www.foundalis.com/res/bps/bpidx.htm
http://nrich.maths.org/

Further reading

Butterworth, B. (1999) *The Mathematical Brain*. London: Macmillan.

Dehaene, S. (1997) *The Number Sense: How the Mind Creates Mathematics*. Harmondsworth: Penguin Books.

Dowker, A. (2005) *Individual Differences in Arithmetic*. Hove: Psychology Press.

Hofstadter, D. R. (1979) *Gödel, Escher, Bach: An Eternal Golden Braid*. New York: Basic Books.

Kasner, E. and Newman, J. R. (1940) *Mathematics and the Imagination*. New York: Simon & Schuster.

Papert, S. A. (1993) *Mindstorms: Children, Computers, and Powerful Ideas*. New York: Basic Books.

Singh, S. (2006) *Fermat's Last Theorem*. London: Fourth Estate.

Research references

Bacon, M., Geake, J. G., Lea-Wood, S., McAllister, H. and Watt, N. (1991) Sum insight: understanding our world through logic, mathematics and philosophy, in M. Goodall and B. Culhane (eds), *Teaching Strategies for a Clever Country*. Melbourne: The Australian Association for the Education of the Gifted and Talented, pp. 114–22.

Boysen, S. T. and Berntson, G. G. (1986) Clever Kermit: arithmetic behavior in chimpanzees, *Scientific American*, 210: 98–106.

Christoff, K., Prabhakaran, V., Dorfman, J. et al. (2001) Rostrolateral prefrontal cortex involvement in relational integration during reasoning, *NeuroImage*, 14: 1136–49.

Eger, E., Sterzer, P., Russ, M. O., Giraud, A-L. and Kleinschmidt, A. (2003) A supramodal number representation in human intraparietal cortex, *Neuron*, 37: 719–25.

Etienne, A. S., Maurer, R. and Séguinot, V. (1996). Path integration in mammals and its interaction with visual landmarks, *The Journal of Experimental Biology*, 199(1): 201–9.

Geake, J. G. (1989) Fractal computer graphics: a window on the world of limits and complex numbers, *Australian Senior Mathematics Journal*, 4(2): 86–98.

Geake, J. G. (2003) Young mathematical brains, *Primary Mathematics*, 7(1): 14–18.

Geake, J. G. (2006) Mathematical brains, *Gifted & Talented*, 10(1): 2–7.

Geake, J. G. and O'Boyle, M. (2000) On educating the very able in mathematics: a sampling of current empirical research, in M. Bulmer, B. McCrae and K. Stacey (eds), *Proceedings of Mathematics 2000 Festival*. Melbourne: University of Melbourne, pp. 153–6.

Geary, D. C. and Widaman, K. F. (1992) Numerical cognition: on the convergence of componential and psychometric models, *Intelligence*, 16: 47–80.

Gleick, J. (1992) *Genius: Richard Feynman and Modern Physics*. London: Abacus.

Haier, R. J. and Benbow, C. P. (1995) Sex differences and lateralisation in temporal lobe glucose metabolism during mathematical reasoning, *Developmental Neuropsychology*, 11(4): 405–14.

Hunter, I. M. L. (2001) Calculating geniuses, in G. Underwood (ed.), *Oxford Guide to the Mind*. Oxford: Oxford University Press.

Jung-Beeman, M., Bowden, E. M., Haberman, J. et al. (2004) Neural activity when people solve verbal problems with insight, *PLOS Biology*, April, 2(4): 13, e111.

Kao, Y. and Anderson, J. (2006) Spatial ability and geometry achievement:

a pilot study. Poster presented at the Institute of Education Sciences Conference, Washington, DC.

Knauff, M., Mulack, T., Kassubek, J., Salih, H. R. and Greenlee, M. W. (2002) Spatial imagery in deductive reasoning: a functional MRI study, *Brain Research: Cognitive Brain Research*, 13: 203–12.

Lee, K. H., Choi, Y. Y., Gray, J. R. et al. (2006) Neural correlates of superior intelligence: stronger recruitment of posterior parietal cortex, *NeuroImage*, 29(2): 578–86.

Livne, N. L., Livne, O. E. and Milgram, R. M. (1999) Assessing academic and creative abilities in mathematics at four levels of understanding, *International Journal of Mathematics Education, Science and Technology,* 30(2): 227–42.

Mamede, E., Nunes, T. and Bryant, P. (2005) The equivalence and ordering of fractions in part-whole and quotient situations, in H. L. Chick and J. L. Vincent (eds), *Proceedings of the 29th PME International Conference*, 3: 281–88.

Motluk, A. (2000) Dicing with Albert, *New Scientist*, 18 March: 43–4.

O'Boyle, M. W., Cunnington, R., Silk, T. et al. (2005) Mathematically gifted male adolescents activate a unique brain network during mental rotation, *Cognitive Brain Research,* 25: 583–7.

Qin, Y., Carter, C. S., Silk, E. M. et al. (2004) The change of the brain activation patterns as children learn algebra equation solving, *PNAS*, 101(15): 5686–91.

Ryan, M. and Geake, J. G. (2003) A study of a vertical curriculum in mathematics for gifted primary pupils, *Australasian Journal of Gifted Education*, 11(2): 31–41.

Singh, H. and O'Boyle, M. W. (2004) Interhemispheric interaction during global-local processing in mathematically gifted adolescents, average-ability youth, and college students, *Neuropsychology,* 18(2): 671–7.

Strange, B. A., Henson, R. N., Friston, K. J. and Dolan, R. J. (2001) Anterior prefrontal cortex mediates rule learning in humans, *Cerebral Cortex*, 11: 1040–46.

Wood, J. and Grafman, J. (2003) Human prefrontal cortex: processing and representational perspectives, *Nature Neuroscience*, 4: 139–147.

Chapter 9

Further reading (music)

Bentley, A. (1966) *Musical Ability in Children and Its Measurement*. London: George Harrap & Co.

Colwell, R. (ed.) (1992) *Handbook of Research on Music Teaching and Learning*. New York: Schirmer Books.

Shuter-Dyson, R. and Gabriel, C. (1968) *The Psychology of Musical Ability.* London: Methuen.

Storr, A. (1993) *Music and the Mind.* London: HarperCollins.

Research references (music)

Andreasen, F. and Geake, J. G. (1988) A differentiated Year 7 music programme for musically gifted and talented students, *Gifted*, 103: 28–30.

Birbaumer, N., Lutzenberger, W., Rau, H., Braun, C. and Mayer-Kress, G. (1996) Perception of music and dimensional complexity of brain activity, *International Journal of Bifurcation and Chaos*, 6(2): 267–78.

Cross, I. (1999) Is music the most important thing we ever did? Music, development and evolution, in S. W. Yi (ed.), *Music, Mind and Science*. Seoul: Seoul National University Press.

Cutietta, R. and Booth, G. (1997) The influence of metre, mode, interval type, and contour in repeated melodic free-recall, *The Psychology of Music*, 24(2): 222–36.

Egner, T. and Gruzelier, J. H. (2003) Ecological validity of neurofeedback: modulation of slow wave EEG enhances musical performance, *Neuroreport*, 14: 1221–4.

Geake, J. G. (1996) Why Mozart? Information processing abilities of gifted young musicians, *Research Studies in Music Education*, 7: 28–45.

Geake, J. G. (1999) An information processing account of audiational abilities, *Research Studies in Music Education*, 12: 10–23.

Geake, J. G. and Gregson, R. A. M. (1999). Modeling the internal generation of rhythm as an extension of nonlinear psychophysics, *Musicae Scientiae*, 3(2): 217–36.

Howard-Jones, P. A. and Demetriou, S. (in press) Uncertainty and engagement with learning games, *Instructional Science*.

Lotze, M., Scheler, G., Tan, H. R., Braun, C. and Birbaumer, N. (2003) The musician's brain: functional imaging of amateurs and professionals during performance and imagery, *NeuroImage*, 20: 1817–29.

Parsons, L. M. (2003) Exploring the functional neuroanatomy of music performance, perception, and comprehension, in I. Peretz and R. Zatorre (eds), *The Cognitive Neuroscience of Music*. Oxford: Oxford University Press.

Parsons, L. M. and Osherson, D. (2001). New evidence for distinct right and left brain systems for deductive versus probabilistic reasoning, *Cerebral Cortex*, 11: 954–65.

Peretz, I. (2003) Brain specialisations for music: new evidence from congenital amusia, in I. Peretz and R. Zatorre (eds), *The Cognitive Neuroscience of Music*. Oxford: Oxford University Press.

Sergeant, D. C. and Thatcher, G. (1974) Intelligence, social status, and musical abilities, *Psychology of Music,* 2: 32–57.

Stewart, L. (2005) Neurocognitive studies of musical literacy acquisition, *Musicae Scientiae,* 9(2): 223–7.

Stewart, L. and Walsh, V. (2005) Infant learning: music and the baby brain, *Current Biology,* 15(21): R882–R884.

Further reading (visual arts)

Berger, J. (1972) *Ways of Seeing.* Harmondsworth: Penguin.

Gardner, H. (1990) *Art Education and Human Development.* New York: The Getty Center for Education in the Arts.

Hughes, R. (2000) *The Shock of the New,* 3rd edition. New York: Thames and Hudson.

Kinder, A. M. (ed.) (1997) *Child Development in Art.* London: National Art Education Association.

Mandelbrot, B. B. (1983) *The Fractal Geometry of Nature.* New York: W.H. Freeman.

Ocvrik, O. et al. (2001) *Art Fundamentals: Theory and Practice,* 9th edn. London: McGraw-Hill.

Research references (visual arts)

Chen, C-C., Kai-Ling, C. K., Kurtosis, L. C. and Tyler, C. W. (2007) Face configuration processing in the human brain: the role of symmetry, *Cerebral Cortex:* 17(6): 1423–32.

Geake, J. G. and Porter, J. (1992) Form in the natural environment: fractal computer graphics and Wassily Kandinsky, *Journal of Art & Design Education,* 11(3): 287–302.

Kay, K. N., Naselaris, T., Prenger, R. J. and Gallant, J. L. (2008) Identifying natural images from human brain activity, *Nature,* 452: 352–5.

Samco, M. R., Caplovitz, G. P., Hsieh, P-J. and Tse, P. U. (2005) Neural correlates of human creativity revealed using diffusion tensor imaging (Abstract), *Journal of Vision,* 5(8): 906.

Solso, R. L. (2000) The cognitive neuroscience of art: a preliminary fMRI observation, *Journal of Consciousness Studies,* 7(8–9): 75–85.

Solso, R. L. (2001) Brain activities in a skilled versus a novice artist: an fMRI study, *Leonardo,* 34(1): 31–3.

Taylor, R. P., Micolich, A. P. and Jones, D. (1999) Fractal analysis of Pollock's drip paintings, *Nature,* 3 June 399: 422.

Tyler, C. W. (1999) Human symmetry detection exhibits reverse eccentricity scaling, *Visual Neuroscience,* 16: 919–22.

Chapter 10

Further reading

Bruer, J. T. (1994) Classroom problems, school culture, and cognitive research, in K. McGilly (ed.), *Classroom Lessons: Integrating Cognitive Theory and Classroom Practice*. Cambridge, MA: MIT Press.

Carskadon, M. A. (ed.) (2002) *Adolescent Sleep Patterns: Biological, Social, and Psychological Influences*. Cambridge: Cambridge University Press.

Geake, J. G. and Cooper, P. W. (2003) Cognitive neuroscience: implications for education? *Westminister Studies in Education*, 26(1): 7–20.

Research references

Blumich, B. (2008) The incredible shrinking scanner, *Scientific American*, 299(5): 68–73.

deCharms, R. C., Christoff, K., Glover, G. H. et al. (2004) Learned regulation of spatially localized brain activation using real-time fMRI, *NeuroImage*, 21: 436–43.

Fardell, R. and Geake, J. G. (2003) Vertical semester organisation in a rural secondary school as a vehicle for acceleration of gifted students, *Australasian Journal of Gifted Education*, 11(2): 16–30.

Fardell, R. and Geake, J. G. (2005) Vertical semester organisation in a rural secondary school: the views of gifted students, *Australasian Journal of Gifted Education*, 14(1): 15–29.

Geake, J. G. (2007) A brainy school of the future? *Learning Matters*, 12(1): 36–40.

Howard-Jones, P. (2007) *Neuroscience and Education: Issues and Opportunities*, Commentary by the Teacher and Learning Research Programme. London: TLRP. Available at: http://www.tlrp.org/pub/commentaries.html

Hyatt, K. J. (2007) Brain Gym®: building stronger brains or wishful thinking? *Remedial and Special Education*, 28: 117–24.

Pickering, S. J. and Howard-Jones, P. (2007) Educators' views of the role of neuroscience in education: findings from a study of UK and international perspectives, *Mind, Brain and Education*, 3: 109–13.

Ryan, M. and Geake, J. G. (2003) A study of a vertical curriculum in mathematics for gifted primary pupils, *Australasian Journal of Gifted Education*, 11(2): 31–41.

Index

APPROACHES TO LEARNING
A Guide for Teachers

Anne Jordan, Orison Carlile and Annetta Stack

"This book provides a really sound grounding in the theories that underpin successful teaching and learning. Without over-simplification it provides accessible introductions to the key learning theories with which teachers and students are likely to engage, and it has immense practical value."
Professor Sally Brown, Pro-Vice-Chancellor,
Leeds Metropolitan University, UK

This comprehensive guide for education students and practitioners provides an overview of the major theories of learning. It considers their implications for policy and practice and sets out practical guidelines for best pedagogical practice.

The book can be read as a series of stand-alone chapters or as an integrated overview of theoretical perspectives drawn from the philosophy, psychology, sociology and pedagogy that guide educational principles and practice. Each chapter contains:

- An accessible introduction to each theory
- A summary of key principles
- Critical insights drawn from the theories discussed
- Examples and illustrations from contemporary research and practice
- Summary boxes that highlight critical and key points made
- Practical implications for education professionals

Approaches to Learning is an invaluable resource for students and practitioners who wish to reflect on their educational constructs and explore and engage in the modern discourse of education.

Contents: *List of figures and tables - Acknowledgements - Introduction - Philosophy of education - Behaviourism - Cognitivism - Constructivism - Social learning - Cultural learning - Intelligence - Life course development - Adult learning - Values - Motivation - The learning body- Language and learning - Experiential and competency-based learning - Inclusivity - Blended learning - The future - Glossary.*

2008   304pp
978-0-335-22670-2 (Paperback)   978-0-335-22671-9 (Hardback)

DEVELOPING THINKING; DEVELOPING LEARNING
A Guide to Thinking Skills in Education

Debra McGregor

"This highly informative book provides a comprehensive guide to the teaching of thinking skills in primary and secondary education."
Learning and Teaching Update

It is now recognised that thinking skills, such as problem-solving, analysis, synthesis, creativity and evaluation, can be nurtured and developed, and education professionals can play a significant role in shaping the way that children learn and think. As a result, schools are being encouraged to make greater use of thinking skills in lessons and the general emphasis on cognition has developed considerably. This book offers a comprehensive introduction to thinking skills in education and provides detailed guidance on how teachers can support cognitive development in their classrooms.

Developing Thinking; Developing Learning discusses how thinking programmes, learning activities and teachers' pedagogy in the classroom can fundamentally affect the nature of pupils' thinking, and considers the effects of the learning environment created by peers and teachers. It compares the nature, design and outcomes of established thinking programmes used in schools and also offers practical advice for teachers wishing to develop different kinds of thinking capabilities.

This is an indispensable guide to thinking skills in schools today, and is key reading for education studies students, teachers and trainee teachers, and educational psychologists.

Contents: *List of figures and tables - Acknowledgements - Introduction - What do we mean by 'thinking?' - What kind of thinking should we encourage children to do? - Thinking and learning - The nature of thinking programmes developed within a subject context - The nature of general thinking skills programmes - The nature of infusing thinking - Effectiveness of thinking programmes - Development of creative thinking - Development of critical thinking - Development of metacognition - Development of problem solving capability - Synthesising the general from the particular - Professional development to support thinking classrooms - School development to support thinking communities - References - Index.*

2007   344pp
978-0-335-21780-9 (Paperback)   978-0-335-21781-6 (Hardback)

MODELS OF LEARNING - TOOLS FOR TEACHING

Bruce Joyce, Emily Calhoun and David Hopkins

Reviews of 1st Edition:

"This powerful book makes many of its points through the use of case studies and examples...Rarely, if ever, has discussion of so wide a variety of approaches to learning been gathered together in a single volume." - British Journal of Educational Technology

This comprehensive, accessible and successful text has been revised and updated to meet the needs of teachers, advisers, inspectors, teacher educators and educational researchers at the beginning of the 21st century.

Key features include:

- **A range of teaching models offering a wide repertoire of strategies for teachers**
- **wealth of practical examples backed up by relevant research evidence and clear guidelines for implementation**
- **A clear, engaging and accessible writing style**
- **A completely new chapter on learning to read and write with the Picture Word Inductive Model**

The purpose of this book is to introduce some of the array of models of teaching that have been developed, polished and studied over the last thirty years. Some of these models have been shown both to accelerate rates of learning and also to bring within reach of pupils types of conceptual control and modes of inquiry which have been almost impossible to generate through traditional chalk and talk teaching. Rather than being formulas to be followed slavishly, each model brings teachers into the study of how students learn thereby promoting reflective action research in the classroom.

Contents

Scenarios - An inquiry into learning and teaching - Families of models of teaching - Learning to think inductively - Learning to explore concepts - Learning to think metaphorically - Learning mnemonically - Learning cooperative disciplined inquiry - Learning to study values - Learning through counselling - Learning through simulations - Learning to read and write with the Picture Word Inductive Model - The conditions of learning: integrating models of learning and teaching - Teaching and learning together - Educational policy and the study of teaching - Appendices - References - Index.

272pp   0 335 21015 5 (Paperback)

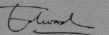
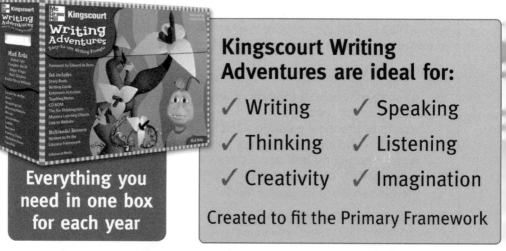